The Preacher's Bible Handbook

The Preacher's Bible Handbook

O. Wesley Allen, Jr., Editor

WESTMINSTER
JOHN KNOX PRESS
LOUISVILLE · KENTUCKY

© 2019 Westminster John Knox Press

First edition
Published by Westminster John Knox Press
Louisville, Kentucky

19 20 21 22 23 24 25 26 27 28—10 9 8 7 6 5 4 3 2 1

Scripture quotations from the New Revised Standard Version of the Bible are copyright © 1989 by the Division of Christian Education of the National Council of the Churches of Christ in the U.S.A. and are used by permission, with some italics added to identify terms and "the LORD" sometimes rendered as "YHWH." Scripture quotations marked GNT are from the Good News Translation in Today's English Version, Second Edition Copyright © 1992 by American Bible Society. Used by permission. Scripture quotations marked NIV are from The Holy Bible, New International Version. Copyright © 1973, 1978, 1984, 2011 by Biblica, Inc.® Used by permission. All rights reserved worldwide. Scripture quotations marked RSV are from the Revised Standard Version of the Bible, copyright © 1946, 1952, 1971, and 1973 by the Division of Christian Education of the National Council of the Churches of Christ in the U.S.A., and are used by permission.

Book design by Drew Stevens
Cover design by Nita Ybarra

Library of Congress Cataloging-in-Publication Data

Names: Allen, O. Wesley, Jr., 1965- author.
Title: The preacher's handbook to the Bible / O. Wesley Allen.
Description: First edition. | Louisville, Kentucky : Westminster John Knox
  Press, 2019.
Identifiers: LCCN 2019001534 | ISBN 9780664263072 (pbk. : alk. paper)
Subjects: LCSH: Bible—Criticism, interpretation, etc. | Preaching.
Classification: LCC BV511.3 .A45 2019 | DDC 220.6—dc23
LC record available at https://lccn.loc.gov/2019001534

Contents

NEW TESTAMENT

Contributors

CHARLES L. AARON
Associate Professor of Supervised Ministry
Perkins School of Theology, Southern Methodist University
Ezekiel, Daniel, Hosea, Joel, Amos, Obadiah

O. WESLEY ALLEN, JR.
Lois Craddock Perkins Professor of Homiletics
Perkins School of Theology, Southern Methodist University
Matthew, Mark, Luke

RONALD J. ALLEN
Professor Emeritus of Preaching and Gospels and Letters
Christian Theological Seminary
John, James, 1 Peter, 2 Peter

LISA MARIE BOWENS
Assistant Professor of New Testament
Princeton Theological Seminary
Ephesians, Philippians, Colossians

WILLIAM F. BROSEND II
Professor of New Testament and Preaching
The School of Theology, Sewanee: The University of the South
Romans, 1 Thessalonians. 2 Thessalonians, Jude

LISA WILSON DAVISON
Johnnie Eargle Cadieux Professor of Hebrew Bible
Phillips Theological Seminary
Exodus, Joshua, Judges, Ruth, Psalms, Song of Songs

STEPHEN FARRIS
Professor Emeritus of Homiletics
Vancouver School of Theology
Acts, Hebrews

JOHN C. HOLBERT
Lois Craddock Perkins Professor Emeritus of Homiletics
Perkins School of Theology, Southern Methodist University
Genesis, 1 Kings, 2 Kings, Job, Jonah, Haggai, Zechariah, Malachi

J. DWAYNE HOWELL
Professor Emeritus of Old Testament and Hebrew
School of Theology, Campbellsville University
Leviticus, Numbers, Deuteronomy, 1 Chronicles, 2 Chronicles

DAVID SCHNASA JACOBSEN
Professor of the Practice of Homiletics
Boston University School of Theology
Galatians, Revelation

MICHAEL P. KNOWLES
George F. Hurlburt Professor of Preaching
McMaster Divinity College
1 Corinthians, 2 Corinthians, Philemon

DEBORAH KRAUSE
Professor of New Testament
Eden Theological Seminary
1 Timothy, 2 Timothy, Titus

KAROLINE M. LEWIS
Marbury E. Anderson Chair of Biblical Preaching
Luther Seminary
1 John, 2 John, 3 John

ALYCE M. McKENZIE
Le Van Professor of Preaching and Worship
Perkins School of Theology, Southern Methodist University
Proverbs, Ecclesiastes

PATRICIA K. TULL
A. B. Rhodes Professor Emerita of Old Testament
Louisville Presbyterian Theological Seminary
1 Samuel, 2 Samuel, Ezra, Nehemiah, Esther, Isaiah

MARY DONOVAN TURNER
Carl Patton Professor Emerita of Preaching
Pacific School of Religion
Jeremiah, Lamentations, Micah, Nahum, Habakkuk, Zephaniah

Introduction

O. WESLEY ALLEN, JR., EDITOR

While there are still some worship traditions that follow the ancient practice of *lectio continua*, reading (and preaching) through a biblical work passage by passage Sunday after Sunday, most do not. The majority of liturgical traditions today jump around the canon (to greater or lesser degrees) week to week in relation to the christological movement of the liturgical year, various pastoral concerns that arise in the congregation, world events that need to be addressed, and the like. Add to this practice the fact that most contemporary approaches to biblical preaching, especially lectionary-based preaching, involve focusing on one individual, isolated passage at a time.

The result of this situation is that preachers, in the rush to prepare a sermon every seven days, find it difficult to study the wider contexts of their focus passages as part of that sermon preparation process. Moreover, the complexity of many biblical writings makes it difficult to know what elements of the wider context should be brought into a sermon and which serve better as background knowledge for the preacher but would be distracting in a sermon. This is especially the case for parts of the canon that do not receive as much attention in the pulpit today as others.

This *Handbook* is intended as an aid for preachers seeking a remedy to this situation. We have gathered a collection of scholars interested in bridging the gulf between the academy's approach to biblical studies and the church's task of proclaiming the gospel in order to provide readers with introductions to each book of the Bible, presented to help preachers contextualize any passage on which they plan to focus in relation to the historical circumstances, literary structure, and theological themes of the book from which the passage is drawn.

The essays are short enough to be read quickly as part of the weekly sermon preparation process without derailing that process. By design, they do not describe all the elements of the sociohistorical background, literary shape, and theological foci of the writing that might be found in the introduction of a critical commentary and which are certainly helpful for understanding the full depth and complexity of the writing. Instead, they focus on only those elements that are essential for the preacher to know as background and literary/thematic context for any of the passages in the work as the preacher interprets it for a congregation for a given worship service. Specifically, the essays focus on information that the authors think worthwhile and relevant for preachers to share in their sermons as they contextualize the passage on which they are preaching for laity.

Hebrew Bible

Genesis

JOHN C. HOLBERT

Whether or not the stories of Genesis contain genuine history engenders vigorous scholarly debate. Surely, any history lies far in the background of stories designed to illuminate and unify Israel at a later date in the life of the community. What we read in Genesis should be named literary/theological history, for the stories, especially for preachers, must be approached as tales well told rather than history recorded. That said, we hardly imply that the stories are any less vital for preaching. The proper questions to raise in our reading have to do more with plot and character than with archaeology and historical dating.

Genesis may be divided into four distinct sections.

PREHISTORY (CHAPS. 1–11)

The first eleven chapters of Genesis are the prologue of the entire biblical story. In them we discover the central themes of the Bible's interests: (1) Who is God? (2) Who are we humans? (3) What are the relationships between God and the humans? Genesis 1–11 displays a rich series of answers.

In chapters 1–2, God is creator of the world, but that act of creation is offered in two distinct accounts. The first suggests that God (*'elohim*) creates all that is solely by the divine voice, displaying a massive power and mysterious hiddenness all at once. The second account, in sharp contrast, shows us God (*YHWH 'elohim*) kneeling in the moistened clay, and with dirty fingers shaping human beings on a potter's wheel (2:7). God then places the created *'adam* (this is not "Adam," but a soil creature) in a garden in order that the creature might serve it and protect it (2:15). This God is intimate, as close as our breath.

After God provides the lonely *'adam* with a partner, built from its side, the first couple is soon engaged in rejection of divine commands, eating the forbidden fruit of the garden, then blaming one another, with the result that they are thrown from the garden and made to live in the world the storyteller knows, one where women give birth in great pain while men attempt to extract a meager living from the rocky soil of Palestine (3:16–19). Despite the grim realities, they proceed to have children. Then the tale turns dark, and fratricide marks the first two brothers when Cain murders Abel. As a result, Cain is forced off the life-giving soil and must wander the earth, ironically settling in "the land of *Nod*," which means "land of wandering" (4:16).

Events move from bad to worse as fruit eating leads to fratricide that leads to Lamech threatening to kill any who dares to strike him (4:23). The massive flood ensues, brought on by the vast "wickedness of humankind" (6:5). The charge against humanity is all-inclusive and terrible: "every inclination of the thoughts of their hearts was only evil all day long" (6:5 alt.). God here is a God who repays bad behavior with universal attack. Yet, after the flood, the tale shifts, as God now acknowledges the weakness of the human creatures and promises never again to destroy them, even though "they are evil from their youth" (8:21 alt.). The same reason that provoked the flood now leads God to vow never to act like that again. In short, the flood's effect is to change the heart of God, not the heart of humanity.

That ongoing human weakness is shown in the person of Noah, the supposed hero of the flood story. After he plants a vineyard, he overindulges in the fruit of the vine, lies naked in his tent, and accidentally is seen as weak and vulnerable by his son Ham. He awakes from his stupor and instead of taking responsibility for his actions, curses his son, and the cycle of separation and family conflict begins again (9:18–25).

The first section concludes with the tale of the tower of Babel, a vast construction designed to create their own unity and to thwart YHWH's demand that they should be "fruitful, multiply, and fill the earth" (the land, 1:28). Though they imagine their tower "has its top in the heavens" (sky), YHWH must "go down" to see it (11:4–5). YHWH then decides to "confuse their language," and they are forced to cease their building, abandoning Shinar to "fill the earth."

The prehistory is an avalanche of evil, from garden to murder to threatened genocide to flood to family destruction to foolish tower building. Through it all, humanity is pictured as bent on evil, creating ingenious ways to reject the demands of their creator God, while that God, first destroying nearly all of them, finally demonstrates a willingness to persist with these recalcitrant humans. Something new is needed, and YHWH acts anew in Genesis 12. This tightly constructed section includes, for the preacher, a changing picture of God, a deeply flawed humanity, and a divine persistence to work with these humans regardless of their actions.

ABRAM AND SARAI (12:1–25:18)

Genesis 12:1–3 is the lynchpin of the entire biblical story. Abram of Haran is called by YHWH to "go from your country, your relatives, and the house of your father to the land I will show you. There I will make of you a great nation, and I will bless you, and make your name great, so that you will be a blessing, . . . and in you all the families of the earth will be blessed" (or, "will bless themselves") (alt.). Abram's task is universal and missional. YHWH will make Abram's name great, and that greatness will be defined as a blessing to all humanity through his own person and his descendants. The definition of greatness is service to the world. This central biblical theme is announced at the very beginning of the story of Israel, and no preacher can miss its prominent power.

Unfortunately, humans are weak and inclined toward evil. Abram is no different. He may be called to be a blessing, but his later actions are anything but a blessing. He soon sacrifices his own wife, Sarai, to the Egyptians in a craven attempt to save his own skin (12:10–16); if not for YHWH's intervention, Sarai would have joined Pharaoh's harem, and Israel's story would have ended before it began.

The ominous fact of Sarai's barrenness drives the remainder of this section's story. YHWH continues to appear to Abram to promise a son, but the years slip by, and the lines deepen on the aging couple's faces. In chapter 15, God promises a child, and Abram proposes that a household slave will be his heir, but YHWH calls him to count the stars, vowing that his descendants will be as numerous as they. In chapter 16,

Sarai takes matters into her own hands and offers her maid, Hagar, as Abram's bedmate in order to create an heir. A boy is born, but Sarai cannot stand the sight of the child and demands his destruction. Abram complies, but YHWH intervenes to save Ishmael and his mother. In chapter 17, God again promises an heir, but this time Abram falls on his face in laughter, and in chapter 18, when YHWH promises again, it is Sarah's turn to laugh at the absurdity of a prune-faced couple giving birth.

But, it happens, and the child is named Isaac, "laughter" in Hebrew (chap. 21). Yet that laughter soon turns to horror, as YHWH demands that Abraham murder that child of laughter on a mountain (chap. 22). Without a word, Abraham prepares to do so, but just as he is about to plunge the knife into the boy's throat, YHWH again appears to stop his hand. The spared child then has his own family, and the story turns to section 3.

This second section tells the story of Abraham and Sarah and the complex births of their sons, Ishmael and Isaac. The themes of human desires to direct the world in their own ways rather than allow God to direct the world in God's way, along with the reality of fractured human relationships created by self-serving hubris, all offer rich fare for any preacher.

ISAAC, REBEKAH, JACOB, ESAU, LEAH, RACHEL (25:19–36:43)

Jacob and Esau are born to Isaac and the previously barren Rebekah; they are twins with very different personalities. Jacob is "Grabby," a colloquial version of his Hebrew name meaning "Supplanter," pictured at his birth as grasping the elder Esau's heel. Esau is "Hairy," literally covered head to toe in hirsute splendor. Rebekah has been told by YHWH that, contrary to societal expectations, her younger child will master her eldest. And so it happens, but not without a maternal push. Esau sells his right to be firstborn to Jacob for a bowl of red stuff (25:29–34), and Rebekah helps Jacob to trick her husband out of the patriarchal blessing (chap. 27).

The themes of irony and trickery continue when Jacob flees his brother and heads to Haran, Abraham's home country. On the way, Jacob confronts YHWH at a lonely place, and receives from his God the promise of land, progeny, and protection. In response, Grabby bargains with YHWH, saying that if YHWH does do all these things, then and only then can YHWH be his God (28:20–22)!

In Haran, he meets Rachel at a well, falls instantly in love, and after seven years of service to his uncle Laban, is supposedly allowed to marry his beloved (chap. 29). But Laban substitutes his eldest daughter, Leah, and hands her, veiled, to the eager embrace of Jacob. When the daylight reveals the truth, Jacob asks Laban about his cruel trick. Laban replies that in this country one cannot marry the younger before the elder. Echoes of earlier tales of deception ring loud.

But Jacob gets his revenge on Laban as he steals the very best of his livestock through magical trickery, despite Laban's ploys (30:25–43). Though Laban works to prevent it, Jacob departs Haran with both of his wives, their servant women, and a vast herd of Laban's finest animals (chap. 31). Upon arriving at the Jabbok River, Jacob wrestles with a man there and claims to have defeated the man (32:28), whom Jacob imagines to be God (32:30). However, he does not actually encounter God until Esau receives him with surprising grace. With all that former trickery forgotten, Jacob is forced to admit that seeing Esau's face is just like "seeing the face of God" (33:10).

This section recounts the story of Jacob and Esau, introducing us to a foolish Esau, who in the end becomes the very face of God in his reception of his rascally brother. God is seen here as the unexpected One, not appearing as humans imagine but showing up in the face of the foolish. This great Bible theme offers a rich resource for the preacher.

JACOB AND JOSEPH (CHAPS. 37–50)

This final section of Genesis is the story of Joseph, the favored son of Jacob and Rachel. Jacob's twelve sons settle again in the land promised by YHWH, but soon strife in the family appears. Joseph is a preening tattletale, living for the opportunity to reveal to Jacob wrongdoing by his brothers (37:2). Nevertheless, Jacob loves Joseph to distraction, because he is a child of his old age with his favorite, Rachel. He thus weaves for him a "long robe with sleeves" (37:3). As a result, his brothers despise Joseph, and after two self-aggrandizing dreams in which Joseph sees himself as master over both his family and the sun, moon, and stars (!) (37:5–11), the brothers plot to kill him.

But instead of murdering Joseph, the brothers throw him into a dry well, imagining that they have seen the last of him. They lie to Jacob that Joseph has been devoured by beasts, but he is pulled from the well by passing traders and sold to an Egyptian nobleman, Potiphar. Soon clever Joseph is running Potiphar's household and attracting the lustful eyes of Potiphar's wife. The woman compromises Joseph, crying rape. Joseph lands in jail; but in no time, he is running the jail, too (chap. 39)!

And there he correctly interprets two dreams. When these interpretations come to the attention of Pharaoh, who is bedeviled by nightmares, he demands that the jailed dream interpreter act for him. Joseph's correct interpretations save Egypt from a severe famine (chap. 41).

Meanwhile, the famine spreads to Israel, and Jacob demands that the brothers go to Egypt to buy grain. Once there, they are ushered into the presence of their brother, Joseph, whom they do not recognize, since he is now Egyptian in appearance and speaks to them through an interpreter. He, however, recognizes them immediately and proceeds to play a cruel game of cat and mouse with them, first imprisoning one as ransom for the rest, after replacing their grain money back into their bags, then secreting his magic cup into the sack of Benjamin. All the while, Joseph weeps in secret (chaps. 42–45).

At last he reveals himself as Joseph, and the brothers are struck mute. Though he attempts to cover his lengthy game with theological niceties–"God sent me before you to preserve life" (45:7 alt.)–no polite phrases can undo the trickery of the revengeful Joseph.

At the very end of the tale, Jacob dies and is buried back in Israel. Yet the brothers still fear that Joseph will gain his ultimate revenge and "pay them back in full" for what they did to him (50:15). So they lie, claiming that the dying Jacob has bidden Joseph to forgive the brothers for their acts against him. The brothers then prostrate themselves before Joseph and cry out that they will be his slaves if he spares them (50:18). Joseph weeps as he hears them, and the weeping here is Joseph's recognition that he has poisoned his family with his cruel games. Then it is that Joseph utters his most famous phrase: "Even though you intended to do harm to me, God intended it for good, in order to preserve a numerous people" (50:20). "Fear not," he concludes, "I will provide for you and your little ones" (50:21 alt.).

Genesis ends in something like reconciliation, but it is a reconciliation fraught with tension. It is a kind of false ending, even when Joseph dies and is buried in Egypt. Unfinished business, both in the family and in the community, marks the conclusion of this tale; with the beginning of the book of Exodus, new tensions break out. God is again called on to struggle with God's chosen ones in new ways. Perhaps Israel, the new name of Jacob at Jabbok, does mean "God wrestles" after all.

The preacher finds the following themes stretching across the stories of Genesis: God's surprising appearances in and employment of unlikely and flawed people; human desires to go their own ways against the commands and will of God; God's final unwillingness to give up on God's sinning yet chosen people.

Exodus

LISA WILSON DAVISON

Exodus recounts the story of how God rescues God's people from bondage and leads them to a new land, just as God had promised Sarah and Abraham. In order to do this, God calls three liberators: Moses, Miriam, and Aaron. The final compilation of the book of Exodus probably took place during the exile (sixth century BCE), but many of the stories contained in the book may be much older. The exilic date reminds us that the book is not trying to accurately recount an actual event, but to tell a story of liberation. Exodus can be divided into three sections, based on different settings: Egypt (chaps. 1–15), the Wilderness (15–18), and Mount Sinai (19–40).

EGYPT (1:1–15:21)

Exodus picks up where Genesis ended, a few generations after Joseph and his brothers moved to Egypt. Joseph not only saved his family from the famine but also saved the Egyptians. He gained a place of power and leadership as the pharaoh's right-hand man. By the beginning of Exodus, however, things have changed. The new pharaoh does not remember Joseph, and the descendants of Sarah and Abraham are now slaves, called "Hebrews" by the Egyptians. By this time, the "Hebrews" have become numerous. Gone are the days of barren women. The Egyptians worry that these "foreigners" will become so powerful that they will rebel and take over the kingdom. Pharaoh uses several tactics to quell the potential threat, escalating the violence to a genocidal level, when slavery and hard labor do not reduce the Hebrews' growth. Two Hebrew midwives (Shiphrah and Puah) are instructed to kill all Hebrew boys at birth. The midwives' civil disobedience thwarts Pharaoh's plan, so he declares that all Hebrew boys be thrown into the Nile.

The story of Moses is both exciting and sad. Moses' survival from infancy, during a time when all Hebrew boys were to be drowned in the Nile, was nothing short of a miracle, orchestrated by his birth mother, his adopted mother, and his sister (2:1–10). The irony of Moses having to flee after murdering an Egyptian in defense of a helpless Hebrew slave (2:11–15a) builds suspense. Moses settles down in Midian, where he marries Zipporah, has a son (Gershom), and works for his father-in-law, Jethro (2:15b–22).

This hero's story pauses to allow an "intrusion note" about God hearing the groaning of the Israelites in their servitude in Egypt (2:23–25). What provokes their crying out? The text does not answer this question, indicating only that the people have managed to find a voice. Their cries prompt God to take action in the story. God has not been mentioned in chapter 2 until this point; suddenly in two verses (vv. 24–25), God is the subject of four important verbs; God "heard," "remembered," "looked," and "took note."

The story returns to Midian. Moses is tending the flocks of his father-in-law on the mountain called Sinai, or Horeb, a sacred place among the Midianites. He sees an incredible sight that the biblical writers could only describe as a bush that was "aflame yet not consumed by the fire" (3:2 alt.). Then, hearing a voice calling his name, he responds, "Here I am," and waits. From the bush comes the voice of God, and God tells Moses to take off his shoes because he is standing on holy ground. Moses does so and hears these words: "I am the God of your father, the God of Abraham, the God of Isaac, and the God of Jacob" (3:6).

The experienced biblical reader will recognize that Moses' fateful words, "Here I am," are a foreshadowing that something dangerous is about to happen. God is sending Moses back to Egypt, where he is a wanted fugitive. God has decided to "make good" on the covenant God made with the ancestors, a promise of land, offspring, and a relationship with God. God wants Moses to convince Pharaoh to let his primary source of slave labor go free (3:7–10). Moses protests against this mission. He cannot see why Pharaoh would listen to him and agree to this crazy idea. God tries to reassure Moses by promising to be with him as he stands up to the sole ruler of Egypt and risks his own life. God even gives Moses a "sign": "when you have brought the people out of Egypt, you shall worship God on this mountain" (3:12).

Still unconvinced, Moses tries another tactic. Feeling a bit daring, he asks God for God's name, and what he gets is a riddle. In the Hebrew Bible, to know someone's name could indicate that you have power over that person. In response to this request, God says to Moses: "'*eyeh 'asher 'eyeh*" (3:14). The traditional rendering of this Hebrew phrase as "I am who I am" only hints at the depth of the divine riddle. The word *'eyeh* is the first-person singular form of the verb "to be." Since Hebrew does not have true verb tenses (e.g., past, present, future, etc.), this word could be translated as "I am, I was, I will be, I have been," and so on. The second Hebrew word, *'asher*, is a relative particle and can mean "that, who, which," and so on. Thus, this "name" of God can be rendered in numerous ways in English, such as these:

> I am who I am.
> I was who I was.
> I will be who I will be.
> I have been who I have been.
> I am who I was.
> I will be who I have been.
> I am that I will be.

Moses cannot have just one word to name God. He, like all preachers and congregations, is reminded that the Divine is beyond human control and comprehension. God's answer indicates that the only way Moses, the Israelites, or anyone else can "know" God is through God's activity in the world or through God's interaction with humanity.

The stories about the dueling between Pharaoh and Moses/God are a key to understanding the function of the plagues (chaps. 5–12). Like all oppressive powers, Pharaoh is unwilling to grant freedom for his slave workforce. The resulting struggle between a God of freedom and human greed reveals that Israel's God is not only more powerful than Pharaoh but also more powerful than the Egyptian gods. Unfortunately, the liberation of an oppressed group of people rarely happens without a level of suffering and violence.

While the plagues are intended to show God's power, they do seem to be an unfair punishment for the Egyptian people. This story reminds us that, most often, the people suffer the consequences of the actions taken by the powerful. Looking at the ten plagues, it is clear that the first nine really did not directly affect Pharaoh. When the waters of the Nile were made unsafe for drinking, the Egyptian people had to dig ditches to find potable water (7:24). Pharaoh, however, had other people to secure his water supply. Likewise, when the locusts ate the crops of the Egyptians (10:1–20), Pharaoh did not go hungry. He had the means and the power to get all the food he wanted, at the expense of the innocent people under his control.

It is only with the last plague, when Pharaoh's son dies, that the repercussions of his oppressive actions affect him directly. Only then does Pharaoh decide to let the Israelites leave. In fact, he sends them away out of fear; he would do anything to appease the Israelites' God and get relief from the curse he was enduring. The killing of the first-born children of the Egyptians, of course, presents some troubling theological questions with which preachers should struggle. What kind of God kills innocent children?

One explanation can be found in the text. When God sends Moses back to Egypt, God tells him to deliver this message to Pharaoh: "Thus says the LORD: Israel is my firstborn son. I said to you, 'Let my son go that he may worship me.' But you refused to let him go; now I will kill your firstborn son" (4:22–23). This is a foreshadowing of how this struggle for liberation will end. From this literary perspective, the tenth plague parallels what Pharaoh has done to the Israelites. The violence continues when Pharaoh realizes what he has done (i.e., just freed his slave labor force) and decides he wants them back. He sends his entire army after the "escaped" slaves, and they pursue the Israelites with the intent of returning them to slavery or killing them. When Pharaoh's army traps the people at the edge of the Sea of Reeds, the Israelites become frightened and blame Moses for leading them out this far only to be killed. As a way of showing the Israelites and Pharaoh that God has the power and is on the side of the oppressed and vulnerable, Moses splits the sea in two parts. Dry land appears, and the Israelites cross safely to the other side.

What happens next is shocking, but it is the only way that the powerless Israelites can be saved from Pharaoh, the powerful. When the Egyptian army enters the dry seabed, in pursuit of the runaways, the waters return to their normal state, and the Egyptian charioteers are drowned. The picture of this watery battlefield evokes memories of other battlefields with dead bodies left where they fell. Pharaoh's campaign to enslave the Israelites again is a vivid reminder of that senseless loss of life.

When we read the Exodus story, it is tempting to identify with the oppressed Israelites. However, many of us today are more like Pharaoh or at least the Egyptians. How do our comfortable lives and participation in the global economy keep others from enjoying a full life? How do we harden our hearts to the suffering of others? What will it take to change our hearts, so we release our grip on power and privilege?

WILDERNESS (15:22–18:27)

The second section of Exodus tracks the Israelites' journey from Egypt to Mount Sinai. These "Wilderness Wanderings" describe a period of getting acquainted. The people learn about this God who liberated them from slavery in Egypt, and the Lord comes to a better understanding of the kind of people the Israelites are. It is a period of "courting," before any firm commitments are made. Having just witnessed God's saving power, the people begin to complain about the less than ideal conditions of their current situation. This story is part of a larger collection of texts in which the Israelites "murmur/quarrel" against Moses and/or Aaron for their plight; in so doing they complain against God.

This section provides several possible homiletical questions about the nature of faith. In what ways do we, like the Israelites, struggle to trust God, others, and ourselves? How often are we not content with what we have? When do we "quarrel/murmur" against God?

SINAI (CHAPS. 19–40)

At Sinai, after all God has done for the Israelites, God lays out their responsibilities of living in covenant relationship. Up to this point, God has been patient and gracious with what often appears to be an ungrateful people. Now they have reached a point of decision making; they must either sign on to a lifelong covenant with God or face a future on their own.

The Ten Commandments (20:1–17) deal with both the vertical relationship between Israel and God (vv. 3–7) and the horizontal relationships between Israel and other parts of creation and among the Israelites (vv. 8–17). In Israel's covenant with God, both aspects were of equal importance: one could not be in right relationship with God without being in right relationship with the rest of creation.

At Sinai, God gave the Israelites an invitation to enter into a covenant and provided a set of guidelines for acceptable behavior in that relationship (20:1–21). The Lord then gives Moses more commandments that expand on the original "Top Ten" (20:22–26; 22:16–31; 23–30). While the Lord provides these other requirements, Moses is gone from the people for a long time. In his absence, they become restless and insist that Aaron make them tangible gods, breaking the second commandment (32:1–2). The Lord had warned them that there was "zero tolerance" for idols and severe punishment for the perpetrators. Aaron does not try to dissuade them from this faithless act. He makes a golden calf (v. 4), makes an altar, and declares a "festival to the LORD" (v. 5). In the morning, the people bring offerings and make sacrifices to the calf, and after eating, they begin to "revel" (v. 6).

Seeing how quickly the people have betrayed the covenant, the Lord is overcome with anger and, perhaps, with disappointment. The Lord no longer wants to claim the Israelites, so the Lord puts the responsibility for them on Moses. So great is the divine anger against the people that the Lord wants to be alone so that the Lord's "wrath may burn hot against the people" (32:10) until it consumes them.

Moses, who had wanted to give up on the Israelites at times when they complained, now defends them. Moses' tactic for persuading the Lord not to destroy the people is very astute. He does not try to gain a stay of execution for the people based on their character or faith; there is too much evidence to the contrary. Instead, he argues on the basis of God's character. Moses appeals to the Lord's ego, reminding the Lord of the covenant made with Israel's ancestors (32:13a). If the Lord kills the people in the wilderness, then the Lord will break the divine promises of many descendants, a land, and a relationship with the Lord (32:13b). Moses succeeds, and the Lord keeps covenant.

As the story of Israel shows, the relationship between Israel and God was never easy. Given that these stories are Israel's self-portrayal, it is amazing that the compilers of the Hebrew Bible have not attempted to "clean up" the people's imperfections. They have painted a picture of a human community struggling to live in right relationship with God, with neighbor, and with self. Sometimes the Israelites succeeded, but more often they failed. Preachers do well to present contemporary people of faith in such an honest light.

Preachers also should recognize that while some of the ancient stories portray a violent Deity, those depictions were not meant to be taken literally; rather, those stories demonstrate the seriousness of breaking covenant and the Lord's passionate expectations of the people, even knowing how often they had messed up. And indeed, even though they did not deserve God's mercy and steadfast love, God chose to grant them forgiveness over and over, while still holding them accountable for their sins.

Leviticus

J. DWAYNE HOWELL

Leviticus is the third book in the Pentateuch and is situated in the Sinai tradition (Exod. 19:1–Num. 10:10). While the book is associated with the priestly class of Levites, it does not name the Levites until 25:32–34 in the purchase of land for the Levitical cities. The Levites, though, are associated with the tribe of Levi, and the setting aside of Aaron and his sons for anointing as priest may be an antecedent to identifying the priests as Levites (chaps. 8–10). Along with being set within the Sinai tradition, Leviticus is also the center of the Priestly Code (Exod. 25:1–Num. 10:10), a series of rituals and narratives portrayed as the giving of instructions for the proper worship of God and the proper relation with one another. The instructions provided in the Priestly Code were intended for the whole congregation of Israel, to ensure against priestly exploitation.

While Leviticus is depicted as being received by Moses during the exodus, it most likely is a collection of material developed through Israel's history that found its final form in postexilic times as priests sought to establish orderly religious practice in the rebuilding of Judah. Preachers should give special attention to the connection between rituals and community since the rituals described in Leviticus sought to express and preserve the basic values that were to be lived out by the Israelites.

Leviticus is primarily a collection of legal material containing only three narrative segments: the ordination of Aaron and his sons and priestly misconduct (8:1–10:20); the institution of the Day of Atonement, *Yom Kippur* (16:1–34); and blasphemy of the divine name and its punishment (24:10–23). The book itself is set up as a series of divine speeches to Moses (cf. 26:46; 27:34). Two distinct sections are identified in Leviticus: In chapters 1–16 is the Priestly section, providing instruction for proper rituals and cleanliness; in chapters 17–26 is the Holiness Code, addressing the community's relation with one another and the world. Leviticus 27 serves as an appendix with additional regulations.

INSTRUCTIONS TO THE PRIESTS (CHAPS. 1–16)

The first seven chapters of Leviticus are devoted to instructions concerning sacrifices in Israelite worship. Practiced throughout the ancient Near East, sacrifices took on various meanings. For some they were a way to sustain the gods or to appease their anger. Other traditions viewed them as a means to encourage fellowship and provide a gift of thanksgiving to the Divine. In Leviticus, the chief duty of the priests is to oversee the sacrifices. Leviticus 1:1–6:7 identifies five distinctive types of sacrifice: the whole burnt offering (1:1–17); the cereal offering (2:1–16); the peace offering (3:1–17; cf. 7:11–12, 28–36); the sin offering (4:1–5:13); and the guilt offering (5:14–6:7).

The participant brings the best animals or produce to be offered and does the primary work of preparing and offering the sacrifice while the priest ensures that it is done properly. Two of the sacrifices, the cereal offering and the peace offering, are freewill gifts intended to express gratitude for divine provision. Both sacrifices had portions given to the priests as a mean of sustaining the priesthood (2:3; 7:28–36). The final two sacrifices deal with the atonement for specific offenses (the sin offering) and offenses that involve restitution (the guilt offering). These two sacrifices were only for unintentional sins and could not be offered for premeditated sins, which were beyond the sacrificial system. Also, the regulations for the sin offering makes allowances for the poor to participate in the sacrificial system, underlining the importance for all in the community to be able to participate.

Leviticus does not present the sacrifices as magical ways to win the favor of God, and the act of offering a sacrifice did not obligate God to the Israelites. Sacrifices could be rejected by God (cf. Gen. 4:3–7). The sacrifice is to represent the changed heart of the participant. Thus, even in the concept of the sacrifice one finds an emphasis on grace over works.

Following the narrative section concerning the ordination of Aaron and his sons in Leviticus 8–10, chapters 11–15 address what is considered unclean and clean to the people of Israel. More than simple dietary regulations, these instructions encompass all that the Israelites may encounter in their daily lives, including bodily fluids, unusual growths on the body, housing, and clothes. These cleanliness laws sought to protect the community, especially the tabernacle, from being separated from God's presence. Leviticus 11–15 seems to be an insertion between chapters 10 and 16. Leviticus 16 begins by recounting the death of Aaron's two sons for an irreverent act (10:1–3). Still, Leviticus 16 offers an apt conclusion for the first portion of Leviticus as it describes the development of the Day of Atonement, *Yom Kippur*, a national day of repentance for Israel (vv. 29–34; cf. 23:26–32).

The rituals described in Leviticus 1–16 provide the preacher not only opportunity to understand the place of ritual in the Old Testament but also the opportunity to discover the place of ritual in today's worship.

HOLINESS CODE (CHAPS. 17–26)

The Holiness Code is the oldest part of material compiled in Leviticus. It addresses the entire congregation of Israel, often using the divine self-introduction ("I am the LORD," "I am the LORD your God") and calling for Israel to be "holy" (set apart), dedicated to the service of God (19:2). While legal requirements are a part of the Holiness Code (chaps. 17, 18, and 20), the section also emphasizes that ritual observance must be accompanied by ethical behavior.

Leviticus 23 provides an example of ritual observance, describing six holy days that serve to remind the community of God's actions in the past and guidance in the present. The Sabbath is to be celebrated weekly and serves as a time of assembly and rest (v. 3). The remaining holy days were to be celebrated annually. The Passover along with the Feast of the Unleavened Bread and First Fruits are reminders of the exodus from Egypt and God's provision in the land (vv. 4–14). The Feast of Weeks celebrates the first summer harvest and provides instruction for care for the poor in the community (vv. 15–22). The last three holy days occur in the seventh month of the year. The Feast of Trumpets marks the New Year on the first day (vv. 23–25). The Day of Atonement on the tenth day is a national day of repentance (vv. 26–32; cf. Lev. 16). Finally, the Feast of Tabernacles begins on the fifteenth day and lasts for a week. The community is to live in tents as a reminder of God's provision in the wilderness and a mark of the end of the harvest season (vv. 33–43).

Chapter 19 lists types of ethical behavior for the community in its relationship with family, servants, and strangers, based on a practical application of the Ten Commandments:

1. Honor father and mother (v. 3)
2. Keep the Sabbath (vv. 3, 30)
3. Have no idols (v. 4)
4. Do not steal (vv. 11, 35–36)
5. Do not lie (v. 11)
6. Do not swear by God's name falsely (v. 12)
7. Maintain appropriate sexual relations (vv. 20–22, 29)
8. Do not hate your brother or take vengeance (vv. 17–18: the word used in the sixth commandment for "not to kill" deals with the idea of blood vengeance)

Readers should note the emphasis on God as being holy throughout the chapter and its changing foci.

Preachers may not expect to find it in Leviticus, but an important homiletical theme to be drawn from the book is its emphasis on social justice. Chapter 19 provides a lens to see such justice in practice. It emphasizes the care for the stranger/immigrant in the land alongside the love of neighbor (vv. 18, 33–34). Such hospitality was vital for survival in the ancient Near East and is still practiced in the Middle East today. Likewise, part of the harvest, the gleanings, is to be left for the poor and the stranger for food. The laborer and the neighbor are to receive fair treatment (v. 13), and female slaves are not to be abused (vv. 20–22). The deaf and the blind are not to be victimized (v. 14). All are to be treated fairly in the community, both rich and poor (vv. 16–17).

Leviticus 25 also addresses the proper treatment of the land and others. This is prime homiletical material in that no other ancient document addresses the connection between the land and its people. The way one treats the land is often mirrored in how the person treats others. If the land is seen as a means to an end, often people are seen the same way. The Sabbath Year calls for the land to remain unfarmed, to rest, every seven years (vv. 1–7). Every fifty years, the Year of Jubilee (vv. 8–17), all debts are to be forgiven and all land is to be returned to its original owners. Such debt forgiveness was to be equitable, so no one would be cheated (v. 17). Both the Sabbath Year and the Year of Jubilee are intended to ensure against the abuse of both land and people and to remind the people that God owns the land and no one else held the authority to use it for selfish purposes (v. 23). Instead, the people are to view the land as a gift to be shared. The proper treatment of others and the land are still pertinent issues today.

Chapter 26 functions as the conclusion for Leviticus (with chap. 27 functioning as an appendix with additional instructions). It offers a choice to the people whether to follow God's instructions or not, showing the conditional nature of the covenant. Two sets of cause-and-effect speeches provide the Israelites with their choices. If the people "follow my statutes and keep my commandments" (v. 3) then God will bless them with prosperity and protection (vv. 4–13). However, if they choose not to obey and honor God (vv. 14 and 15) then God will bring destruction on the people (vv. 16–39). Even if the Israelites refuse to repent, the land will keep its sabbaths (v. 34; cf. v. 43). Mercy may be found, though, and God will remember the covenant with the patriarchs if Israel confesses its sins (vv. 40–42). Still, God will remember the people even in times of punishment (vv. 43–45).

Leviticus has often been misconstrued by preachers as no more than a series of outdated rituals and prooftexts for debates regarding sexuality. Instead, it offers insight into what it means to be the people of God. The instructions include all the people and are not just limited to the religious leaders. Rituals are to be expressions of changed lives and gratitude, not a way to make God obligated to the Israelites. Sacrifices are to be an offering of a part of themselves.

Community plays a significant role in Leviticus. Cleanliness laws are to provide protection for the whole community. The rituals are open to all to participate, no matter social and economic position. The Israelites are to live out the ritual in the ethical behavior expressed toward others. People can easily take advantage of others, but the teaching of Leviticus emphasizes that all are to be treated fairly, just as God deals with Israel fairly.

Numbers

J. DWAYNE HOWELL

Numbers is the fourth book of the Pentateuch, named for the censuses that are taken in chapters 1–4 and 26. While depicting the exodus period, it is composed of a variety of material dating between 950 and 450 BCE. The Hebrew name for the book, *Bemidbar,* "In (the) Wilderness" is based on the first verse of the book, "The LORD spoke to Moses *in the wilderness* of Sinai." "In the Wilderness" is an apt name for the book because the entire book is spent in the wilderness as the Israelites journey from Sinai to the Plain of Moab, moving toward the Promised Land, continuing the Sinai tradition beginning in Exodus 19. However, this journey takes a generation. Whereas, Numbers begins, "on the first day of the second month, in the second year after they had come out of the land of Egypt," Deuteronomy begins, "in the fortieth year, on the first day of the eleventh month" (1:3). Something happens in the book of Numbers that stalls the entry into the Promised Land for almost thirty-nine years. Numbers shows the tension between God's guidance and the people's rebelliousness and the cost it will impose on the Israelites. The wilderness also represents chaos in Hebrew thought, and special attention should be given to the chaos that arises as Israel constantly challenges God's guidance.

DEPARTURE FROM SINAI
(CHAPS. 1–12)

The first four chapters deal with four different censuses in Numbers:

> 1:2–54, every male twenty years or older except for those in the tribe of Levi
> 3:14–39, the counting of the Levites
> 3:40–51, the numbering and redemption of all firstborn males
> 4:1–49, the division of the Levites among the Kohathites, the Gershonites, and the Merarites, each with specific area of service

Chapter 2, the tribal arrangement around the tabernacle, is inserted in the census narratives after the counting of all males over twenty years old, those of military age. The tribes are set up as regiments on the east, south, west, and north sides of the tabernacle, with the Levites stationed with their assigned tribes. The dominant tribes in Israel's later history, Judah and Ephraim, are positioned in two central areas. Judah is placed on the east side at the entrance of the tabernacle, while Ephraim is placed on the west side, the side of the Holy of Holies. Judah's favored location at the entrance may be a reference Judah's later favored position because of its association with the Davidic line.

Numbers 5:1–10:10 deals with final preparations before leaving Sinai. Chapter 5 emphasizes the need to place unclean people, those with leprosy and those who have touched a corpse, outside the camp. The regulation is put in place to protect the camp because ritual uncleanness was thought to be contagious (cf. Lev. 15:31).

Numbers 6 introduces the role of the Nazirite vow in Israel (vv. 1–21). Though elsewhere it is portrayed as a lifetime commitment (Judg. 13:2–7; 1 Sam. 1:9–11, 22), here the Nazirite vow is stated to be a limited commitment (vv. 5, 13). The chapter closes with the Aaronite Blessing (vv. 24–26):

> The LORD bless you and keep you;
> the LORD make his face to shine upon you, and be gracious to you;
> the LORD lift up his countenance upon you, and give you peace.

Numbers 7:1–10:10 tells of the final preparations for leaving Sinai, including the celebration of the Passover (9:1–14).

As the Israelites leave Sinai, the first of several revolts occurs in Numbers 11, despite the preparation and worship described in the previous chapters. The Israelites complain about having only the manna to eat and long for the food they had in Egypt. In response, God sends a feast of quail, but it is quickly followed by a plague as a punishment for the Israelites' lack of faith (vv. 31–35). In the narrative Moses delegates his authority to seventy elders, who begin to prophesy when they are empowered by the Spirit of God (vv. 16–25). Elsewhere Moses also delegates his authority (Exod. 18:13–27, under Jethro's guidance; Deut. 1:9–18, under God's guidance). In the Numbers narrative, Joshua becomes concerned when two additional men, Eldad and Medad, begin to prophesy though they are not part of the seventy (vv. 26–28). Moses responds to Joshua, "Are you jealous for my sake? Would that all the LORD's people were prophets, and that the LORD would put his spirit on them!" (v. 29). Moses' words serve as a challenge in the church today as some would want to deny others the opportunity to speak because of their gender or sexual orientation/identity.

The second act of rebellion occurs within Moses' own family as Miriam and Aaron try to assume Moses' authority (Num. 12). Since Moses had married a Cushite woman, they attack his qualifications to lead the Israelites. (While some scholars locate Cush as Ethiopia, it can also refer to Midian, and be a reference to his wife, Zipporah.) Aaron and Miriam believe he is incapable of mediating for the people because of this marriage. God sides with Moses in the conflict and strikes Miriam with leprosy (vv. 5–12). The one who wants to become a leader, therefore, now becomes an outcast. Upon Moses' intercession, Miriam is healed, but she will remain outside the camp for a time of repentance (vv. 13–16). This story and the story of the manna and the quail emphasize for the reader the importance of trust in God.

TRAVELS AROUND KADESH-BARNEA
(CHAPS. 13–21)

A third rebellion occurs as Israel prepares to enter the Promised Land (Num. 13–14). In this story, Israel is to enter Canaan from the south soon after leaving Sinai. Twelve spies are selected, one from each tribe, to travel and investigate the land for forty days. When the spies return, they tell of the abundance of the land. However, ten of the spies believe that the Israelites cannot conquer the land due to its strong inhabitants.

The two remaining spies, Joshua and Caleb, offer a "minority report" saying that God will provide the victory if they remain faithful (13:30; 14:6–9). Instead, the Israelites listen to the majority of the spies and rebel against Moses. Despite God's intent to destroy rebellious Israelites, Moses mediates for them and turns God's anger back (14:13–19). The Israelites attempt to take the land after they have forsaken God's guidance. In response, God punishes the Israelites for their insurgence by not allowing any from this generation to enter the Promised Land (14:26–45). They will wander in the wilderness one year for every day the spies were in the land (14:34). The only exceptions are for Caleb and Joshua, who had remained faithful (14:24; 32:12; cf. Josh. 14:6–15).

The primary location for the wilderness wandering centers on Kadesh-Barnea. The people continue to revolt against Moses' leadership. In Numbers 16, Moses is challenged by 250 men led by Levitical leaders Korah, Dathan, and Abiram (vv. 2–3). In response, God destroys the insurgents (vv. 31–35). The Israelites revolt because of these deaths, and only the intercession of Moses and Aaron spares their lives (vv. 41–50).

As the Israelites prepare to leave Kadesh-Barnea, they begin to complain about the lack of water (20:1–13). Though Moses is commanded to speak to the rock to bring forth water, he instead strikes the rock, and water begins to pour out from it. Yet, since Moses had not honored God's instructions exactly, he will be forbidden from entering the Promised Land. The place is called Meribah (contention) since the people did not honor God because of their strife. A parallel Meribah story is told in Exodus 17 when the people complain about thirst on the way to Sinai. In this account Moses is told to strike the rock (vv. 5–7).

As they continue toward the Promised Land, the Israelites persist in their complaints. God sends fiery serpents as punishment, to bite them (Num. 21:4–9). Many become sick and several die. Moses once again intercedes for the people and is commanded to fashion a bronze serpent and hold it up on a pole. All who look up at it are healed. (The bronze serpent, Nehushtan, becomes a religious relic that will be worshiped by Israel, and King Hezekiah will destroy it during his religious reform; 2 Kgs. 18:4.) The forty-year wilderness wandering represents the loss of a complete generation. Similarly, it may take a church a complete generation to recover from poor decisions.

ENTRY INTO THE PLAIN OF MOAB
(CHAPS. 21–25)

God provides victories for Israel as they advance toward the Plain of Moab (21:21–35). Attempting to turn back the Israelites, Balak, a Moabite king, hires Balaam, a Mesopotamian holy man, to put a curse on the Israelites (Num. 22–24). Though Balaam refuses at first to come to Moab, he finally agrees, but with the caveat that he will only speak what the Lord tells him. In a series of humorous stories, including a talking donkey (22:21–35), Balaam gives a series of oracles that blesses Israel and curses all of Israel's enemies (23:1–24:25).

Trouble again emerges as Israel is encamped on the Plain of Moab (chap. 25). Some of the men begin to associate with the sacred prostitutes of Moab and take part in the worship of Baal of Peor. A plague ensues on the Israelites (v. 8; cf. 31:16). God instructs Moses to kill the leaders of Peor and all the Israelite men who worshiped Baal of Peor. Numbers 31 tells of the destruction of the Midianites, associated with Peor, by the Israelite army. Balaam is among those killed, being accused of introducing the sacred prostitutes to the Israelite men (31:16). All the people are put to death or enslaved: men, women, and children.

MATTERS THAT ARISE DURING THE
WANDERING (CHAPS. 26–36)

Numbers 26–36 serves as an appendix and includes additional information about the Israelites in the Plain of Moab. An additional census is taken in Numbers 26. Joshua is named as the successor to Moses (27:12–23). Instructions for sacrifice and the celebrations for holy days are in Number 28–29. The tribes of Reuben and Gad request land in the Transjordan (chap. 32). Israel's history from the exodus out of Egypt to its arrival in the Plain of Moab is recounted in Numbers 33. Numbers 34–35 sets out the boundaries of Canaan and the placement of Levitical cities and cities of refuge.

Since a generation has passed away, new laws are established for issues that have emerged. Many of these deal with the rights of women. Since over time many had become widows, what would be the right to their husbands' property, and what are the rights of women in general? Women are allowed to keep the property, but it must remain in the deceased husband's family if sold (27:1–11; 36:1–12). Likewise, any vow made by a woman could be overruled by her husband (30:1–16).

Numbers is the story of Israel's journey from Sinai to the Plain of Moab. Preachers should note the contentiousness of the journey as the Israelites struggle against God's guidance and the underlying theme of a lack of trust and faithfulness. Moses serves as a mediator between God and Israel, which sins throughout the story. The obstinance of Israel leads to a generation dying in the wilderness. As the story ends in the Plain of Moab, anticipation awaits as a new generation readies to cross the Jordan River into the Promised Land.

Deuteronomy

J. DWAYNE HOWELL

The name "Deuteronomy" means "second law." The developed nature of its theology and legal interpretation places its final form in the seventh century BCE. Deuteronomy is one of the most influential books in the Bible and provides the preacher with a resource for understanding Hebrew Bible traditions and interpretation.

Narratively speaking, it serves as both a conclusion of the Pentateuch and a link to Israel's history in the Promised Land. The book retells the story of Israel's time in the wilderness, its preparations to enter the Promised Land, and the transition of authority from Moses to Joshua, providing a conclusion to the Pentateuch. However, it is also a link to the book of Joshua as it anticipates the conquest of the Promised Land.

Theologically speaking, Deuteronomy shares an outlook (and writing style) found in the books that follow: Joshua, Judges, 1–2 Samuel, and 1–2 Kings, which are referred to as the Deuteronomistic History. The theology of Deuteronomy is also important for many of the Prophets and it is believed to be the scroll of the law associated with the reforms of Josiah (2 Kgs. 22:3–23:27) and Ezra (Neh. 8). Finally, Jesus often refers to Deuteronomy. In the temptation in the wilderness, Jesus responds to the three temptations by quoting from Deuteronomy each time (Matt. 4:4 and Deut. 8:3; Matt. 4:7 and Deut. 6:16; Matt. 4:10 and Deut. 6:13). Also, when Jesus is asked about the greatest commandment, he cites the Shema (Matt. 22:37–38; Deut. 6:4–5).

The book is arranged as three final speeches by Moses to the Israelites.

1:1–4:40, a retelling of the events of the exodus
4:41–26:19; 28:1–68, the giving of the Law
29:1–30:20, a call for the Israelites to renew their covenant
    with God

Two additional sections complete the narrative. First, inserted into the second speech, Moses gives instruction for a covenant-renewal ceremony to be held at Shechem once the Israelites have settled into the land (27:1–26; cf. Josh. 24:1–28). Second, the conclusion of the book (chaps. 31–34) give the details of the final events of Moses' life and then his death.

A theme that runs throughout the whole of Deuteronomy, to which preachers should attend, is that Israel has a choice to make: follow God and be blessed, or reject God and be cursed.

RETELLING THE STORY OF THE EXODUS (1:1–4:40)

Moses' first speech is a historical review reminding the people of God's guidance through the wilderness. The Israelites are now in the fortieth year of their journey because of the previous generation's failure to trust God (1:19–45; cf. Num. 13–14). Moses recounts the conflicts and battles that Israel has faced on its journey (2:1–3:29). The historical review emphasizes God's guidance throughout the wilderness, despite the Israelites' stubbornness. Recounting God's provision and appeals to Israel's faithfulness as the people enter the Promised Land is an important theme. Another emphasis in Deuteronomy with homiletical potential is that the Lord is the only God: all other gods are false deities. In Deuteronomy 4:35 the writer states, "To you it was shown, that you might know that the LORD is God; there is no other besides him" (RSV).

GIVING THE LAW (4:41–26:19; 28:1–68)

The second Mosaic speech retells the giving of the law. In 5:1, Moses calls to the assembly, "Hear," which is another common theme in the book of Deuteronomy upon which preachers should draw. To "hear" is more than just the auditory reception of sound: it is to be obedient and take appropriate action. For example, 6:4–5 is called the "Shema" (Hear), based on the command "Hear, O Israel." It is a prayer calling for Israel to remember that there is only one God and that they are to love "the LORD your God with all your heart, and with all your soul [being], and with all your might [strength]." (Jesus called this "the greatest and first commandment" in Matt. 22:37–38.) The Israelites are to live out the Shema daily by making it a part of their daily prayers, remembering it in all their travels, and teaching it to their children. They are to wear it on their foreheads and forearms in leather boxes known as phylacteries. They are also to put it on their doorposts as a reminder of the Shema in their coming and goings. Today, little boxes called mezuzahs, containing the Shema, can be found on the entry doors of Jewish homes.

Why would there be such an emphasis on hearing and obeying in Deuteronomy? First, the history recounted in the first four chapters tells of the people's disobedience and distrust of God in the wilderness. Now, as they are about to enter a land already inhabited, they are to remember their fidelity to God. The temptation will be to adopt the false worship practices of the land and forget God. Thus, they are to remember the laws they have been taught and are to teach them to their children (6:6–25). Also, they will be tempted to forget their dependence on God as they become prosperous in the land, and thus they need to continue to be faithful. Chapter 9 reminds the people that the land is not a reward for their faithfulness: they have been disobedient. Only by Moses' intercession can they now enter the land. Thus the Israelites are reminded to remain faithful to God so that they will continue to be blessed (8:1–10; cf. 7:12–26; 11:1–31; 28:1–14). However, if they reject God's guidance, they will be cursed (8:11–20; 28:15–68).

An important chapter for all ministers is Deuteronomy 18, the promise of a prophet like Moses to serve as a mediator for the people (vv. 15–22). The chapter serves as both a call and a warning. The prophet will be from among the people and will speak the words of God (vv. 17–19). However, if the prophet speaks on their own accord or of false gods, the prophet is to die (v. 20). Such an action may seem extreme, but when ministers speak on their own today and do not speak the word of God, they also die, perhaps not physically but by reputation, losing the trust of those they lead.

Deuteronomy 27 is an independent element that the author inserted into the giving of the law, providing instructions for a covenant-renewal ceremony at Shechem. Moses addresses first the elders (vv. 1–8), then the priest (vv. 9–10), and finally the people (vv. 11–26). The words to the people consist of twelve curses for disobedience. The covenant-renewal ceremony is to be celebrated once they are in the Promised Land at Shechem (cf. Josh. 24:1–28). Shechem plays a vital role in the history of Israel; it is where Abraham first entered the land (Gen. 12:6) and where the covenant with Abraham is completed by the Israelites' conquest and settlement of the Promised Land.

CALL TO RENEW THE COVENANT (29:1–30:20)

Moses' third speech begins with a covenant ceremony on the Plain of Moab. Once again, he reminds the people that they must choose between two ways.

The first way, the good way of obedience, will bring blessing and life (30:1–16, 20). There will be a new sign of the covenant, not the circumcision of the male foreskin, but a circumcision of the heart (cf. 10:16; Jer. 31:33; Ezek. 11:19; 36:26–27). No longer will they have an outward sign of the covenant, but now they will have an inward sign of a changed heart as evidence of God's blessing. Also, no longer is the covenant limited to males, but all can participate in it.

The people are likewise reminded that the second way, the way of disobedience, will bring only destruction and death (30:17–18). If they decide to serve other gods, they will not survive long in the land. Only by remaining loyal to God will the Israelites be secure in the land.

CONCLUSION (31:1–34:12)

The final chapters detail the concluding events of Moses' life. Joshua is named as his successor (31:1, 3, 7). Joshua had been introduced in Exodus as a leader in the battle against the Amalekites (Exod. 17) and became an assistant to Moses at Sinai (Exod. 24:13; 32:17; 33:11; Num. 11:28; 27:12, 18, 22). His actions remind the people of what it means to be faithful to God.

Moses instructs that the law be read to the people every seven years at the Feast of Booths as a reminder to each generation of Israel's covenant with God (31:9–29). The public reading of a covenant is a part of ancient Near Eastern treaties. Already in Deuteronomy Moses has reminded the people of their history in the wilderness and how their disobedience brought failure and punishment (1:1–4:40). Each generation needs to be reminded of God's call to obedience. To neglect the practice of teaching the law to the next generation can be disastrous (cf. Judg. 2:10).

The Song of Moses (31:30–32:43) praises God for divine faithfulness but chastises Israel for its unfaithfulness. The poetic piece reminds us that other songs in the Hebrew Bible are attributed to Moses (the Song of the Sea, Exod. 15; a Psalm of Moses, Ps. 90). The Song of Moses in Deuteronomy is presented as a covenant lawsuit against Israel. The people have been protected by God, yet they have continually turned away from God. Moses uses the poem as a warning to the people preparing to enter the Promised Land. And they are to take it "to heart" and teach it to their children as well (Deut. 32:44–47).

As Moses prepares for his death, he blesses each one of the tribes (33:1–29). God instructs Moses to go to the top of Mount Nebo and to look toward Jericho in the land of Canaan. There he will die since he is not allowed in the land because of his sin at Meribah (32:48–52). Deuteronomy 34 recounts Moses' journey to Nebo and his death. Verses 10–12 provide his epitaph:

> Never since has there arisen a prophet in Israel like Moses, whom the LORD knew face to face. He was unequaled for all the signs and wonders that the LORD sent him to perform in the land of Egypt, against Pharaoh and all his servants and his entire land, and for all the mighty deeds and all the terrifying displays of power that Moses performed in the sight of all Israel.

Deuteronomy places Israel at a crossroads. They are on the Plain of Moab, preparing to enter the Promised Land. In the past is their enslavement in Egypt, the exodus event, and a forty-year journey to reach this place in time. Their journey has often been marked by their distrust of God. Only by the faithfulness of God and the intercession of Moses have they been able to arrive at this point. Now the challenge is placed before them: trust God and be blessed in the land, or reject God and face destruction.

Joshua

LISA WILSON DAVISON

The book of Joshua follows on the heels of Moses' farewell in Deuteronomy. It contains stories about how the Israelites took over the Promised Land, or at least parts of it. About half of the book is about the "conquests" of different cities in Canaan, and the other half focuses on how the Promised Land will be divided among the tribes of Israel. Several themes of homiletical importance are found within Joshua: God keeps promises (e.g., the ancestral promise of a land); a concern for "insiders" and "outsiders" (e.g., Rahab was an "outsider" who became an "insider" because of her protection of the Israelite spies in Josh. 2); and the achievement of "rest" (11:23).

While the overall impression of the biblical story is that the Israelites conquered the whole of Canaan, destroying the inhabitants of the land, there is very little evidence (e.g., archaeological, extrabiblical, etc.) to support a violent taking of the land by an outside group. Even the biblical texts indicate some exceptions to the massive conquest (13:1–6). Many scholars argue that the Israelites emerged within the Promised Land as a mix of current inhabitants and some immigrants to the area. Yet even if the genocide of the people in Canaan never happened, we are still left with troubling texts of a seemingly violent God.

In the ancient Near East, war was a constant threat, and belief in warrior deities was commonplace. Israel relied on one God, who was responsible for all of life. When war was unavoidable, Israel understood it as sacral, with God as the guiding force behind human efforts. Any victory was not their doing; they should always give God the credit. God's desire for justice and righteousness oftentimes required the elimination of the forces that would thwart the establishing of shalom. During the "conquest of the Promised Land," Israel understood themselves to be the instruments of their Warrior God. (Later, however, the Israelite prophets would show the two-edged nature of this divine metaphor. When they perpetrated injustice and unrighteousness, Israel also could be the recipients of the Warrior God's effort to make shalom a reality.)

Israel's "Warrior God" may not be our preferred image of the Divine. There is an inherent danger in connecting religion and violence. This, however, is not the most prominent image of the Divine within these sacred texts. Like all the language used for God, describing God as a "warrior" is metaphorical and should not be understood literally.

This book begins what scholars commonly refer to as the Deuteronomistic History, which includes Joshua through 2 Kings. In the first half of the twentieth century, biblical scholars theorized that these books were the work of one writer/composer, who sought to record a history of Israel during the Babylonian exile. In more recent years, scholars have come to envision the creation of this "history" as being the work of more than one person, perhaps a "school" or at least a group of theologically like-minded people. Utilizing a variety of sources, the Deuteronomistic Historians retold Israel's story, from emergence in the Promised Land until the fall of Jerusalem, pointing out where the people "went wrong" and made mistakes that eventually led to the exile (e.g., choosing a human ruler over God, worshiping other gods, failing to care for the vulnerable, etc.). Since this recounting was done through hindsight, the compilers could clearly identify the bad decisions and the ways that the people broke covenant with God and with each other.

It is important to remember that this version of Israel's "history" was told from the perspective of the powerful, and thus it represents only one view of how the events leading to the exile unfolded. What the Deuteronomistic History presents for the reader is an act-consequence ("You reap what you sow"; cf. Gal. 6:7) understanding of God's interaction with Israel (humanity). When the Israelites were faithful to the covenant, God "blessed" their lives. However, when the people broke the covenant, God "punished" them. A sample cycle goes like this: the Israelites break a commandment; God punishes them by not giving the Israelites a victory over an enemy; the Israelites repent;

God grants them another chance and a victory. This is seen in the story of Achan (Josh. 7). Because Achan did not abide by God's command to utterly destroy everything in the city of Jericho, the Israelites are unable to conquer the city of Ai. Once Achan and his household are properly punished, the Israelites are able to take Ai. Even when Israel breaks covenant, most often God forgives the Israelites and gives them another chance.

ENTERING THE PROMISED LAND (CHAPS. 1–4)

In the first chapter, God reiterates information that Joshua should know: "Moses is dead." God then charges Joshua with leading the Israelites into the Promised Land. However, before this crossing into the land can take place, something is required of the community. The people are told to prepare themselves for this upcoming experience. Joshua says to the community, "Sanctify yourselves" (3:5). The Hebrew word translated as "sanctify" comes from the root word with the basic meaning of "holy" and is often used to describe God and God's holiness. The form used here indicates that the people are to make themselves "holy as God is holy." In order for the people to gain the full benefit of what God is about to do, they must prepare their whole selves to stand in the presence of the Divine and to be transformed by God's presence and a promise of an unknown future.

In the next few chapters of Joshua, the Israelites cross the Jordan River, via a path formed when the waters cease flowing for a time, and encounter the native peoples of the land. It is clear that the writers are intent on making connections between the exodus from Egypt and the entering of the Promised Land. Thus, just as the Sea of Reeds split in half for the Israelites to escape Pharaoh's army and cross from oppression to freedom, the Jordan River miraculously provided safe passage into the Promised Land, marking a transition from uncertainty to security (Josh. 3). Joshua is paralleled with Moses as the people's leader for this next step of their journey. In his final address in Deuteronomy, Moses has already identified Joshua, son of Nun, to be his successor as leader of the people (Deut. 31). Thus on one level, the first part of the book of Joshua is about God ordaining Joshua as the divinely recognized leader of the Israelites. On another level, however, it is about Israel's transformation from wandering in the wilderness to settlement in the Promised Land.

LIFE IN THE PROMISED LAND (CHAPS. 5–23)

Once the Israelites have a presence in the Promised Land, they observe an early form of the Passover (5:1–10), as directed in Exodus 12. However, before this ritual can take place, all the Israelite males, who were born in the wilderness, must be circumcised to keep the covenant established with Abraham (cf. Gen. 17). This all took place at Gilgal, making it one of the first holy sites in the Promised Land. On the day after the Passover, we are told that the Israelites ate food made from crops grown in the land that God had promised to their ancestors. On the day that they partook of the abundance of the land of Promise, the daily sustenance of manna provided by God throughout the wilderness journey ceased. This is an important marker for the biblical audience. It is at this point in Israel's story that the Israelites transition from a people without a home to a settled people. God has granted them a land for them to grow and harvest, so they can feed themselves. There is no more need for the manna. A new phase of the relationship between Israel and God is beginning, and the future stretches out with unknown possibilities.

COVENANT RENEWAL (CHAP. 24)

The book of Joshua concludes with another key event of Israel's emergence in the Promised Land. Joshua gathers the Israelites at Shechem for a covenant-renewal ceremony. This complies with the instructions God gave Moses and the people at Mount Sinai to take the commandments out of the Ark of the Covenant and read them aloud for the whole community to hear on a regular basis. Then the Israelites would be given the opportunity to affirm/reaffirm their commitment to the covenant. This would be particularly important for future generations, allowing them to decide, for themselves, whether they were willing to enter into the covenant that God made with their ancestors (Exod. 24:7).

Having survived the wilderness wanderings and the "conquering" of Canaan, the Israelites are offered a chance to "get right" with God. After reminding the people of all that he and God have done for them, Joshua asks the people to choose whether they will be faithful to the God who brought them this far or follow other gods. Not just once, but twice the Israelites affirm their commitment to serve God and to keep the covenant at all costs (Josh. 24:16, 18). With the relationship renewed, Joshua sends the people back to their homes and can die in peace. Whether the Israelites remain true to the covenant is yet to be seen.

The idea of a covenant-renewal ceremony may seem strange to us today; however, this text provides important insights for the twenty-first century. While we want to believe that the promises we make (to God or to one another) are sincere and will not be forgotten, the complications of life have a way of making those promises fade. What would it be like if we had opportunities to renew our commitments on a regular basis? This text from Joshua is an opportunity to preach about the importance of making and keeping covenants (with God and with others).

CONCLUDING REFLECTIONS

A great deal has changed over the millennia that separate us from the writers of Joshua. Our modern world has helped us to know many things. We can explain why the sun rises and sets each day, and how carbon dioxide becomes oxygen. Diseases that long ago would have wiped out an entire population are now either preventable or treatable. We have twenty-four-hour access to events happening around the world and can chat online to loved ones in faraway places.

All of our knowledge and technology, though, have not made life any more certain or the future any less unknown. The fears and hopes of a group standing on the eastern shore of the Jordan River bear a great similarity to those of our postmodern society. What does the future hold for us? What awaits us on the other side of our "river"? Will we keep covenant with the Holy One? Questions such as these will drive sermons based on Joshua.

Judges

LISA WILSON DAVISON

The book of Judges claims to recount the stories of ancient Israel from the time of settling in the Promised Land until right before the beginning of monarchy. During these early decades of life in the Promised Land, the people are led by charismatic and mostly military leaders called "judges." In Judges, the role of a "judge" (Hebrew *shophet*) does not match the role of judges today (i.e., presiding over the proper application of law in the legal system). The primary function of the biblical judges is to be a military hero and overthrow whatever outside power is controlling Israel. Then, usually, the judge leads the people for a certain period of rest. A few times these "judges" do have a more traditionally judicial role (e.g., Deborah), but that is never their primary function.

According to the text, there are twelve "official" judges of Israel, those who are actually identified by this title. Each of them is identified as God's choice to deliver the Israelites from a foreign oppressor. Once this is accomplished, there is a time of "rest" for Israel. The numbers connected to the majority of the judges' reigns reveal a chronological scheme; all are factors of ten (20, 40, 80, etc.). Here is a list of the judges and the chapters in which their story is told:

Othniel (3:7–11)
Ehud (3:12–30)
Shamgar (3:31)
Deborah (chaps. 4–5)

Gideon (chaps. 6–8)
Abimelech (chap. 9)
Tola (10:1–2)
Jair (10:3–5)
Jephthah (10:6–12:7)
Ibzan (12:8–10)
Elon (12:11–12)
Abdon (12:13–15)
Samson (chaps. 13–16)

This book is the second in what scholars commonly refer to as the Deuteronomistic History, which includes Joshua through 2 Kings. In the first half of the twentieth century, biblical scholars theorized that these books were the work of one writer/composer, who sought to record a history of Israel during the Babylonian exile. In more recent years, scholars have come to envision the creation of this "history" as being the work of more than one person, perhaps a "school" or at least a group of theologically like-minded people. Utilizing a variety of sources, the Deuteronomistic Historians retold Israel's story, from emergence in the Promised Land to the fall of Jerusalem, pointing out where the people sinned and made mistakes that eventually led to the exile (e.g., choosing a human ruler over God, worshiping other gods, failing to care for the vulnerable, etc.). Since this recounting was done through hindsight, the compilers could clearly identify the bad decisions and the ways that the people broke covenant with God and with each other.

What the Deuteronomistic History presents for the reader is an act-consequence ("You reap what you sow"; cf. Gal. 6:7) understanding of God's interaction with Israel (humanity). When the Israelites are faithful to the covenant, God blesses their lives. However, when the people break the covenant, God punishes them. The act-consequence theology of the Deuteronomistic History comes into full view in Judges, which follows a consistent circular pattern of apostasy-oppression-repentance-salvation.

The book is set in a time in Israel's history between entry into the Promised Land and the beginning of the monarchy, the "time of the Judges." From a literary perspective, some scholars have identified the materials in Judges as "historical romances," with "historical" referring to the literary setting (not that they are meant to be reliable sources for history) and "romances" indicating the important role that

heroes play in the stories. The stories are more concerned with recording the legends surrounding the leaders of different groups than with
recording historical events. The collection also serves as a reminder
of the importance of keeping covenant with God. There were always
temptations to follow other gods, to be like other nations, but Israel
is given the challenge and the opportunity to worship only their God.

Judges describes a time of turmoil, in which the Israelites are portrayed as living in tribes who have a loose association, usually centered
on worship and/or necessity for survival (e.g., water, military support,
etc.). No permanent human leader ruled in the land because the people were to understand God as their only ruler. However, the people
continually break covenant with God and, as a result, suffer under the
hands of foreign powers. Only when the people repent of their sin and
call out to the Lord does God send a means of deliverance in the form
of a leader (judge), who acquires the needed victory over the enemy.
The reader can easily see that many of the judges' traits are not what
would be considered today as valuable or ethical. One such example
is the story of Jephthah (chap. 11). This military hero is remembered
not only for his victory over the Ammonites but also for sacrificing
his daughter because of a bargain he made with God before going
into battle.

One of the best-known judges is Deborah. She is the only female
judge named in the Bible. Her story appears in a prose version (chap. 4)
and then in a poem (chap. 5). Deborah is first introduced as a prophet
who is "judging Israel," and as *eset lappidoth* (4:4). This last phrase is
usually translated as "wife of Lappidoth" but may be better rendered
as "a women of flames." When Deborah takes up her position under
a palm tree in the "hill country of Ephraim," the Israelites go to her
for adjudication of their disputes. In this first encounter, then, Deborah actually fulfills the role that we envision for a "judge" today. She
is also identified, however, as a "prophet" and as a "warrior" leading
the Israelites into battle. God visited Deborah, giving her a message
for her military commander, Barak. She tells him that the time has
come to defeat Sisera and Jabin's army and put an end to the Israelites'
oppression. Barak is not eager to take on this mission, given that the
Canaanites' military is described as more advanced in weaponry than
the Israelites' army: they had "nine hundred chariots of iron" (4:3).
Even though God has promised to give Barak and the Israelites the
victory, he tests Deborah's sincerity and honesty. Only if she will go,
too, will Barak take on the mission. She agrees to accompany Barak

and the army into battle. The Israelites are victorious, and the poem in chapter 5 celebrates Deborah's leadership in the battle, along with the assistance they gain from Jael, who assassinates the Canaanite general Sisera. This deliverance is followed by forty years of peace in the land.

Deborah's story provides preachers the opportunity to lift up the different roles Israelite women could fulfill and to show that God calls women, as well as men, to important roles that require faithfulness, intelligence, and boldness. If, as suggested above, Deborah is not married (and never described as a biological mother), then her story demonstrates that women can be leaders and make a difference in the world without having to fill the traditional roles of "wife" and "mother." Deborah is valued for her wisdom and her role as a prophet

Another well-known judge is Samson, a legendary character who seems to have had more brawn than brains (chaps. 13–16). His birth story contains an angelic announcement to his mother that her son should be a Nazirite (13:1–5; cf. Num. 6:1–21) and will deliver the Israelites from the hand of the Philistines. The adventures of Samson include demonstrations of his strength and sexual prowess, alongside his breaking the Nazirite vows and losing a wife. Samson does wreak violence on the Philistines, but his ego and impulsiveness lead to his ultimate capture by this enemy, thanks to Delilah. In what amounts to a suicide attack, Samson does throw the last blow, killing thousands of Philistines by tearing down their temple. His family recovers his body and buries him in the family tomb. The summation of Samson's career is that "he judged Israel twenty years" (Judg. 16:31).

Judges ends with the statement: "In those days there was no king in Israel; all the people did what was right in their own eyes" (21:25). This sets the stage for why a monarchy, or at least a centralized government, was needed to bring order to the Israelites and aid in their keeping the covenant with God and each other. However, Israel's having a human monarch turned out to have its own set of problems, as described in Samuel and Kings (cf. Deut. 17:14–20).

The book of Judges frightens many contemporary readers and often is used as evidence about how the "God of the Old Testament" is vengeful and not the "loving God of the New Testament." While the presence of disturbing stories in Judges cannot be denied, much of the fear and misuse of the book stems from skewed and misinformed interpretation, from the belief that every story in the Bible has been recorded as something to be emulated. In spite of, dare one say because of, those texts, this biblical book offers many lessons and insights to

preachers and congregations who are willing to give the time and attention needed for a faithful reading.

The story of the Levite's concubine (Judg. 19) is an example of a
story that elicits the question of how it is helpful to one's faith. This
chapter recounts the story about a man who throws his concubine to
a mob in Gibeah. She is gang-raped all night and left, nearly dead, at
the doorstep of the house where the Levite is staying. The man is so
angry at what has been done to his "property" that he cuts her into
twelve pieces and sends them to all Israel as a motivation for war. This
horrible story seems to have no homiletical possibility. However, the
story of the Levite's concubine, perhaps, can serve as a mirror, helping
modern communities of faith to ask where human lives are being torn
apart in humanity's desire for vengeance. Likewise, what if the story
of Jephthah's daughter is remembered not as an example to follow but
as a way to shock contemporary readers into wondering who are the
daughters of Jephthah in our world? How are children being sacrificed
on the altar of our desires for power and success?

Judges reflects a time in Israel's story when life was extremely precarious, when violence was the preferred way to settle disputes, when
wars were waged in the name of God, and human lives were traded
for protection and political power. Unfortunately, things are not that
different today. Maybe that is the real reason we do not want to preach
these texts; they hit just a little too close to home. In confronting them,
we might also have to confront our own injustice and violence. We are
blessed that our spiritual ancestors did not preserve only the "pretty"
stories of their faith struggles. Their willingness to record the not-so-
pretty tales of the human condition provides us the opportunity to
confront our faults and unfaithfulness.

Ruth

LISA WILSON DAVISON

Although it is set in the time of the Judges, most scholars believe Ruth was written during the postexilic period (after 538 BCE) as a response to the extreme prejudice against "foreign" wives reflected in the book of Ezra. Its "historical vagueness" gives the story a timeless quality. The only chronological "anchor" in the book is the genealogy in chapter 4, which some scholars think was a later addition to the text in order to connect Ruth and David.

Ruth is a short story characterized by elevated prose, a well-developed plot, a satisfying denouement, and great irony. This genre was often used in ancient Israel to entertain and to teach, somewhat like a parable. While God does not explicitly appear in the narrative until the last chapter, the clear sense is that God has been at work throughout the story. This biblical book seems to make the claim that the divine is found in the ordinary rather than in the extraordinary.

Ruth has two settings: Bethlehem and Moab. The opening chapter moves quickly between Bethlehem and Moab, setting up the main plot for the entire book. The geographical shifts (Bethlehem to Moab to Bethlehem) also reflect the different moods of the story. The characters move from scarcity (1:1–2) to emptiness (1:3–18) to despair (1:19–22) to hope (chaps. 2–3) to fulfillment (chap. 4).

The story opens in Bethlehem, where Naomi and Elimelech live with their sons, Mahlon and Chilion. There is a famine in the land (1:1), a first ironic twist of the story: *Beth-lechem* translates from Hebrew as

"house of bread," yet there is no bread in the "house of bread." Elimel-
ech moves his family to Moab, where there is food. To the ancient
Israelite audience, this decision signals possible danger. According to
Genesis 19:36–37, the Moabites are the descendants of an incestu-
ous relationship between Lot and his eldest daughter. For Naomi and
Elimelech, living in Moab is a foreshadowing of the coming disasters.

Soon after settling in Moab, Elimelech dies, and Naomi is left a
widow in a foreign land with two sons, who marry Moabite women:
Orpah (wife of Chilion) and Ruth (wife of Mahlon). The ancient audience would have also viewed the intermarrying with foreign wives as a
bad move, and not much time passes before both Mahlon and Chilion
also die, without producing a male heir. Naomi is in the unenviable
position of being a childless widow in Moab with two childless foreign daughters-in-law (1:5). Having heard that the famine is over back
home, Naomi decides to return to her homeland.

Orpah and Ruth, having left their homes and married foreign men,
assume that they should follow their mother-in-law to Bethlehem. As
childless widows, they are in a situation similar to Naomi's, so they
start with her on the journey to what will be a foreign land for them.
Realizing that she has nothing to offer the women and they could cause
trouble for her (Naomi may not be welcome in Bethlehem if she is
accompanied by two Moabite women), Naomi encourages Orpah and
Ruth to stay in Moab, each to return to her "mother's house" (Ruth
1:8). When the women are not persuaded, Naomi tries a more forceful
approach, reminding them that she has no more sons to offer them.
Even if she were able to birth more sons, Orpah and Ruth would not
want to wait for the boys to reach a marriageable age. With this argument, Orpah decides to take her chances back home.

Ruth is not convinced. She makes a covenant with Naomi, a commitment to be with Naomi, no matter what it costs her (1:16–17).
By leaving her homeland, her religion, and her people, Ruth becomes
Naomi's companion for the remainder of their life's journey. In the
ancient world, women without husbands and sons were in one sense
quite vulnerable, but they also had a certain level of freedom. Naomi
and Ruth's relationship no longer has to be about competition; now it
needs to be based on cooperation. After Ruth's pledge of loyalty, there
is nothing left for Naomi to say. The women travel together. When
Naomi and Ruth arrive in Bethlehem, the women of the town hardly
recognize Naomi. She declares that her name is no longer Naomi, but

that they should call her Mara ("bitter," 1:20). Blaming God for the tragedies of her life, she settles in Bethlehem with Ruth.

Although Naomi is not pleased to have Ruth follow her back to Bethlehem, her daughter-in-law turns out to be her salvation. Naomi, consumed with bitterness at her lot, decides to wait for death. Ruth refuses to let her give up and goes to find them some food (2:1–3), seeming to know about the Israelite practice of leaving the edges of a field unharvested to leave that grain for widows, orphans, and strangers (cf. Deut. 24:17–22). Either by happenstance or divine providence, Ruth finds the field of Boaz, Elimelech's kinsman, and begins to glean the leftover grain. When Boaz learns who Ruth is, he shows her great generosity and respect. He tells his servants to watch out for Ruth and to let her gather extra grain (Ruth 2:4–17).

Ruth returns home and tells Naomi about being in Boaz's field. It is now the elder woman's opportunity to pass on wisdom to Ruth. She tells Ruth to stay with Boaz's female servants; a woman gleaning alone in the field would have been easy prey for attackers (2:22). Naomi also realizes it is her responsibility to help Ruth (and herself) find future security. Because of the patriarchal culture of Israel, Ruth and Naomi need a male protector, and Naomi develops a plan to help secure that necessity. She instructs Ruth to go to the threshing floor, after the celebration of the barley harvest and threshing, to make Boaz an offer that hopefully he will not refuse. When Boaz has drunk too much and falls asleep on the threshing floor, Ruth will capitalize on his weakness and "convince" him to marry her. Naomi instructs Ruth on how to dress, where to go, and what to do when she meets Boaz (3:3–4). The plan works like a charm. Boaz agrees to marry Ruth, as long as the closer relative of Elimelech does not want to do so, and sends her back to Naomi with some extra grain (3:7–18).

At the city gate, where legal matters are settled by the elders, Boaz confronts the other relative. Upon realizing that redeeming Elimelech's property requires him to marry a Moabite woman, the relative releases his right of redemption, and Boaz receives the elders' approval to marry Ruth (4:1–10). Then the people and the elders offer a blessing that references Rachel and Leah, wives of Jacob, and Tamar, the daughter-in-law of Judah who tricked Judah into impregnating her. All three of these women went to great lengths to secure justice for their families and to make certain that the ancestral covenant of Israel survives for a new generation.

Boaz and Ruth marry, and she gives birth to a son. Boaz, having fulfilled his role as redeemer (essentially a sperm donor), disappears from the story. In the closing scene (4:14–17), we are provided with a beautiful consummation of the partnership formed between Naomi and Ruth. Naomi is holding her grandson, and the women of Bethlehem vocally affirm the importance of her relationship with Ruth. The story concludes with the genealogy showing that Ruth is the great-grandmother of King David.

Naomi and Ruth face incredible obstacles to gaining the justice a patriarchal society denies them; they are two women in a man's world. They do not let their lack of authority, however, stop them from ensuring their future and that of their people. As the final scene closes on this love story, Ruth and Naomi, along with Obed, can live together, just the three of them, as a complete family.

As one of only two books named for women, Ruth provides the opportunity to preach about women living in patriarchal society. While many might say there is little parallel between the male-dominated society of ancient Israel and twenty-first-century cultures, there is ample evidence that patriarchy is alive and well. Today, too many women are forced to take great risks in order to secure their futures. Often, they must "work" the system to attain justice and equality, only to be criticized for behavior that is valued in men. Ruth is the embodiment of God's faithfulness and demonstrates the inherent worth of all people, regardless of gender or ethnicity.

1 Samuel

PATRICIA K. TULL

As part of the narrative sequel to the Pentateuch, which extends from Joshua through 2 Kings, 1 and 2 Samuel relate Israel's transition from a tribal society led by various regional "judges" to the dynastic Davidic monarchy. First Samuel begins with the birth of the final judge, Samuel himself, and extends through the kingship and death of Saul. Interwoven with Saul's story is that of young David, who will succeed him in 2 Samuel.

Temptations besetting leaders emerge throughout the books, as successive figures rise, encounter obstacles, and succumb. Two leaders—one on his way out of favor and one on his way in—are often set side by side as if to offer contrasts for readers' examination. The book of 1 Samuel explores the human heart's knowability, the ambiguities of political and military actions, the tense relationships between personal and public matters, the challenge of facing failure and success with dignity, and the tragedies of mental and familial instability. Besides the four leaders—Eli, Samuel, Saul, and David—many memorable secondary characters appear, from Samuel's mother, Hannah, to the widowed and dying daughter-in-law of Eli, the giant Goliath, Saul's offspring Michal and Jonathan, the ill-fated priest Ahimelech, the surly Nabal and his quick-thinking wife Abigail, the trusting but misled Philistine Achish, the frightened but compassionate woman of Endor, and the devoted inhabitants of Jabesh-gilead who rescue Saul's body from Philistine disgrace.

In addition, God plays a mysterious and often troubling role, communicating through direct speech, prophetic messages, casting of lots, meteorological phenomena, astounding coincidence, and the possessing of characters by spirits, whether helpful or harmful. A God who is clearly independent of humanity will nevertheless shows surprising receptivity to human initiative, continually adapting to unfolding events, showing favor and disfavor at will for reasons often left unstated. Such a characterization of God reflects understandings found in ancient literature of surrounding nations, of divine beings as powerful, immortal, but not necessarily irreproachable. To a remarkable degree, however, circumstances reflect a recognizable universe that does not operate on fairness but can be influenced by human behavior.

Eight semicontinuous passages from 1 Samuel appear in the Revised Common Lectionary during Year B in Ordinary Time. In addition, Hannah's song in chapter 2, the story of Samuel as a boy in chapter 3, and David's anointing in chapter 16 occur out of context in other parts of the year. Though the Lectionary only uses chapters 1–3 and 8 (regarding Samuel) and chapters 16–18 (regarding David), omitting the vast majority of Saul's fascinating story, 1 Samuel is not a series of isolated events but one interlinked saga. Thus preachers may choose to expand the sequence throughout a season to explore more fully the book's psychological and theological richness and will certainly need to place any passage on which they preach in the larger narrative context.

ELI AND SAMUEL (CHAPS. 1–3)

First Samuel opens with the family of Elkanah, who travels yearly to worship at a shrine in Shiloh, where the priest Eli officiates. Not uncommonly for the time, two women share one husband. Tragically, one of them remains childless. When Hannah goes alone to the shrine to pray (1 Sam. 1:9), she is at first mistaken for a drunkard by the physically and spiritually unperceptive priest Eli. When she clarifies her distress, he blesses her. She leaves comforted and, sure enough, becomes pregnant. Revealing to her husband her vow to dedicate this child to God's service, she returns the young boy to Shiloh, entrusting him to Eli.

Hannah's exultant song, following in chapter 2, announces themes prevailing throughout Scripture, down to Mary's Magnificat in Luke 1.

A series of parallel clauses that portray the just God as defeater of the powerful and defender of the powerless is summed up in the statement "Not by might does one prevail." The final verse leaps ahead, foreshadowing that God "will give strength to his king, and exalt the power of his anointed" (2:10).

Hannah's song celebrates her own reversal of fortune, but other reversals quickly follow. Eli's sons, barely mentioned before, receive a scathing review as cheating scoundrels. Their story alternates with affectionate portrayals of Samuel as chapter 2 prepares for the boy's call by God to speak up against Eli and his sons, providing crucial context for an episode that is more fraught than selective reading would suggest.

The familiar story follows of God's calling the young Samuel by night and being mistaken three times for Eli. Obeying Eli's instructions, Samuel responds to God and hears God's message condemning Eli. Eli demands to know the message and responds with resigned acceptance. Harshly judged for his sons' abuses, he becomes the first of the book's rejected leaders. Undiscerning as he is, Eli shows himself decent, kind, and God-fearing, setting an example that later failed leaders will not find grace to follow. As Samuel grows up, he is established as a reliable prophet and leader in Eli's stead.

THE ARK OF THE COVENANT (CHAPS. 4–6)

First Samuel 4 links the above story with that of the ancient symbol of God's presence, the ark of God, which resides at Shiloh, and unfolds disasters already foreshadowed: the battlefield deaths of Eli's sons and the ark's capture by Philistine foes. Upon hearing the news, Eli likewise dies. But in later chapters, the ark has a story of its own, overcoming its captors through its direct threats both to human health and to the Philistine god, Dagon, whose statue is repeatedly found fallen before it. The Philistines send the ark away, and it is joyfully welcomed at Israel's border.

SAMUEL AND SAUL (CHAPS. 7–15)

In chapter 7, Samuel is found twenty years later, calling the people to recommit to God. Their faithfulness ensures victory when the Philistines attack, demonstrating the effectiveness of Samuel's leadership. By chapter 8, however, times have changed. He has grown old and, like Eli, placed his two sons in charge. But like Eli's sons, they prove to be dishonest. So the people ask for a king. Samuel reacts badly, but God's response is mixed, telling him to listen, because it is not Samuel, but God, whom they are rejecting. Warning them against royal acquisitiveness and violence, Samuel reluctantly acquiesces.

Saul is introduced in chapter 9 as a young man seeking his father's donkeys. Approaching Samuel for help, he is instead anointed to be king. Samuel foretells a series of signs confirming God's participation. Samuel then summons the people, scolds them again, and proceeds to choose a king by lot. When Saul is picked, he is discovered hiding. Almost immediately, though, he zealously defends the threatened city of Jabesh-gilead, sealing his kingship.

In chapter 12 Samuel calls everyone to Gilgal, where he delivers a chapter-long speech rehearsing his fair dealings with all, reviewing their ancestors' sins, and once again scolding the people for requesting a king, setting up Saul's reign for the failure it will soon become. Twice in succeeding chapters (13 and 15) the two men quarrel over unclear orders disobeyed, resulting in Saul's rejection by Samuel, but not in his immediate removal from the throne.

From chapter 13 onward, Saul's own blunders help undermine his reign. Snared in conflict between Samuel and the people, Saul cannot help but fulfill Samuel's warnings. Yet his sin is not greed, as Samuel predicted, but misplaced zeal. In chapter 14 he quarrels with his brave son Jonathan and loses face when his troops support the son against him.

God's turning point comes in chapter 15, when Saul defeats the Amalekites but captures their king alive, failing to execute him. Samuel confronts Saul, and they again argue. The chapter concludes with God expressing regret over Saul.

Thus Samuel shows himself to be an unyielding leader, unable to apprentice another. Saul is portrayed as a trainee willing to please, whose confidence erodes with every scolding. He will subsequently seesaw between rigidity and humility, savagery and nobility, losing ground not only in God's eyes but also in the eyes of his followers and readers. Thus Saul's story exemplifies the tragedy of leaders undermined and finally undone by others who refuse to cede control.

SAUL AND DAVID (CHAPS. 16–31)

At God's initiative, Samuel anoints another monarch in chapter 16. From this point onward, attention will alternate between two parallel narratives, the painful story of Saul's downfall and the winsome story of David's rise. Tradition has preferred to focus on the latter, more sanguine narrative, in which providence prevails for good rather than ill. But this is no simple tale.

The well-known story of David's anointing follows the biblical trope of favoring the younger sibling. This anointing results in God's spirit departing from Saul and staying with David, and Saul being tormented by "an evil spirit from God" (16:14). Saul's condition ironically leads him to hire David to play music to soothe him. Thus David enters Saul's court as musician.

The challenge by the Philistine warrior Goliath in chapter 17 occasions David's second introduction to Saul. Displaying both ambition and zeal, David inquires about Goliath until he is brought to Saul. David assures Saul that he can defeat the giant, then does so with a single stone. Thus David appears as a nimble warrior, outwitting stronger opponents—capacities he will soon need in relation to the king himself.

Saul's son Jonathan is captivated with David. In a gesture signaling his coming abdication, he gives David his own robe and weapons. Envying David's growing popularity, though, Saul tries four times in chapter 18 to murder him. The lectionary departs from 1 Samuel in the midst of this story, with tensions between the two anointed kings mounting, and only resumes in 2 Samuel 1 with news of Saul's death.

But there is far more to the story. While chapters 16–18 have furnished insight into Saul's nature, readers do not yet know David. Nor are we likely to understand him well without paying close heed to what remains unsaid by and about him. Whereas the narrator often speaks directly about what Saul is feeling and thinking, David's inner life remains hidden, leaving a blank that Saul fills in with the worst of conjectures and that readers aware of David's later prominence tend to fill in with more grace. As the story shuttles back and forth between Saul's and David's locations, both men are endangered by enemies without, but preoccupied by their own rivalry. The ironic twists of this increasingly Shakespearean tragedy, unfolding in a few pages, issue finally in David's flight to seek refuge with the Philistines while boldly betraying them, and in the deaths of Saul, Jonathan, and Saul's two other sons in battle against these same enemies. Saul's years of missteps offer David time to grow into leadership, as well as opportunity to consider how he will do the job better. Second Samuel will show whether the next leader handles success more gracefully than his predecessors have handled failure.

2 Samuel

PATRICIA K. TULL

As part of the narrative sequel to the Pentateuch, which extends from Joshua through 2 Kings, 2 Samuel continues the story from 1 Samuel of Israel's transition from a tribal society to David's reign. David was first introduced as a rival to Saul's throne in 1 Samuel 16. Following Saul's death at the end of 1 Samuel, David becomes king.

Second Samuel is occupied throughout with David as ruler. It describes David's rise to kingship, the consolidation of his power, and the disastrous events arising from his acts of sexual misconduct and murder. Its sparely narrated but thickly woven plot resounds with ironies and psychological acuteness. Shifts in David's psyche are revealed as events unfold, and he moves from an unshaken confidence in his partnership with God to a more profound recognition of God's independence. God's portrayal in 2 Samuel remains understated, visible only at certain dramatic junctures, creating a sense of a just order working itself out despite, and sometimes even through, human evil.

Besides David and God, one character present throughout is David's nephew and military leader, Joab. A ruthless pragmatist loyal to the throne, Joab carries out campaigns, assassinations, and retaliations, some authorized by David and many not. His violence helps bring David's inner conflicts into sharper relief. Many other characters also appear, including members of Saul's and David's families, prophets, military leaders, and friends. The famed Bathsheba remains a mysterious figure whose feelings and motives have eluded centuries of curiosity.

Seven semicontinuous passages from 2 Samuel follow the 1 Samuel readings in the Revised Common Lectionary in Ordinary Time of Year B, and one more occurs on the Reign of Christ. Second Samuel 7 also appears in Year B's Advent lectionary readings.

Since 2 Samuel is one continuous narrative, it is crucial for preachers to know what precedes and follows in order to resist oversimplifying individual scenes. Tradition's wish to admire a leader who is, in fact, portrayed as ruthlessly violent presents ethical challenges that contemporary preachers should not ignore. Realism about human nature, and about limits in comprehending divine nature, can help preachers read the stories through ethical eyes. David is neither saint nor villain.

DAVID REIGNS IN JUDAH
(CHAPS. 1–4)

After Saul's death in 1 Samuel 31, an Amalekite messenger arrives whose story conflicts with the version previously told, in which Saul committed suicide. The messenger attempts to play the middle, both lamenting Saul and bringing his crown and armlet to David. He claims to have killed Saul, but only at his request. Readers know this is a fabrication; David does not.

David's reaction to the news is violently indignant. He has the man executed for having destroyed "the LORD's anointed" (1:14), and laments for Saul and his son Jonathan. David's reasons for mourning Saul are economic, but his grief for Jonathan is personal, reflecting the two young men's friendship.

David immediately begins maneuvering himself into power, gaining rule first in chapter 2 over the southern tribes. Meanwhile, Saul's commander, Abner, crowns as king a surviving son of Saul named Ishbosheth (Ishbaal). This man's insecure position crumbles when he accuses Abner of sleeping with Saul's concubine Rizpah. Abner indignantly vows to support David but learns that he must first bring to David Saul's daughter Michal, who was long ago deserted by David and given to another man. That pure politics has overrun familial affection is underscored in the snapshot of Michal's husband, Paltiel, weeping behind her until Abner orders him away (3:16). In quick succession Abner and Ishbosheth are murdered (3:27; 4:6), but David stands aloof from these deeds.

DAVID REIGNS OVER ISRAEL (CHAPS. 5–10)

Chapter 5 inaugurates several events consolidating David's kingship. With the field of potential rivals cleared, the Israelite tribes who followed Saul now woo David and anoint him king some twenty chapters after his secret anointing by Samuel in 1 Samuel 16. David attacks the Jebusite town of Jerusalem, situated between the north and south, and makes it his capital.

In chapters 6 and 7, David seeks to unite church and state: first, by bringing into Jerusalem the ancient symbol of divine presence, the ark of God, and second, by housing it permanently near his palace. In both cases God weighs in. When David tries to bring the ark from Abinadab's home, where it resided throughout Saul's reign, it proves no safer for human manipulation now than before: Abinadab's son Uzzah attempts to steady it on the cart and dies—a reminder that despite David's political genius, God still remains powerfully in control.

Enraged and fearful, David leaves the ark stored elsewhere, retrieving it three months later in a great pageant of music and dance. This story is upended by a quarrel with Michal. Having been traded to him by her father, Saul, for Philistine foreskins, then abandoned, and later extradited from a kindly marriage, Michal exhibits righteous disdain for David as passionate as her love had once been. David is no better feminist role model than Saul. His retort emphasizes dismissiveness toward her and a sense of freedom to do as he pleases. Whether Michal's subsequent childlessness results from her choice, David's, or God's is left unstated. She is one of several female figures, including Bathsheba and Tamar, unwillingly dominated by powerful men.

In contrast to the childless Michal, David immediately receives a transgenerational divine promise. Chapter 7 is a theological centerpiece not only of 2 Samuel but of Israel's story overall. David tells the prophet Nathan about his wish to build God a "house." God relays through Nathan that, on the contrary, it is God who will build David's house, his dynasty. God says of David's future heir: "I will not take my steadfast love from him, as I took it from Saul. . . . Your house and your kingdom shall be made sure forever before me" (7:15–16). Eli, Samuel, and Saul all have failed to see their sons succeed them. This time, succession is assured. Along with several royal psalms and Isaianic royal poems, this passage will eventually underlie later hopes of a messiah from the Davidic line reflected in New Testament passages.

Subsequent events illustrate David's ruthlessness and grace. David welcomes Mephibosheth, a remaining grandson of Saul. This transaction is couched in royal magnanimity, but it benefits the king, giving him oversight of potential rivals. Chapter 10 shows him attempting to extend friendship to neighboring Ammonites and retaliating when his envoys are humiliated. The ensuing war becomes the setting of King David's most famous conquest, which occurs at his career's pinnacle.

SINS AND CONSEQUENCES (CHAPS. 11–23)

The story of Bathsheba in chapter 11 is well known but widely misinterpreted. Renaissance paintings focus on the woman bathing, smiling seductively, on her own roof or in an open square. But the storyteller's eyes are on David, who spies her from his own roof. Movies detail a love affair, but the terse narrative could hardly show less romance. David strolls; he sees; he inquires. The woman is wife of one of his fighters and daughter of another. Nevertheless, the king sends, takes, and lies with her. Her reaction is understated: she goes to him, returns, and conceives. Her single independent act is a two-word message preventing David from standing aloof: "I'm pregnant" (11:5 alt.). What confession would have cost the king, we cannot know; his futile cover-up costs many lives, beginning with Bathsheba's husband. Sovereignty has limits: a king can take a body but can control neither biological processes nor human or divine reactions to his actions.

Bathsheba's palace visit lasts four words. Her husband, Uriah's, lasts four days, 128 words unfolding suspense. Despite coercion, Uriah is too loyal to the army to enjoy his wife and home. His uprightness contrasts with the king's irresponsibility and foils his cover-up. So David sends Joab orders to have him killed in battle.

Joab cannot follow these orders without others' help. Instead, he deliberately botches the campaign, killing many other soldiers. Rage permeates his report to David, but this is nothing beside the scathing message Nathan brings in chapter 12. Nathan's main points are not rape and adultery, but murder and wife stealing. He uses a story inviting royal judgment to indict a man of thoughtless killing. When David takes the bait, Nathan's pronouncement, "You are the man!" (12:7), forces him to recognize his deeds. God has given him much, but he cannot take everything. Divine judgment follows in a blunt series of parallel clauses describing God's prior actions for David, David's actions against God, Uriah, Bathsheba, and God's planned actions against David, including the death of Bathsheba's child, violence in his household, and sexual usurpation.

Children should not need to suffer for their parents' sins, and yet they do. The storyteller leaves the links between David's deeds and the ensuing family tragedies inferred but inescapable. Most of this story is omitted from the lectionary: the baby's death, David's daughter Tamar's rape and ruin by her half brother Amnon, who is then murdered by her brother Absalom, who flees to a foreign country for several years; he returns, amid superficial reconciliation with his father, and foments rebellion on grounds that are both justified and foolhardy. David is forced to flee his throne and his capital, and his followers are divided, some betting on him, others on his son. But the clash between loyalties in his realm pales before the clash between interests within: David wishes to regain the throne he waited so long to obtain. But he also wishes to save his seditious son. It falls on the pragmatic Joab to slay the young man. Suspense builds as David awaits word from the battle and readers await David's reaction. In the end it is Joab who orders a grieving father to gesture gratitude toward his warriors.

Unlike Eli, Samuel, and Saul, David has emerged triumphantly from troubled years, with every resource firmly in hand and great potential to rule well. Yet his own success undoes him. Preachers should note that although biblical prophets often rail against greed, violence, and abuse of power, few stories portray more vividly the devastation wreaked by these than does David's story. Few accounts show more forcefully the heartbreaking consequences, not least of which is the squandered opportunity to use power to benefit rather than destroy. By the time we reach David's poetic reflection on kingship in chapter 23, it reads ironically, for like most politicians David has not lived up to his youthful idealism, nor to the image he wishes to project.

Many ethical and theological themes in 2 Samuel resound in contemporary events: those who lead should serve rather than abuse their followers; power does not reside in armies, wealth, strategy, talent, or prior promise, but is given by God. And justice, even divine justice, appears in no predictable or wooden fashion, but unfolds slowly through the twists and turns of human events. The book of 2 Samuel invites readers to sharpen our moral vision, beckoning no simplistic formulas or easy pronouncements, but demanding full recognition of the many-sided nature of human existence before a God whose plans intersect but by no means coincide with our own.

1 Kings

JOHN C. HOLBERT

Selections from the books of Kings rarely show up in the Revised Common Lectionary. This slighting may be due to the fact that readers have characterized the books either as hodgepodges of disparate materials or as a series of vignettes slavishly constructed and constrained within a rigid ideological theology, allowing for little creativity or literary individuality. That theology is said to be Deuteronomic, from a seventh-century BCE writer who depicts sin as always visibly punished and proper worship as done only in Jerusalem. Though there is truth in these suggestions, both of these characterizations are simplistic and not helpful to the would-be preacher of these texts. There is a recognizable rationale for the structure of these two books: the enumeration of the subsequent reigns of the kings of Israel and Judah. Originally the two books may have been one, and their subsequent division is perhaps no more than the result of the length of available scrolls. Yet each of the two presents unique features for the preacher that bear careful attention.

First Kings may be divided into two main sections: the reign of Solomon (1:1–11:43) and the beginning of the history of the divided monarchy, with Israel in the north and Judah in the south of the country (12:1–22:53), a history that continues into 2 Kings. Both books together comprise some four hundred years of literary/theological history.

THE REIGN OF SOLOMON (1:1–11:43)

The narrator of 1 and 2 Samuel's portrait of David and his exploits is obviously still at work in 1 Kings 1–2; these two chapters bear all the marks of the subtle literary skill of the earlier tales of David. Though the literary/historical goal of the chapters is to recount Solomon's accession to the throne of Israel after the death of David, the storyteller presents us with enough clever material to make the choice of Solomon highly problematic. Of course, Solomon is the child of Bathsheba, David's wife acquired through scandal and violence, and as such stands to achieve the throne at the expense of any number of royal sons, most especially Adonijah, David's surviving firstborn.

Solomon's accession is far from simple. Bathsheba first admonishes a dying David to make her son king, claiming that David had in fact promised just that to her, swearing by YHWH that it was to be so (1:17), though nowhere earlier in the story has David promised any such thing. Nonetheless, Nathan, David's chief prophet, quickly reaffirms Bathsheba's claims about her son, adding that Adonijah has declared himself king at a nearby tent, while Bathsheba, Nathan, and Solomon have not been invited to the party. With that, David rises from his bed and demands that Solomon ride on the sacred mule and become king of Israel. In effect, Solomon's reign begins on a shaky foundation of partial truth. Upon hearing of the new reality of Solomon's coronation, all of those who have followed Adonijah to the tent now leave his sinking ship. Solomon consolidates his power on a river of blood, and 1 Kings 1–2 spares us none of that reality.

Following that harrowing beginning, 1 Kings offers us a portrait of the reign of Solomon in chapters 3–11. We first hear of the wise Solomon, an appellation that has been connected to the man for nearly three millennia. The king first prays to YHWH for wisdom, rather than wealth and power. YHWH welcomes such a selfless prayer and gives Solomon great wisdom, adding wealth and power into the bargain (3:1–14). Immediately, Solomon demonstrates his wisdom by deciding an especially intractable case involving two prostitutes and two children, one living and one dead. He discerns who the real mother of the living child is by threatening to hack the boy in two, and then watching the two reactions of the women, one saying to hack away, the other crying that she will give the child to the other to save its life. The king observes that only the actual mother would give up her child in like manner, and hands the living child to that woman. "All Israel heard of the judgment . . . and stood in awe of the king, because they perceived that the wisdom of God was in him" (3:28).

And his wisdom was matched by his astonishing skills in poetry, proverb, and song. "People came from all the nations to hear the wisdom of Solomon" (4:34). Soon he builds the temple to YHWH. His great wisdom leads him to hire Hiram, ruler of Tyre, to get the needed materials for the temple (5:1–12). A note of irony now appears in the tale as Solomon "conscripts forced labor out of all Israel," some thirty thousand men who head to Lebanon to aid Hiram in the cutting and securing of the great trees of Lebanon (4:13). These conscripts work one month in the north and have two months at home. When Solomon eventually dies, we see that a building foreman, Jeroboam by name, will lead a vast crowd of overworked Israelites back north to form a new nation (chap. 12).

In 1 Kings 5–6, the temple is built and filled with glorious objects for worship, and then in chapter 8 Solomon dedicates the building with a long and fulsome prayer wherein he lavishes praise on the temple, but affirms that no building can contain the mighty YHWH. Chapters 9–10 describe more examples of Solomon's wisdom and might: YHWH appears to him with a warning to follow YHWH's ways always lest YHWH "cut Israel off from the land . . . given them" (9:7); the queen of Sheba is amazed by the king's wealth and wisdom (10:1–13), leaving Israel with a huge quantity of gold and precious objects; and Solomon expands the power of his kingdom with chariots and horses stationed strategically throughout the land (10:26–29).

Finally, chapter 11 gives us the picture of Solomon the Foolish. Though YHWH has earlier warned Israel, "You shall not enter into marriage with [foreigners]" (11:2), Solomon "loved many foreign women" (11:1), indeed married 700 (!), and had 300 concubines to boot (11:3). He "clung to these in love," and sure enough, "his wives turned away his heart," just as YHWH had warned. As a result, YHWH vows to "tear the kingdom from [him]" and "give it to your servant" (11:11). This pronouncement foreshadows the disaster to come at Solomon's death.

Due to Solomon's dalliance with all these foreign women, YHWH brings enemies to confront the now distracted king: Hadad from Egypt, Rezon of Damascus, and most importantly, Jeroboam, a building foreman who led all the forced laborers of the king (1 Kgs. 11:14–40). Under the call of the prophet Ahijah, Jeroboam leads a rebellion against Solomon, and though the king tries to murder him, Jeroboam escapes to Egypt.

In this section on Solomon, the preacher will find many of the themes so memorably offered in other biblical books. The great kings David and Solomon are both loved by God and are deeply flawed human beings, yet God works with them in the attempt to fulfill the divine will for the chosen people. In addition, the temple is described at such length, because it will be a formative symbol around which Judah will coalesce down to its final destruction.

THE DIVIDED MONARCHY (12:1–22:53)

After Solomon's death, his son Rehoboam ascends the throne, but his rule is marked by a rash decision that will change Israel forever. The exiled Jeroboam returns to Israel and urges Rehoboam to ease the burdens that Solomon has laid on his subjects (12:4). Though the new king's older advisers urge him to accept this sound advice, his younger courtiers urge the king to use his new power, causing him to utter one of the Bible's most regrettable phrases: "My father disciplined you with whips, but I will discipline you with scorpions" (12:14)! Immediately, Jeroboam calls for open rebellion and leads vast numbers of his followers north to form a new kingdom of Israel, leaving Rehoboam as king only over Jerusalem and Judah. For the next two hundred years, Israel is a divided nation.

Now the narrator begins a synchronized history of the divided nation, focused on the reigns of the kings of each kingdom. That history is, however, recounted through the lens of "the sin of Jeroboam," his decision to establish two worshiping shrines: at Dan in the far north and at Bethel near the border with Judah. Each shrine is marked by a golden calf to separate northern worship from the temple in Jerusalem (12:25–33). Because the teller of the history is clearly a southerner, whose proper worship can only be in Jerusalem, Jeroboam and all northern kings who follow him can be nothing but sinners. This represents the distinct ideology of the one who is writing: southerners (Judeans) are mostly good; northerners (Israelites), bad. A preacher will need to be clear about the unfortunate confusion of the term "Israel," which in these books refers only to the northern, breakaway kingdom founded by Jeroboam.

The theme of prophetic presence in the larger monarchical story becomes especially prominent with the saga of Elijah. It should be noted that prophets do not become significant in the land until kings appear. Samuel confronts Saul, Nathan confronts David, Ahijah confronts Rehoboam, and an unnamed "man of God" confronts Jeroboam (chap. 13). But the Elijah cycle of stories generally outstrips its predecessors in scope and power. The cycle extends into 2 Kings, but the bulk of the narrative appears in 1 Kings, due especially to the rise of King Ahab in the north and his supremely evil consort, Jezebel of Tyre. It could be said that up to the appearance of Elijah in the narrative, prophets are only secondary characters to the kings, but upon Elijah's arrival, the kings take a backseat to the more powerful prophetic figures.

The Elijah stories consist of several miracle tales (lifting of the three-year drought, the raising of the widow's son from death, the huge contest with the 450 prophets of Baal on Mount Carmel) along with a story of justice for the poor, the episode of Naboth's vineyard (17:1–19:21; 21:1–29). In addition, there are prophetic stories surrounding the Syro-Israelite wars, especially that of prophet Micaiah and his confrontation with the false prophets of a king (22:1–40).

First Kings ends on a sour note, as the foul Ahab of Israel dies in battle with the Arameans, while his ally, the Judean Jehoshaphat, reigns in Judah a few more years, refusing to remove "the high places" of pagan worship, allowing his people "to offer sacrifices and incense" at these shrines; he is thus little better than so many of the kings, both north and south, who preceded him. He dies, leaving a very tenuous alliance with Ahaziah of Israel, himself described as a servant of Baal, and following in the sinful way of Jeroboam, son of Nebat. As the great Samuel had warned centuries before (1 Sam. 8 and 10), kings tend toward greed, corruption, and lust for power. And the literary history of 1 Kings demonstrates that truth again and again.

Across the vast royal and prophetic canvas of 1 Kings, the preacher can find the following themes: all human figures, no matter how storied their memories, are flawed and dangerous; the rise of kings inevitably leads to the coming of prophets whose role it is to call those kings' actions into question. This raises the modern question of the role of the church over against the state. God often appears in the unlikely person as opposed to the publicly powerful.

2 Kings

JOHN C. HOLBERT

The books of Kings narrate the long story of the kingdoms of Israel and Judah from the death of David in the middle of the tenth century BCE to the exile of Judah in the middle of the sixth century. First Kings recounts the separation of the nation after the death of Solomon into two realms, Israel in the north and Judah in the south, and 2 Kings tells of the dissolution of Israel at the hands of the Assyrians in the eighth century and the exile of the leaders of Judah to Babylon in the sixth century. The overarching interest in 1–2 Kings in searching for God's mysterious engagement in the long history of Israel and Judah creates in the preacher a richer vein of homiletical material.

The narrative in the opening chapter of 2 Kings is a prelude of sorts to Elijah's vivid departure and the introduction of his successor Elisha (chap. 2). Ahaziah, successor in Israel to King Ahab, has had an accident and is confined to his bed in the capital city of Samaria. He sends some messengers to ask Baal-zebub (meaning "Lord of flies") whether or not he can expect to recover from his injuries. But YHWH's angel reports to Elijah about Ahaziah's delegation and commands him to proclaim that Israel's God is not Baal-zebub. Ahaziah's messengers return to the king, who sends fifty soldiers to demand that Elijah appear before him. Elijah calls down fire from the sky (see also 1 Kgs. 18:20–40) to consume the fifty. And he does the same to a second cohort. Finally, a third cohort *entreats* the prophet not to destroy them, but to come to the king. Elijah appears, announcing to Ahaziah that he will die of his

injuries. And he does. As was seen several times in 1 Kings, prophets
are forever thorns in the flesh of wicked and pagan kings of Israel and
Judah. The preacher may again find here the role of the prophet in the
face of power politics.

The rest of 2 Kings that follows can be divided into three sections:
(1) stories surrounding Elisha the prophet (2:1–8:29); (2) stories of the
divided monarchy to the fall of Israel (9:1–17:41); and (3) stories of
Judah to the Babylonian exile (18:1–25:30).

ELISHA THE PROPHET (CHAPS. 2–8)

The transfer of prophetic power from Elijah to Elisha is unique in the
Hebrew Bible. Elijah demands that his successor, Elisha, let him go
alone to wherever YHWH has called him, but Elisha attends his master
each time (2 Kgs. 2:1–12). Finally, Elisha witnesses Elijah's end as he
is whisked into the sky in a storm wind. Elisha watches Elijah's ascent
until he disappears, and tears his clothes in mourning. But then he sees
Elijah's prophetic mantle, his cloak of power, and rushes to pick it up.
To test his own power, he goes to the bank of the Jordan River, shouting, "Where is YHWH, the God of Elijah?" (v. 14), striking the water,
which divides, just as Elijah had done a few verses earlier (v. 8). The tale
affirms the presence of a new prophet in Israel and harkens back to the
story of Moses at the Sea of Reeds (Exod. 14–15).

Many of the stories of Elisha are quite similar to those of Elijah: he,
too, creates a miraculous quantity of oil for a widow (1 Kgs. 17:8–16
and 2 Kgs. 4:1–7); he, too, raises a widow's son from death (1 Kgs.
17:17–24 and 2 Kgs. 4:18–37), with the added feature that Elisha
makes possible the birth of the son in the first place to a very aged
couple in the manner of Abraham and Sarah (Gen. 12–22). The stories of Elisha are in the main more focused on miraculous power than
the stories of Elijah: he sweetens brackish water (2 Kgs. 2:19–22),
curses impudent children (2:23–25), purifies a pot of stew (4:38–41),
feeds a hundred men with twenty loaves of barley and a few ears of
grain (4:42–44), and makes a lost ax head float (6:1–7). This miracle-
working capability is demonstrated at length in the memorable tale
of the healing of the Syrian general Naaman of his leprosy (chap. 5).
In short, Elisha is remembered and presented primarily as a worker of
miracles. When a preacher addresses such miracle stories, it is important to focus less on the miraculous quality of the event itself than for

whom they are performed. To be sure, the curse on the shouting children is a story of pure power for its own sake, but the others appear to help various persons and groups in need.

Still, as with the prophets who preceded him, Elisha was involved politically as well, as the second section of 2 Kings makes clear.

HISTORY OF THE DIVIDED MONARCHY TO
THE FALL OF ISRAEL (CHAPS. 9–17)

Elisha's political involvement is seen when he conspires to make Jehu king of Israel (chap. 9). Jehu is a commander of the armies of Israel under King Joram, son of Ahab. Elisha has determined that every trace of the house of Ahab be wiped away from Israel; he chooses Jehu to exact the terror. Jehu kills the wounded Joram; Joram's ally, Ahaziah of Judah; and in the most grisly of scenes, Jezebel, a named wife of Ahab. Finally, Jehu sets out to massacre all of Ahab's descendants (chap. 10), but unfortunately his zeal for the ways of YHWH is not complete enough: "Jehu was not careful to follow the law of YHWH the God of Israel with all his heart" (10:31). That terrible "sin of Jeroboam" in the person of the golden calves that the first king of northern Israel had ensconced in Dan and Bethel trips Jehu up, as it does all the northern kings before and after him.

Following Jehu's death comes the six-year reign of the only woman to rule over one of the kingdoms, Athaliah of Judah (chap. 11). Though she tries to wipe out all of her royal rivals, one, Joash, is secreted away in a temple bedroom. Jehoiada, a priest of the temple, shares no love for Queen Athaliah. He has Joash crowned king under military protection and has Athaliah executed in the palace (11:1–16).

These violent scenes of the slaughters of Jehu and the palace intrigues and murders surrounding the short reign of Athaliah are indicative of the chaos that the royal successions in both kingdoms present in chapters 12–16.

Finally, in chapter 17, the last king of Israel, Hoshea, is captured by the Assyrians and deported. The fall of the northern kingdom elicits from the author a rationale for the collapse. "This occurred because the people of Israel had sinned against YHWH their God. . . . They had worshiped other gods and walked in the customs of the nations whom YHWH drove out before the people of Israel, and in the customs that the kings of Israel had introduced" (17:7–8). This sweeping generalization summarizes the author's lens whenever he speaks of northern monarchs. They were idolaters, every one, since they "followed in the ways of Jeroboam," who "set up the golden idols in Dan and Bethel" and did not worship YHWH in Jerusalem, the only place of true worship (cf. 17:22; 1 Kgs. 12:25–33, my trans.). Thus, for the author the end of Israel is made inevitable by the rulers' paganism, characterized most vividly by Ahab and Jezebel. Two issues for the contemporary preacher are these: What constitutes proper worship of God? Just where may God be worshiped?

THE KINGDOM OF JUDAH FROM HEZEKIAH TO THE BABYLONIAN EXILE (CHAPS. 18–25)

The final years of Judah, the southern kingdom, are detailed in the rest of 2 Kings. These times, as narrated, are marked by a recurring juxtaposition of hope and despair, of attempted reform and ultimate disaster. Hezekiah brings reform to the land of Judah, cleansing the land of its many pagan altars. But in his zeal he rebels against the Assyrians and their king Sennacherib, who had just laid waste to Israel and Samaria. Hezekiah's refusal to pay tribute to the Assyrians soon brings their armies to the cities of Judah. The threat forces Hezekiah to strip the temple of all its gold and silver in an attempt to stave off Assyrian wrath. Rabshakeh, spokesman for the Assyrian king, in a lengthy speech near the walls of Jerusalem (18:19–35) warns Hezekiah and his people not to rely on any gods to save them from the might of Assyria, because the Assyrians have been victorious everywhere.

In terror, Hezekiah consults the prophet Isaiah for advice in the face of possible annihilation. Isaiah counsels complete trust in YHWH, and despite the increasingly dire threats of King Sennacherib, the Assyrian army is decimated and the king leaves for home (chap. 19). The author tells us that Sennacherib is murdered by two of his sons after he returns to Nineveh (19:37), but this report is not confirmed by the Assyrians' own account of the death of this king. The more dramatic account serves well the story of the reforming Hezekiah, whose purification of the worship of Judah leads to the salvation of the land and city.

The next great reformer is Josiah, who also institutes religious reforms in the land (chaps. 22–23). During his rebuilding of the temple in Jerusalem, a scroll is discovered in the year 622 BCE. This scroll has often been connected to our book of Deuteronomy. The scroll is authenticated by Huldah, a female prophet, and its commands are instituted by Josiah. All worship is henceforth centralized in Jerusalem, and all high places of pagan practice are proscribed. However, though Josiah is long remembered as Judah's greatest reformer, he is killed in 609 BCE in a foolish attempt to prevent a pharaoh from marching through Judah.

The last two chapters of 2 Kings narrate a series of kings ascending the Judean throne after Josiah's death. This series of rulers is capped by the last king of Judah, Zedekiah, who is at first a Babylonian puppet ruler. After an ill-fated rebellion against the Babylonians, however, he witnesses the sack of Jerusalem (587 BCE), just before being blinded and dragged to Babylon in chains (24:18–25:7).

Second Kings ends with the anticlimactic note that Jehoiachin, king before Zedekiah, who has been captured in an earlier Babylonian assault, is released from his Babylonian prison, placed under house arrest, and given a regular allowance by the Babylonian king as long as he lives (25:27–30). According to the theology of the narrator, all this tragedy for the southern kingdom has occurred for the same reason that Israel in the north fell to Assyria: "[they] did what was evil in the sight of YHWH, just as [their fathers] had done" (2 Kgs. 24:9).

Preachers might conclude that the authors of the books of Kings had a simple view of the movement of history: unfaithfulness inevitably leads to judgment and downfall. But it should be recognized that much of the material of 2 Kings belies that simplicity and is marked by significant complexity, reflecting what history often teaches: one cannot understand human actions by means of simple explanations. A modern preacher will need to recognize this surprising fact: while the books of Kings on their surface offer a simple rule of sin and judgment, many of their stories call into question that very rule.

1 Chronicles

J. DWAYNE HOWELL

First and Second Chronicles offers a history of Israel from Adam to the Decree of Cyrus and was written in the postexilic period (after 538 BCE). It was intended for a community in disarray, providing hope and order to those returning from Babylon to Judah as they try to reestablish their lives and their faith. Originally one scroll, 1 Chronicles covers the period from Adam to Solomon's transition to the throne, and 2 Chronicles begins with Solomon's reign and the building of the temple, then continues through the kings of Judah, the exile, and concludes with the Decree of Cyrus. The Chronicler places emphasis on David and his lineage to create hope for the exiles returning home in that one like David will usher in a new united kingdom. An important aspect of 1–2 Chronicles for the preacher is the retelling of stories of the past to help bring hope and comfort in the present.

A profitable approach to getting a handle on the Chronicler's writings is to contrast them with the approach of the Deuteronomistic Historian (Joshua, Judges, 1–2 Samuel, 1–2 Kings). They are considered as part of the primary history of Israel (Genesis–2 Kings sans Ruth), covering the history of Israel to the exile, containing preexilic and exilic material. The Historian's writing about the monarchy (1 Sam. 8:1–2 Kgs. 25:30) emphasizes the role of the prophets and Israel's failure to follow God as reasons for the exile. The Chronicler, on the other hand, writes during the postexilic period and uses material from the Historian, expanding some of the stories and abbreviating or eliminating other stories. The Chronicler emphasizes the role of the priests, who reestablish the rituals and worship of Israel in the postexilic period. The Historian and the Chronicler help to provide different historical and theological perspectives for the reader.

First Chronicles 1–9 gives a series of genealogies that cover the family lineages from Adam through Saul. At the heart of these genealogies are those associated with the reestablishment of the southern kingdom after the exile and the hoped-for reuniting of the entire kingdom of Israel: David and his descendants, the Levites, and the tribe of Benjamin. It would be easy for preachers to dismiss the genealogies as unimportant. However, they are significant for establishing David in a direct line from Adam through his son Seth. When Saul's reign is discussed, it is described as a failure, and he and his family are quickly eliminated (10:7–14). Unlike the Deuteronomistic History's lengthy account of the rise and fall of Saul (1 Sam. 8–25), the Chronicler chooses to bypass the call narratives and court history of Saul. While there are parallels between the reports of Saul's and his sons' deaths on the battlefield in both the Chronicler (1 Chr. 10:1–12) and the Historian (1 Sam. 31:1–13), the Chronicler emphasizes the unfitness of Saul for the kingship:

> So Saul died for his unfaithfulness; he was unfaithful to the LORD in that he did not keep the command of the LORD; moreover, he had consulted a medium, seeking guidance, and did not seek guidance from the LORD. Therefore the LORD put him to death and turned the kingdom over to David son of Jesse. (1 Chr. 10:13–14)

The Chronicler also bypasses the early stories of David's call (1 Sam. 16–17) and moves directly to David's ascension to the throne at Hebron upon Saul's death (1 Chr. 11:1–4). David's time before the kingship is described in a recollection of the increasing support for him even among Saul's own troops in chapter 12. David quickly consolidates his power and centralizes his government in Jerusalem (11:5–9; cf. 2 Sam. 5:6–10). He then moves to centralize the worship in Jerusalem by having the Ark of the Covenant brought to Jerusalem. Despite tragedy on the first attempt to deliver the ark (13:9–14), on the second attempt it is brought into Jerusalem with great celebration (15:1–16:6). The narrator here presents David as offering a psalm of thanksgiving (16:7–36) that parallels psalms in the book of Psalms (vv. 8–22//Ps. 105:1–15; vv. 23–33//Ps. 96; vv. 34–36//Ps. 106:1, 47–48). The arrival of the ark in Jerusalem lays the foundation for the

Davidic covenant. Both the Chronicler and the Historian recount the story, with minor variations, and center on the concept of a "house" (1 Chr. 17:1–25; 2 Sam. 7:1–29). Seeing that he dwells in a house (palace) while God dwells in a tent, David wants to build a house (temple) for God. David enlists the aid of his court prophet Nathan to fulfill his building plans. However, in a dream, Nathan is told by God that a house (temple) is not needed. God instead honors David by making a house (dynasty) out of his lineage and by allowing David's son to build a house (temple) for God. Both accounts end with a prayer of thanksgiving by David.

Two stories are especially important in contrasting the Chronicler's and the Historian's accounts of David. The first story is about David's taking of a census, subsequent punishment by God, and the offering from David to turn the punishment (1 Chr. 21; 2 Sam. 24). First, the Chronicler reports that it is Satan who incites David to take a census (1 Chr. 21:1), not God as the Historian reports (2 Sam. 24:1). Second, to turn God's wrath away from the people of Israel, David purchases a threshing floor and offers a sacrifice. The name of the property's owner differs in the two accounts (1 Chr. 21:18 names Ornan the Jebusite; 2 Sam. 24:18 says Araunah the Jebusite). The account of the purchase concludes 2 Samuel. However, the story is continued by the Chronicler and emphasizes that the land will become the site for the temple built by David's son (1 Chr. 22:1).

The second story involves the list of David's mighty men (1 Chr. 11:10–47; 2 Sam. 23:18–38). One major difference is noted between these lists. The Chronicler places Uriah the Hittite in an inconspicuous place in the middle of the list (1 Chr. 11:41), whereas it is prominently last in the Historian's list (2 Sam. 23:39). Perhaps this was the Historian's way of saying that while David was a beloved king, not all was as it seems in the kingdom. Likewise, the Historian reports David's affair with Bathsheba and the murder of her husband, Uriah, to cover up Bathsheba's subsequent pregnancy (2 Sam. 11). This account is completely absent from the Chronicler's narrative of David's reign. Similarly, absent from the Chronicler's account are stories of David's family problems, inner kingdom turmoil, and the revolt by his son Absalom against his father (cf. 2 Sam. 13–20). The Chronicler places David and his descendants in a better light, seeking to draw support for the resettlement of the land and the reestablishment of Israel by one like David. The slanting of David's story makes sense when we remember that the Chronicler is writing after the exile. Israel has no king, is under foreign rule, and is in ruins. The Chronicler tells the stories of an idealized instead of flawed David to provide hope that another such "David" will come and lead the people to victory and world glory.

First Chronicles concludes by transitioning from David's rule to Solomon's rule (22:1–29:30). The Chronicler and Historian also differ in their narrations of this story. The Historian portrays David as senile and being tricked into placing Solomon on the throne by Nathan and Bathsheba. Solomon's eventual claim to the throne emerges after a very violent purging of his political enemies (1 Kgs. 1–2). The Chronicler, on the other hand, describes a strong transition between David and Solomon. In 1 Chronicles, David charges Solomon with building the temple, providing plans and supplies (22:6–19). Following lists of temple officials and their responsibilities (chaps. 23–27), chapters 28–29 narrate the public anointing of Solomon as king (29:22b–25) and the recognition of Solomon's responsibilities for temple construction and a freewill offering for its construction (28:1–29:9). These stories of Solomon's ascension to the throne and his commission to build the temple would have stirred up for the original postexilic readers anticipation for the restoration of the temple.

The stories of 1 Chronicles are intended to bring hope to a people in disarray. Retelling the stories of the past can bring hope to people in disarray in our congregations today.

2 Chronicles

J. DWAYNE HOWELL

Second Chronicles is a continuation of the story begun in 1 Chronicles, the establishment of the reigns of David and Solomon. The two books originally comprised one scroll and are placed last in the arrangement of the Hebrew version of the canon. The two books of Chronicles provide an overarching history of Israel from Adam to the Decree of Cyrus. They were written in the postexilic period as the people were returning from the Babylonian exile and attempting to reestablish their faith and their lives. The people are coming back to a desolate homeland, without a king, and under foreign rule. The Chronicler offers idealized pictures of the former reigns of David and Solomon to offer hope for the reuniting of the kingdom by one like them.

Second Chronicles may be divided into three parts. Chapters 1–9 focus on Solomon's reign and emphasize the building and construction of the temple. Chapters 10–28 record the history of the kings of Judah after Solomon and the division of the kingdom into Israel in the north and Judah in the south. Chapters 29–36 record the history of the Judean kings after the fall of the northern kingdom, the exile, and the Decree of Cyrus allowing the exiles to return home. While 2 Chronicles addresses the division of the kingdom into north and south, it does not report the history of the kings of the northern kingdom as found in the Deuteronomistic History (1–2 Kings). The northern kingdom rejected the Davidic line, and thus the Chronicler is not concerned with its history. However, the Chronicler does look to a time when all the tribes of the kingdom will be reunited under a Davidic ruler.

SOLOMON'S REIGN (CHAPS. 1–9)

Second Chronicles opens with the story of Solomon's request for wisdom from God (1:1–13). Because of his humble request he is also granted wealth and honor from God (vv. 14–17). The wealth underlines his ability to undertake the building of the temple. The Chronicler views Solomon as being actively involved in the building of the temple, having received its details and provisions from his father, David (3:1–5:1). Solomon brings the ark into the temple upon its completion (5:2–14). His dedication of the temple reminds the people of God's mercy in the exodus and how God has not chosen a city or ruler to build a temple until now, choosing Jerusalem and honoring the Davidic line (6:3–6). Such language exhibits the importance that the David-Solomon story plays in encouraging the exiles returning from Babylon. As they enter a decimated Jerusalem and see the temple in ruins, they are reminded that the city and the temple once represented God's presence among them. Emphasis on the temple also elevates the importance of the priests in 2 Chronicles since they are the ones directing the worship of Israel. Stories from the past allow the preacher to sustain others in times of trouble and discouragement.

KINGS OF JUDAH (CHAPS. 10–28)

Rehoboam succeeds Solomon upon his death (9:29–31). Unlike Solomon, Rehoboam does not act with wisdom in using his power. When he refuses to ease the burden upon the people, a revolt ensues, and the kingdom divides, with Jeroboam leading the northern tribes and Rehoboam left to rule over Judah and Benjamin (10:6–11:12). Even though the clergy supported Rehoboam (11:13–17), Rehoboam led Israel away from God. Only the threat of an Egyptian invasion would lead him to repentance (12:1–12).

After the division of the kingdom, the Chronicler only records the history of the Davidic kings in the south, while making little reference to the kings to the north who had revolted (chaps. 11–28). Each king is remembered according to his faithfulness to God. Kings who are blessed for their faithfulness are often portrayed with long reigns. Two of the early kings are Asa (41-year reign; 14:1–16:14) and Jehoshaphat (25-year reign; 17:1–20:37). Both of their reigns are noted for religious reforms and strengthening of their forces. However, Asa sinned by entering an alliance with Aram, which led to his death. Jehoshaphat, on the other hand, is celebrated for his devotion throughout his reign: "The LORD was with Jehoshaphat, because he walked in the earlier ways of his father"(17:3).

Jehoshaphat does enter an alliance with Ahab of Samaria, with the eventual outcome of Athaliah's usurpation of the throne (22:10). She is the only woman to reign over Judah, but the Chronicler considers her reign illegitimate due to an absence of any royal pedigree. She is eventually murdered, and Joash is placed on the throne (23:12–21).

Joash, the son of Ahaziah, is only seven years old when he is placed on the throne; he has a long reign, like Asa and Jehoshaphat, forty years (24:1). The Chronicler emphasizes the importance of the priesthood: Joash is mentored by the priest Jehoiada, and a mark of Joash's reign is religious reforms (24:4–14). However, after Jehoiada's death, Joash begins to adopt false worship practices and is eventually assassinated by his own servants (24:15–27).

The prophets do not serve in as prominent role in 2 Chronicles as in 1–2 Kings, but they are not absent. In the Jehoshaphat narrative, Micaiah's prophecy against Ahab and Ahab's eventual defeat and death are included by the Chronicler (2 Chr. 18). The prophet Elijah sends a letter to Jehoram, condemning him for adopting the ways of the northern kingdom, actions that bring a plague on Judah and lead to Jehoram's death (21:9–20). Unlike the Deuteronomistic Historian, who emphasizes the role of the prophet, the Chronicler instead views the role of the priest as being important for the rebuilding of the land and the reestablishing of the proper worship of God.

AFTER THE FALL OF THE NORTHERN KINGDOM (CHAPS. 29–36)

This section begins with Hezekiah's reforms of the worship of Judah after the fall of the northern kingdom in 722 BCE (29:3–31:21). The reforms include the cleansing of the temple and the land of false images and shrines and reorganizing the priests and Levites. The Chronicler provides an extended account of the reform that is lacking in the Historian's account (2 Kgs. 18:1–8). On the other hand, the Chronicler's account of Sennacherib's invasion lacks the active role that Isaiah plays in calming Hezekiah and telling of Sennacherib's retreat and eventual death, as in the Historian (2 Kgs. 19:1–7).

Isaiah is only mentioned three times, with no dialogue, in the Chronicler's account (2 Chr. 26:22; 32:20, 32). Again, the Chronicler describes the religious reforms but downplays the role of the prophets, showing its emphasis on the emerging role of the priests.

Hezekiah is succeeded by his son Manasseh, who begins to dismantle his father's reforms by adopting false worship practices. This creates a major problem especially given that he reigns for fifty-five years! The Chronicler recounts a time of captivity and repentance for Manasseh to account for the long reign (2 Chr. 33:10–17). The Prayer of Manasseh in the Apocrypha purports to be his prayer of repentance. However, the Chronicler only mentions the prayer without providing any content (2 Chr. 33:18–19), and Manasseh's son Amon continues in the false worship that his father has begun (2 Chr. 33:21–25).

Josiah rises to the throne at the age of eight and guides Israel through a time of religious reforms (2 Chr. 34). After a scroll of the law is found in temple renovations, Josiah has it interpreted by the prophetess Huldah (vv. 8–28). When Huldah shares how Israel is far from the will of God, Josiah leads in religious reform and abolishes false worship practices and worship sites (34:29–35:19). Josiah is killed by the Egyptians (35:20–27), and his death signals the beginning of the fall of the southern kingdom through a quick succession of kings in the Chronicler's account. Eventually Judah falls to the Babylonians (587 BCE), and many are taken into exile to Babylon; Jerusalem and the temple are destroyed (36:1–21). The Chronicler does not offer a history of the exile but does conclude with the Decree of Cyrus (the king of Persia who conquered Babylon), which allows captives to return to their homeland and rebuild their lives and worship (36:22–23).

The construction and destruction of the temple serve as bookends to 2 Chronicles. Under Solomon's attention the temple is built with great celebration. Through the line of succession to Solomon, kings are judged according to their faithfulness to God. Finally, as the people move further away from God, Jerusalem and the temple are sacked by the Babylonians. Second Chronicles ends with a note of hope as the Decree of Cyrus allows the exiles to return home and begin again. The Chronicler retells the history of Israel to emphasize that just as God has blessed David and Solomon and allowed Solomon to build the temple, the same can happen for those returning from the exile if they remain faithful. The use of stories from the past to guide people in the present is important for preaching today.

Ezra

PATRICIA K. TULL

The books of Ezra and Nehemiah offer the only narrative glimpse of Jerusalem's story during the time of Persian rule, mostly set long after Babylon's defeat by Persia in the mid-sixth century BCE and the beginning of Jerusalem's restoration, yet clearly continuing that restoration. Part annals, part lists, part autobiography, part narration, the books are compiled around the subject of Jerusalem's reconstitution under new management. Jerusalem is no longer ruled by the kings of Judah, but by the absentee landlords of Persia.

The end of 2 Chronicles and the beginning of Ezra share a key feature: 2 Chronicles 36:22–23 and Ezra 1:1–4 cite a written edict by King Cyrus of Persia, the conqueror of Babylon and self-styled liberator of Babylon's captives, declaring that Judah's God "charged me to build him a house [i.e., a temple] at Jerusalem," and enjoining Judeans to return to that city. Until recently, most scholars thought Ezra and Nehemiah had been composed by the same author as Chronicles, as its sequel. There is less agreement on that argument today. What is clear is that Ezra and Nehemiah provide much of the scant information available about events in Judah during Jerusalem's Persian-period renewal. Yet the great many writing forms found in the two books, the overlaps and disparities between them, and ongoing questions about the time period in which the priest Ezra was active leave many gaps in our ability to read these books as a continuing and informative, historical narrative. Instead of giving us a direct view of Judah's society in the

Persian period, the books afford a sense of how some of Jerusalem's literate society wished to remember themselves and their relationship to their God.

The two figures, Ezra and Nehemiah, are both leaders of the Judean community and representatives of the Persian rulers, who sent them to provide spiritual and political governance for the struggling Jerusalem community. The two rarely appear together, and there is some speculation that they may have been active at differing times. Ezra the priest is introduced in Ezra 7 as returning from Babylon during the reign of Artaxerxes, and his presence continues through the book's conclusion. He reappears in Nehemiah 8. The name Nehemiah appears in a list in Ezra 2:2, but otherwise he inhabits only the book named after him.

The Revised Common Lectionary includes no readings from Ezra, but preachers should not ignore the book. The first six chapters concern the rebuilding of the temple in the late sixth century BCE, while chapters 7–10 primarily concern the actions of Ezra, who arrives in a later generation.

REBUILDING THE TEMPLE (CHAPS. 1–6)

As mentioned above, chapter 1 begins with Cyrus's edict of liberation and return. Those who heed this call are aided by a freewill offering given by Jewish neighbors in Babylon, as well as by Cyrus, who provides the temple vessels that Nebuchadnezzar of Babylon had captured decades before. Sheshbazzar appears at this point, identified as a prince and leader of this returning community. Chapter 2 lists the returnees by family, concluding with the figure of 42,360, as well as 7,337 servants and 200 singers. Chapter 3 narrates the rebuilding of the temple's altar and the keeping of the Festival of Booths, or Sukkot, and then, several months later, the ceremonial laying of the temple's foundation. Poignantly, the narrator notes that while most of the assembly rejoiced, some of the elders who remembered the prior temple wept, "so that the people could not distinguish the sound of the joyful shout from the sound of the people's weeping" (v. 13).

Difficulties arise in chapter 4, when people who had remained in the land offer to join in the rebuilding. Their words, as quoted by the returnees, position them not as Israelites but as foreigners who have been settled in the land by the Assyrian conquerors after the destruction of the northern kingdom, Israel. Oddly, the descendants of Judeans who had never left the land after the Babylonian destruction seem to go unmentioned (an ambiguous reference to "separated themselves from the pollutions of the nations of the land" in 6:21 may or may not refer to this group). These Judeans are described as being only a few in 2 Kings 25:12, but they were likely most of the population that survived the war, a group certainly responsible for such poetry as the book of Lamentations. This chapter makes it clear that the returnees from Babylon view themselves as exclusive insiders, not to be confused with worshipers of Israel's God whom they find in the land. Ezra 4:5 identifies the interference of such others as the reason for the delays in the temple's rebuilding.

An account follows that evidently occurs years later, during the reign of Artaxerxes, and concerns not the temple's construction but that of the city. It continues the theme of opposition, however, describing a letter that the "people of the land," as the account calls the opposition group, wrote to the Persian king accusing the returnees of intending revolt, resulting in an order to discontinue building.

Chapter 5 introduces the prophets Haggai and Zechariah, who urge resumption of the temple's construction. Most of the chapter relates a letter from Tattenai, the province's governor, sent to King Darius of Persia (son-in-law to Cyrus, successor of Cyrus's son Cambyses) requesting confirmation of Cyrus's original approval of this project. In chapter 6 Darius has the edict found, repeats its essence, and orders Tattenai to support the project. The temple is completed and dedicated and Passover is celebrated, completing this section of the book.

EZRA THE SCRIBE (CHAPS. 7–10)

Ezra first appears in the book named for him in chapter 7, when he sets out from Babylon to Jerusalem during the reign of Artaxerxes of Persia. He is described as "the priest Ezra, the scribe, a scholar of the text of the commandments of the LORD" (Ezra 7:11). He is sent with money from the emperor and others for temple offerings, and he comes to teach the law of the Judean God and of the king. The imperial text authorizing his mission is offered in full in Ezra 7:12–26.

Beginning in the next verse, the story is presented as if told by Ezra himself. Chapter 8 lists the families who return with him. Discovering that no descendant of the priestly family of Levi is among them,

Ezra sends leaders to bring a retinue of Levites. The rest of the chapter recounts his actions as they travel and arrive in Jerusalem.

In Ezra 9, in a scene reminiscent of some of the Pentateuch's darker texts, Ezra receives the disturbing news that the people have intermarried with Canaanites, Hittites, Perizzites, and all the other "-ites" known so well from Deuteronomy's injunctions to slay them. His reaction shows how steeped he is in the ancient story. Fortunately, what follows, while drastic and unsettling, is not the mass murder usually associated with these prior inhabitants. Ezra recounts his own confessional prayer concerning the situation. Chapter 10 reverts to third-person narration, describing the assembled Jews' agreement to separate themselves from their foreign wives. The book ends with the returned exiles dramatically and painfully dismissing wives and children, revealing their depth of concern to maintain identity and boundaries.

While preachers may judge the sensibilities displayed in Ezra to be foreign and even unintelligible to moderns for whom inclusivity rightly trumps racism, they will also find in those sensibilities the struggles of identity-making, particularly to a community whose future appears insecure. This element of the book affords much homiletical potential in a day when the church struggles with its identity in relation to and over against contemporary culture. Indeed, Ezra affords us a glimpse into groups living under imperial pressure to maintain peace, unity, and purity, even at great cost to individuals.

Nehemiah

PATRICIA K. TULL

The books of Ezra and Nehemiah offer the only narrative glimpse of Jerusalem during Persian rule, mostly set long after Babylon's defeat by Persia in the mid-sixth century BCE. Including annals, lists, autobiography, and narration, the books are compiled around the subject of Jerusalem's reconstitution under new management. Jerusalem is no longer ruled by Judah's kings, but by Persia's absentee landlords.

Ezra and Nehemiah are Judean community leaders and representatives of Persian rule, sent to provide spiritual and political governance for the Jerusalem community. The two rarely appear together and may actually have been active at different times. Ezra the priest is introduced in Ezra 7 as returning from Babylon during the reign of Artaxerxes, and his presence continues through the book's conclusion. He reappears in Nehemiah 8. Nehemiah's name appears in a list in Ezra 2:2, but otherwise he inhabits only the book named after him.

Together, the books provide much of the scant information available about Persian-period events in Judah. Yet their many genres, the overlaps and disparities between them, and ongoing questions concerning when Ezra was active—all render it difficult to read these books as an informative historical narrative. Instead of giving us a direct view of Judah's society at this time, the books show how members of Jerusalem's literate society wished to remember themselves and their God.

Nehemiah's only passage to appear in the Revised Common Lectionary is 8:1–3, 5–6, 8–10, during Epiphany in Year C, alongside Luke 4's account of Jesus' reading in the synagogue from Isaiah. The Nehemiah passage comprises a precedent for reading Scripture in an assembly, as Ezra the priest and scribe reads to Judean listeners at length from the book of the law and other leaders help interpret what is read. This chapter will be described below.

NEHEMIAH'S MEMOIR (CHAPS. 1–7)

The first seven chapters are presented as Nehemiah's first-person memoir. In the Persian city of Susa, he hears about troubles in Jerusalem, a city lacking walls and gates. He recounts his intercessory prayer requesting success in an unspecified mission. Readers begin to detect his intent in the first chapter's final line as he reveals himself to be a Persian official.

Chapter 2 describes ensuing events: Seeing Nehemiah's sadness, King Artaxerxes inquires what troubles him. Nehemiah asks to be sent to rebuild Jerusalem and is given letters from the king to the provincial governors. Suspense builds when he names certain individuals (Sanballat and Tobiah) who are unhappy to see him.

Soon after his arrival in Jerusalem, he rides out quietly to inspect the walls and gives orders to begin rebuilding them, encountering verbal opposition for unspecified reasons from Sanballat, Tobiah, and an Arab named Geshem. After naming those who work on the wall (chap. 3), chapter 4 resumes the opposition narrative, with Sanballat and Tobiah first mocking their stonework without effect and then plotting to fight. Nehemiah has the workers arm themselves and stay within the city at night to guard the walls.

Chapter 5 concerns the poor's outcry over debt slavery, which Nehemiah shames the city's nobles into resolving. Nehemiah recounts his own generosity as he repairs the city. Chapter 6 involves further failed efforts of Nehemiah's enemies to discredit and even harm him as the walls are completed. Finally, in chapter 7, with the walls completed, Nehemiah puts his brother Hanani in charge, ordering that the gates be opened only in full daylight under armed guard. Genealogical lists of returnees (largely identical to Ezra 2) are repeated, along with some who claim to be Israelites but cannot prove it.

EZRA (CHAPS. 8–10)

Chapters 8–10 concern not Nehemiah but Ezra. Nehemiah makes only a cameo appearance in 8:9, where he is listed alongside Ezra and the Levites as instructing the people. But textual evidence suggests that later scribes may have added Nehemiah and Levites to a verse originally crediting Ezra alone as speaking. This section more properly follows Ezra's story in Ezra 8 or 9.

In Nehemiah 8, Ezra appears in a role both innovative and strangely familiar: reading and expounding Scripture. The passage emphasizes that this audience at this occasion includes not only the priests and Levites, but also all the people, men and women. Indeed, it asserts that Ezra reads at the request of the people themselves. They gather on the first day of the seventh month, which today is the fall new year, Rosh Hashanah, in the Jewish calendar, traditionally followed by Yom Kippur and the Festival of Sukkot, or Booths. They gather not at the temple but at the Water Gate. The location of this gate is uncertain, but its name suggests proximity to the Gihon spring, Jerusalem's only water source, on the city's eastern side (cf. 3:26; 12:37). The significance of this location it that while not all people were admitted to the temple, they were all welcome at the Water Gate, and thus Scripture was made accessible to all.

The narrative does not specify which parts of the Torah Ezra read, nor can we be sure whether it was already in the form that became canonical. In fact, variation between pentateuchal prescriptions for the Sukkot festival (Lev. 23:33–43; Num. 29:12–38; Deut. 16:13–15) and the festival as described in Nehemiah 8:14–18 may suggest differences, as may the placement of the penitential day after the festival rather than before it. But more important than the specifics is the practice that Ezra institutes of reading Scripture to others as authoritative directives from God, and then interpreting Scripture so that all understand. Ezra's readings continue throughout the festival week (v. 18). Here is a story that preachers ought to highlight in that for later readers, this early glimpse within Scripture itself of the faithful reading Scripture, an early precedent for scriptural interpretation, carries a picture-within-a-picture quality. It resembles finding an ancestral village or grave, a marker of the place from which we came.

The occasion could have been marked by dismay, as in King Josiah's earlier story in 2 Kings 22:11–13. Instead, when the people begin to weep, Ezra tells them to rejoice because "this day is holy to the LORD" (v. 9). They are told to feast and share their food, taking strength from "the joy of the LORD" (v. 10). Celebration of Sukkot follows, during which Ezra continues to read to the people.

Chapter 9 describes a subsequent day of penitence, with Ezra recounting Judah's ancestors' miraculous escape from Egypt and journey through the wilderness with God, who gave them success despite repeated rebellions, until they were finally exiled. They continue, Ezra says, "slaves to this day" (v. 36) in their own land. All the officials then agree to follow God's law.

CONCLUSION (CHAPS. 11–13)

Chapter 11 seems to resume Nehemiah's memoir, describing how Jerusalem was populated. But it is quickly interrupted by a series of lists of residents of Jerusalem and of surrounding repopulated cities and villages. Finally, beginning in 12:27, Nehemiah describes the city wall's dedication. Chapter 13, like the conclusion of Ezra, concerns the problem of foreigners, as well as further troubles that Nehemiah encounters from opponents, and his struggle to prevent commerce on the Sabbath. Nehemiah does not, like Ezra, recount an orderly disposal of the problem of mixed marriages, but tells his own attempts to prevent further infractions. The book concludes with a summary of his work, which goes well beyond restoring the city to temple reform and organization, offering modern readers a glimpse of the complexities of human rule even among our ancient forebears.

Esther

PATRICIA K. TULL

The book of Esther narrates the actions of two Jewish heroes, Esther and her older cousin Mordecai, who save their people from genocide during the reign of Ahasuerus of Persia. Its ten chapters display humor, irony, reversals, and broad coincidence. Parallels and contrasts between heroes and antiheroes are rife, as is skepticism over human power structures. Jewish communities read the book every year during the Festival of Purim, which is associated with this story. Otherwise we have no clear indication of the historical circumstances in which the story was written and no records of why it was originally included in the canon.

Esther is one of only two biblical books named after women (cf. Ruth). It is also one of two books without any reference to God (cf. Song of Songs). Despite this lack, and the absence of other common motifs such as the Sinai covenant, central Israelite traditions and history, the land of Israel, its capital Jerusalem, or its temple, Esther offers an incisive exploration of courage and faithfulness, exemplifying biblical writers' talent for narrative suspense and ethical critique.

Esther appears only once in the Revised Common Lectionary. The reading from chapters 7 and 9 relates the story's climax and denouement, in which Esther accuses her foe, Haman, of treachery, and he is hanged; and Mordecai proclaims the annual Festival of Purim, commemorating Jewish survival. This reading, embedded in Year B's post-Pentecost semicontinuous readings, seems to invite telling Esther's whole story, since the verses do not make sense on their own.

While the story can be overviewed in one sermon, its many twists and turns are better suited for a series, or a Bible study in which participants can relish for themselves Esther's character development, dark humor, and ironies. The book provides opportunity to explore the hidden nature of providence, as well as themes such as greed, jealousy, courage, and wit during politically fraught times.

Events unfold in Persia's capital, Susa, where Jews have settled after the Babylonian exile. The book commences with an improbable six-month banquet thrown by King Ahasuerus for officials, followed by a weeklong public banquet. Opulent settings and unrestrained revelry are described in breathless detail. On the climactic day, the drunken king, wishing to show off his queen's beauty, sends seven eunuchs to summon her. But she refuses. He angrily consults seven sages, who advise him that she should never appear before the king again and should be replaced by a "better" wife.

The king's advisers later suggest that all the land's beautiful virgins be gathered to undergo yearlong beauty treatments and that the king choose a new queen from among them. Esther is introduced as one of these women, along with her cousin Mordecai, who is her guardian. Hiding her Jewish identity, she wins favor first from the eunuch supervising the harem and then from the king, who makes her his queen. Mordecai meanwhile foils an assassination plot, saving the king's life.

In chapter 3, the king elevates a new character, Haman, to power. All are commanded to bow before Haman, but Mordecai refuses. Furious, Haman bribes the king to order the slaying of all Jews on a day eleven months hence. The king agrees, uses the bribe to bankroll the slaughter, and allows Haman to send letters to this effect throughout the kingdom.

Mordecai and the Jews mourn this edict. When he appears before the palace in sackcloth, Esther hears though a messenger his request for her to plead on the Jews' behalf. She hesitates, since going to the king unbidden could mean death, but when pressed she agrees. This conversation includes two lines that some see as the theological center of the book with the most homiletical potential. Mordecai says, "Who knows? Perhaps you have come to royal dignity for just such a time as this" (4:14), and Esther responds that after the Jews and she herself fast for three days, "I will go to the king, though it is against the law, and if I perish, I perish" (4:16).

Chapter 5 initiates Esther's actions. Dressing in finery, she approaches the king, who immediately pledges whatever she asks, up to half his kingdom. Surprisingly, she invites him and Haman to a banquet. During the feast the king again pledges to grant a request, and she invites them to a second feast the next day, promising to disclose her request then. Haman's ego is bolstered by these exclusive invitations, but he is still frustrated by Mordecai's indifference. His wife and friends suggest erecting a tall gallows and demanding Mordecai's execution.

Ironic coincidence fills the pivotal next chapter. The sleepless king has his own annals read to him, where he is reminded that Mordecai has not been rewarded for saving his life. When Haman enters to demand execution, Ahasuerus instead asks what to do for someone the king wishes to honor. Thinking himself the intended honoree, Haman constructs an extravagant display: a parade through Susa on the king's horse, in the king's robes, led by his highest official. Ahasuerus enthusiastically orders him to honor Mordecai so. Humiliated, he carries this out. His wife and friends, yesterday's supporters, now predict his downfall.

The lectionary passage comes in here. At the second banquet, Esther requests that her people be spared. Blindsided, the king asks who is threatening them, and she accuses Haman. Enraged, the king walks out. Begging, Haman throws himself on her couch. The returning king accuses him of molesting her, and at a servant's suggestion has him hanged on the very gallows he had erected for Mordecai.

The rest of the book is denouement. Ahasuerus gives Haman's property to Esther and trusts Mordecai with his own signet ring (8:7–8), the ring he had given Haman to seal the edict against the Jews. Esther begs him to revoke that edict, but he says not even he can do so, inviting them instead to compose a counteredict. Mordecai decrees permission for Jews to defend themselves.

The day both edicts come into force arrives in chapter 9, and the Jews prevail. Ahasuerus asks Esther's further wishes, and she requests a second day of fighting in Susa. Mordecai enjoins the Jews to keep these days as an annual celebration called Purim and is last seen inheriting Haman's job.

Preachers may rightly wonder why, long before Christian anti-Semitism, the book attaches particular weight and danger to Jewishness. Proceeding from the same Jewish wisdom tradition that developed Proverbs and Jesus' reversal sayings, Esther illustrates poetic justice, not only in the large-scale reversal of Haman's wishes, but also more subtly, such as in the king's first order that wives obey their husbands, then followed by his eagerness to obey his new wife, and Haman's wish for elevation eventuating in his being raised to the high gallows instead.

The theme of written words appears throughout as one edict after another is published. Consequences hang on following various commands, some amusingly illogical. The king's written annals likewise figure in, reminding him of debts unpaid and turning the tide in Mordecai's favor.

Ethical issues are highlighted in the book's stark character contrasts. Haman represents insecurity, blind greed, ambition, and violence. The king displays extravagant, unstable power, dangerously susceptible to whim and suggestion. Mordecai and Esther act with dignity, equanimity, and good faith. In addition, Esther grows from a pliant youth to a courageous queen who utilizes her personal power, including sexual charm, to save lives.

Job

JOHN C. HOLBERT

Preaching from the book of Job is difficult. The problem begins with the original Hebrew, which is extremely complex, possessing over two hundred words that occur only in this book. Translators have struggled with the vocabulary for centuries, leaving non-Hebrew readers to access the text from very dissimilar translations.

Also, scholars have tried in ways innumerable to suggest places in the text of Job that are misplaced or "secondary" interpolations (that is, added into the original by some scribe or two over the years). However, nearly every ancient manuscript includes all forty-two chapters of the book. Preachers need to account for the whole book.

Moreover, there are the powerful themes that the book is mistakenly said to contain. For example, "Job is the story of an innocent sufferer"; to be "like Job" is to be plagued with painful and unexplained disasters. But do not fear: "Job repents at the last in the face of the whirlwind of God and ends his days old and content." The moral? "Accept the pain of life, trust God, admit your sin, and all will be well."

A variation of this misinterpretation is the famous "patience of Job," promoted by the KJV of James 5:11. In the face of his profound suffering, Job is ever "patient," providing us with a model for our own faithful behavior. The NRSV, however, reads "endurance" at James 5:11 rather than the KJV's "patience," and that catches the fuller nuance of the word. "Endurance" is not quite the same thing as "patience." Any cursory reading of the story of Job makes it plain that Job's "patience" lasts at best two chapters (!), while his endurance persists to the very end. Job most certainly complains impatiently; beginning with chapter 3 he complains with language unbridled!

A third misguided interpretation says, "In the face of the universe's assaults (chaps. 1 and 2), and unmerciful attacks by his so-called friends, Job complains and cries out in anguish, but he never denies his God. He almost blasphemes, but, due to his superior faith, he does not reject the Almighty. And because of that mighty faith, Job is accepted again by God at the end and lives a long and happy life with his new family and with God (42:7–17)." The fact is, however, that Job does reject God quite directly and with nothing less than appalling language (e.g., 9:22–24). It may well be that this God of Job and his friends needs to be rejected, which is perhaps one of the basic reasons for the book. A preacher can use Job as the beginning of a very basic examination of the nature of God.

PROLOGUE (CHAPS. 1–2)

Another element of the text that has generated great curiosity and mis-interpretations is the appearance of Satan in YHWH's court of gods. Instead of "Satan" as a name, the Hebrew in Job is more accurately rendered as "the satan." When this denizen of the heavenly court appears in Job 1 and 2, he is never called "Satan," despite the continual mistranslations. Even the NRSV continues to read Satan (with a capital "S"), though it offers a note suggesting "the Accuser" (capital "A") and says the Hebrew here is *ha-satan*. *Ha* in Hebrew is the definite article, hence "the satan" is the correct reading. The word is a title, not a name. The satan's role in the court of YHWH is to observe human behaviors on the earth and come to report those to YHWH; he is not the demon with the horns and tail, urging sinners off to a fiery hell. He is a member of the "children of the gods" (1:6 alt.; 2:1 alt.), the heavenly crew presided over by YHWH. In other words, the association of the satan in Job with the Devil, as tradition came to understand Satan, should be avoided.

Job's trip to the ash heap, brought on by the assaults of the satan, with the apparent collusion of YHWH, are the means by which the tale of Job begins. If the reader begins by "blaming Satan," the story is in fact over. "The devil made me do it" gets both YHWH and Job off the hook of the story's dilemma. Similarly, if YHWH is the "bad guy," then the story is also over, driven strangely by YHWH alone. We must see chapters 1 and 2 as prologue for the drama about to unfold; we cannot give the game away in the top half of the first inning. This prologue to the book is written in prose, as is the brief epilogue of Job 42:7–17. The rest of the book is all in poetry. It has been suggested by many scholars that the author of the poetry borrowed the prose story, which may be an older account, to frame the long poetic tale, creating what we now have.

JOB'S DIALOGUE WITH "FRIENDS" (CHAPS. 3–37)

Any quest for the historical Job is doomed to failure. The book of Job is a tale, a story, about the nature of God: just who is the God of the universe? That question was asked especially in the exile of Israel, that sixth-century-BCE removal of all the intelligentsia of Jerusalem to Babylon. The question of the nature of God was alive in the exile. What did they think now that all they had counted on in their faith—the land of Israel given to Abram, the king directly descended from the great David, the magnificent temple, the sacrifices of that temple—was gone? Who is YHWH now?

The book of Job raises that question sharply. What if I could portray a man who was wonderfully pious in every way, but who lost everything, ending up with nothing but questions? What do you suppose God had to do with him? And how would he react to that unfair experience? And how would other persons react to him?

The character Job is fabulously pious, but then loses everything. God has something to do with the loss, but exactly what is not clear. Job then rails against his fate in increasingly harsh language. He first speaks generally of the unfairness of things (chap. 3). But after his friends come, supposedly to "comfort him" (2:11), while assaulting him as a foul sinner, fully worthy of his place on the heap (for the most egregious of their attacks, see 4:7; 8:4; 11:6), Job becomes more specific and more personal. He first wishes he were dead (e.g., 3:20–21; chaps. 7, 10), but then turns in fury to an attack on God. Those who claim Job "almost blasphemes" have not read 9:22–24, where Job offers a full-blown accusation against God as both an equal opportunity destroyer and a sadist to boot! The dialogue goes on like this, becoming increasingly rancorous, reduced to name-calling and invective.

Always, it should be remembered that Job and his three friends agree that God rewards the righteous and punishes the wicked—a basic tenet of the wisdom tradition. The difference is that for the friends, God has done just that in the case of Job: they assume Job must be a foul sinner who is getting what he deserves. For Job, his own case proves that God does not act this way, though Job's exemplary piety demands that God reward his exemplary behavior. The intrusive fourth friend, Elihu (chaps. 32–37), adds little to advance the discussion.

YHWH'S DIALOGUE WITH JOB (38:1–42:6)

Finally, YHWH shows up. And here we find the key to the tale: just who is this YHWH? At first, it sounds as if YHWH is speaking about another set of problems entirely! What is all this talk about snow and rain and wind and ice and lions and eagles and ostriches (38:1–40:2)? Job did not hear carefully what YHWH first said to him at 38:2: "Who is this who obscures my design with words without knowledge?" (my trans.). YHWH has carefully listened to a debate that has served to "obscure the design" (a better translation than the NRSV's "darkens counsel") of YHWH. That design includes all the vast workings of weather as well as all the wild animals, including even the foolish ostrich that cannot fly like any sensible bird (39:13–18), but can run like the wind. Every animal mentioned is wild (including the warhorse of 39:19–25, far more than a typically tamed horse), and thus must be cared for by YHWH and remain dangerous to humans.

Job's first response to this catalog of weather and creatures is open disdain for YHWH's speech: "Look! I am trivial; how can I answer you? I lay my hand on my mouth [in terror of a powerful enemy]. I have spoken once, and I will not answer; twice, but will proceed no further!" (40:4–5, my trans.). Essentially Job says, "You win, you big bully! It was just as I said earlier, 'If I summoned God, and God answered me, I do not think God would listen to my voice!'" (9:16).

But YHWH is not through with Job yet. Job 40:8 draws the issue tighter and clearer. "Will you even put me in the wrong? Will you condemn me that you may be justified?" Do you think that the universe is a zero-sum game, Job, asks YHWH? If you are right, then I must be wrong? I will stand over here and watch you while you act like you think I act. Go on! "Tread down the wicked where they stand; bind their faces in the world below. Then I will acknowledge you, that your own right hand can give you victory" (40:12–14 alt.). Preachers might imagine a twinkle in YHWH's eye as YHWH issues this challenge to Job because that is precisely how God does *not* operate in the world, and Job cannot act like that either.

Then from the divine throne room rumble two giant mythological creatures, Behemoth and Leviathan. These beasts would have been familiar to ancient readers as part of the Canaanite pantheon of creatures, but what is important is the divine claim in 40:15: "Look at Behemoth, which I made just as I made you." Behemoth is the giant creature of the land that arches his back to cause earthquakes so common in Israel. No one would call Behemoth a benevolent creature. But he is a creature of God just as much as humans are.

The world that Job thought he knew, a simple world of reward and punishment, does not exist. And the God who makes and sustains that world is not the simple God of creed and bumper sticker, who acts in easily understandable and predictable ways. This God presides over a world of grit, horror, surprise, beauty, and wonder all at once.

When Job responds in 42:1–6, he can now admit that he did not know what he was talking about as he railed against God. "I had heard of you by the hearing of the ear, but now my eye sees you; as a result I now recant [what I said], and I change my mind in dust and ashes" (42:5–6, NRSV alt.). The NRSV's "despise myself," translated here as "recant," has no root in the Hebrew text and is a poor translation. Moreover, the NRSV's "repent" implies a trip to the mourner's bench. But "to change one's mind," as the Hebrew is translated above, is to see the world in a different way and to determine to live in that world with different eyes. That is repentance in the fullest sense of the word, a key element of Job deserving of preachers' attention.

EPILOGUE (42:7–17)

Throughout the poetic dialogue, YHWH has spoken to Job, the supposed foul sinner, and not to the friends who speak as if they know all about God. Finally YHWH does speak to one of the friends, Eliphaz, but only to rebuke the friends for not being like Job! "My fury is kindled against you and your two friends, because you have not spoken to me what is right, as my servant Job has" (42:7 alt.). Preachers should ask, "What has Job spoken that is 'right'?" He has shouted and complained and attacked with angry words, and God likes that honesty, however ill-informed it proved to be. In short, God would rather have a

loud-mouthed truth teller than a pious know-it-all any day! A preacher
will do well to explore the theme of how an appropriate relationship to
God may be constructed, well beyond the "unquestioning" kind.

One final note is needed. As demonstrated above, the entire book
of Job is a rejection of the simple and false idea that God rewards the
righteous and punishes the wicked. Hence, the epilogue (42:7–17) cannot be allowed to undercut that notion. Job 42:10 must be translated
correctly to make that certain. "YHWH restored the fortunes of Job,
and he prayed for his friends; and YHWH gave Job twice as much
as he had before" (my trans.). The NRSV reads the italicized "and"
above as "when," implying that Job's prayer caused YHWH to respond
with divine goodies. That will plainly not do in this story; the Hebrew
merely has "and" there, without cause-and-effect sense. YHWH gives
back to Job, because that is what YHWH chooses to do.

Does the book of Job provide easy answers to the question of the
nature of God for preachers to offer today's congregations? Certainly
not. Instead, it invites preachers to go about the much-needed task
in today's world of clearing the decks of the overly easy theology that
presents God as One who rewards and punishes in some strict calculus.
Not only is the world a rich, rare, and strange place, but so is the God
who made it. We can never know all of the ins and outs of God, but we
can know that God desires our questions and is eager for our searching
for the truth of things. That is an important message to preach in and
of itself.

Many congregants come to church with a central question in mind:
who is the God I have come to worship? The book of Job both counters
the common idea of simple divine rewards and punishments, based on
human behavior, and opens up the possibilities of a larger and freer
God, a God not bound by what we do, but a God who is both more
mysterious and more anxious to hear the genuine pains and hopes of
the people whom God has created.

Psalms

LISA WILSON DAVISON

The book of Psalms is unique among the books of the Hebrew Bible because it is the only one that consists of nothing but prayers. While other books contain prayers, they are usually set within the context of a narrative. The psalms stand on their own, without any supporting story. The name "Psalms" comes from the Septuagint's (LXX) Greek title, *Psalmoi,* suggesting songs sung with musical instruments for accompaniment. In the Hebrew Bible, the title is *Tehillim,* meaning "praises." It reflects Israel's concept that all prayer (regardless of topic or tone) is a way of praising God. This concept of praise is key to understanding, appreciating, and preaching from the Psalms.

ORIGINS

The Psalter is often referred to as the "hymnbook of the Second Temple," reflecting the scholarly argument that the book of Psalms got its final shape in the period of rebuilding the temple under the leadership of Zerubbabel (ca. 520–515 BCE). Regardless of when the collection was compiled, however, we are basically ignorant about the date of composition for most of these psalms (except Ps. 137, which could not have been written prior to the beginning of the Babylonian exile, 586 BCE). It is possible that some were actually composed in the preexilic period or even earlier. In fact, some of these prayers are probably very ancient.

The book of Psalms is of great importance for the church because of its influence on hymns, theology, worship, understandings of God, and prayer from the early church onward. The Psalms also provides a rich resource of prayer and worship materials for today. They reflect the gamut of human emotions and experiences. It is a shame that while psalms play such an important role in liturgy, preachers rarely focus sermons on them.

SUPERSCRIPTIONS

All but thirty-four psalms begin with superscriptions. These titles, though, yield little historically reliable information, and many are difficult to understand. The superscriptions seem to represent an effort to classify these psalms by those who assembled and edited them. There are three types of information included in the superscriptions: proper names associated with the psalm, musical/liturgical notes, and literary genre of the psalm.

Seventy-three psalms with superscriptions contain *ledavid* in Hebrew, which could mean *of, for,* or *to* David, as in dedicated to or in honor of David. Other psalms begin with a similar structure yet with other names of biblical characters (e.g., Moses, Solomon, Jeduthun, Heman, Ethan, Korah, and Asaph). These should not be taken as bylines of authorship.

The tradition of claiming Davidic authorship for many, if not all, of the psalms in the Psalter has led to the rather common conclusion that this collection of prayers is decidedly "masculine." Scholarly consensus has been that these psalms concern primarily male interests and therefore were composed by men. Outside of the Psalter, however, prayers of both men and women are found throughout the Hebrew Bible, though the number of prayers placed on the lips of females is certainly fewer. Still, given the patriarchal context out of which the stories of ancient Israel developed, it is quite surprising to find eleven women (in the Protestant canon; there are three more in the Apocrypha) whose prayers have been recorded in the biblical texts. Even though some of their prayers consist of only a line or two, they are portrayed as women of faith who were free to address their concerns and joys directly to God without the "assistance" of a man (e.g., Hagar, Rebekah, Deborah,

Hannah, and others). Add to Scripture's portrayal of women praying the prominent use of first-person pronouns (I, we) found throughout the 150 psalms, and it is impossible to know if the author of this or that psalm is male or female. Indeed, even psalms that grammatically indicate a male subject are not limited to the experiences and concerns of men. The emotions, joys, and concerns found throughout the Psalter are those shared by both men and women.

Liturgical instructions are found in fifty-five psalms. They begin with "to the leader," followed by a variety of words and phrases, the majority of which we do not understand (e.g., "the deer of the dawn," "lilies," etc.). More than likely they indicated moods, modes, or melodies to accompany the singing of certain psalms.

Genre designations found in the superscriptions include *mizmor/*psalm or song, *sir/*song, *tehillim/*praises, and so on. These distinctions are also mostly unclear to scholars today.

TYPES OF PSALMS

One traditional approach to studying the Psalter that is helpful to preachers is to identify different types of psalms or psalm forms. Based on structure and/or content, early scholarship divided the psalms into five broad categories: Community Laments, Individual Laments, Hymns of Praise, Psalms of Thanksgiving, and Royal Psalms. Later scholarship has identified other types, including: Enthronement Psalms, Songs of Zion, Liturgical Psalms, and Wisdom Psalms. All scholars agree that the most common psalm type is Lament, accounting for 60 of the 150 prayers (43 individual and 17 communal). Looking at a few of these types of psalms can aid preachers in recognizing both common elements shared by a form and features unique to individual psalms.

Lament

Laments are prayers of complaint. They express experiences of the depths of loneliness, frustration, and fearfulness, thus portraying a world out of order. Typically, this situation is blamed on God, who has failed the psalmist(s), or on enemies who are triumphing unfairly. Usually the psalmist claims innocence. Most laments are characterized by a sixfold structure:

—address to God
—complaint
—confession of trust
—petition
—words of assurance
—vow of praise

Psalm 13 is an example of a brief lament, sans the words of assurance.

These ancient prayers often present theological concepts and express strong emotions, with which many contemporary readers struggle. In particular, "imprecatory psalms" (a subset of laments) contain desires for vengeance and violence against one's enemies. Psalm 137, with its closing words expressing desire for the infants of the psalmist's enemies to be killed violently, is an especially graphic example of an imprecatory psalm. While these prayers might be difficult to read, preachers should recognize that they are one of the greatest gifts of the Psalms. They teach us that expressing our anger and pain, even our desires for revenge, in conversation with God is an act of great faith, even an act of praise.

Too often, Christian tradition has taught that it is inappropriate even to have vengeful feelings, much less pray for God to carry out such wishes. Not only do the laments assure us that it is normal to have such feelings; they also demonstrate that the best thing to do with them is to give them to God in prayer. Relinquishing these toxic desires over to God is healthier than denying them or holding on to them. Eventually they will surface, usually in ways that are harmful to others and/or to ourselves. Even with such desires for retribution, a prayer of lament is a great statement of faith. The community is making the claim that God actually cares about what happens to human beings and that God is still involved in the world, even when all the evidence seems to deny such a claim. The psalmists believe that prayer has the power to change reality, and that includes the potential to change the ones praying and how they see the world.

Hymns of Praise

Fifteen psalms are identified as Hymns of Praise. These prayers typically celebrate God as creator and as sustaining controller of history. They are mountaintop celebrations of wondrous faith in a reliable, trustworthy God.

Often Hymns of Praise follow a threefold A-B-A pattern:

— an opening call to worship
— the motive/reason for praise
— a concluding recapitulation of the opening

Psalm 117 is an example of this type. In two short verses, this prayer reflects the ABA pattern. These hymns employ imperative verb forms, expressing the mood of certainty that God's creation and order for the world is sure and worthy of praise.

Prayers of Thanksgiving

There are seventeen Prayers of Thanksgiving in the Psalter. Many appear to be words spoken on the other side of a lament. Here, God is praised for delivering a person or group from distress. They often include expressions of confidence and gratitude. The occasion and experience of deliverance is remembered by telling the inspiring story of how God has transformed distress into gladness. They are similar to what we might call "witnessing" or a "testimony." Psalm 116 reflects these sentiments.

Some Prayers of Thanksgiving do not address a previous situation of distress. Rather, they are prayers that express a complete trust in the Holy. The much-beloved Psalm 23 falls in this category.

THEMES

As we looked at some common types of psalms found throughout the Psalter, similarly preachers will do well to recognize recurring themes found throughout those different psalm forms.

Covenant

While it might be surprising that 40 percent of this book's "praises" are laments, which often contain expressions of anger and desires for vengeance, this kind of honest prayer provides insight into a key concept of Israel's faith that is a foundation for the Psalter. That concept is Israel's understanding of their relationship with the Holy as a covenant, a contract between two parties in which both sides have obligations.

Just as the covenant allows God to call the people to account for failure to keep their part of the agreement, Israel feels confident in telling God when it feels that God is failing to keep covenant. This covenant is also the basis for Israel's trust that God is always present and cares about their lives.

Khesed

Another key concept in the Psalms, related to the covenant, is found in the Hebrew word *khesed*, which is often translated as "steadfast love." This translation, however, does not do justice to the concept of *khesed*, which is used most often in describing God's relationship with humanity. The term does not imply a cotton-candy kind of love that is decorated with hearts and Cupid's arrows; *khesed* refers to a fierce, passionate love.

God's "steadfast love" is strongly protective and requires a strict exclusivity on Israel's part. While God's *khesed* may demand a great deal of the people, the returns on their investment are incredible. The consistent motivation for God's deliverance of Israel (individually and as a people) is God's *khesed*. Without this strong love, God might have left them to suffer and abandon the covenant.

Metaphors for God

No other book in the Hebrew canon challenges us to expand our vocabulary about God more than the Psalter. Some psalms describe God as the Creator and Sustainer of all. No matter how much seems to be wrong with the world, these psalms make the bold claim that God is always in control. On the other hand, in addition to portraying God as transcendent, the psalms also use images of the Holy being intimately involved with humanity and all creation.

Like all human language, the psalms utilize metaphors to speak about God, using common images to describe the indescribable, such as inanimate objects (rock, fortress, etc.) and human roles (such as shepherd, teacher, ruler, etc.). It is this second category where preachers can help congregations overcome misunderstanding the role of a metaphor. While it is quite clear that God is not actually a rock, some want to claim that God really is (literally) father or king. Since Israel claimed that the Holy could not be captured in just one image (see Exod. 3:13–14), the Psalms contain a wide variety of metaphors to indicate that God is not a human or an object. Sometimes the psalmist asks, "Who is like the LORD our God?" (113:5). The expected answer is a resounding "No one!"

Images of Humanity/*Nephesh*

There are also a variety of ways that humans are portrayed in the psalms, some positive and some negative. Psalm 8 is a bold statement about the inherent worth and value of human beings. It proclaims that God cares about us amid all the marvelous things God has to consider. Even more, it declares that human beings are created in the image of God and given special responsibility to care for the rest of God's creation. Psalm 8 is a celebration of the goodness present in every human being, and it serves as a wonderful counterweight for the image of humanity found in Psalm 14. This prayer proclaims that there is not one single good person to be found on earth. Humanity is a sorry lot. In this psalm, God's voice (perhaps a prophet's voice on God's behalf) laments the ignorance and injustice of God's people. While God has provided humanity with a clear set of instructions about how to live in the Torah, humanity fails to keep covenant. The whole of the Psalter provides the reassurance that God always offers forgiveness without requiring anything in return; God keeps covenant.

Another important anthropological concept for reading the psalms is the Hebrew word *nephesh*, a term that has no appropriate English equivalent. The tendency of most translators has been to render it as "soul." Unfortunately, the Western concept of "soul," as part of the dichotomy between body and soul, is misleading when used in the Hebrew Bible. Israel thought about humans in a more holistic way and not as dualism of flesh and spirit. In Genesis 2:7, the first human is simply a clod of dirt until God breathes God's breath into the clod. Only then does it become a "living being" (*nephesh*). The idea is that our *nephesh* is that which makes us alive and who we are.

The Psalms reflect the understanding that a human should also pray with one's whole self. The faithful must be open to God in their prayers, realizing that every experience is an opportunity to experience the divine. In the Psalms, one seeks to bring one's heart into congruence with the divine will. Prayer is not about learning to say the right words or to use the right name for God; it is not to give an accurate definition of the divine nature. Rather, prayer is about finding a person's connection to the Divine, about finding God in conversation and in all of life's experiences. Prayer is remembering one's past, naming one's struggles and joys, and listening for the Holy.

CONCLUSION

Reading through the entire Psalter (and since the Revised Common Lectionary assigns a psalm for every Sunday of its three-year cycle, the majority of psalms are read in lectionary-based congregational worship) can feel like an emotional roller-coaster, with hills of confidence and drops of doubt all done at a confusing and chaotic speed. Within these 150 prayers, we find the full gamut of human experiences (e.g., joy, sadness, fear, trust, anger, and thankfulness). The individual psalms often seem to ramble, shifting with the passing thoughts of the psalmist. Too often, we think that our prayers must be ordered and eloquent. We struggle when our prayers are disjointed and faltering because the needs of the world keep interrupting our train of thought.

This biblical book (and preaching from it) reminds us that prayer is a mix of focused pleading and random conversation with the Divine. Sharing whatever is weighing on our mind with God is a legitimate form of prayer, as is reminding God (and ourselves) of God's steadfast love and faithfulness.

Proverbs

ALYCE M. MCKENZIE

The book of Proverbs is part of the Bible's Wisdom literature, so called because these books (Proverbs, Ecclesiastes, and Job) feature far more occurrences of the Hebrew words *khakam* (wise) and *khokmah* (wisdom) than do any other portion of the Hebrew Bible. Proverbs' wisdom teachings are more optimistic about ordering one's existence toward positive outcomes than Job and Ecclesiastes. All three books, however, are attempts to answer the question "What is the best way to live?" They offer different answers but use the same method: the keen observation of patterns in human relationships and the natural world.

A common misconception that causes many preachers to avoid preaching on Proverbs is that individual proverbs have no historical, literary, or theological context. When preachers discount proverbs' historical, literary, and theological settings, they miss out on its "apples of gold" (25:11), practical wisdom for daily living. There are only six passages from Proverbs in the Revised Common Lectionary, and they conform to the rubric of lengthier passages (1:20–33; 8:1–4, 19–21, 22–31; 9:1–6; 22:1–2, 8–9, 22–23; 25:6–7; and 31:10–31). In other words, the shape of the lections bypasses the historical, literary, and theological function of individual proverbs to illuminate contemporary situations.

HISTORICAL CONTEXT

Tradition has attributed Proverbs to King Solomon (died ca. 931 BCE). While he may have composed a few of the proverbs, the collection actually contains sayings from multiple contexts across the centuries of Israel's history: clan, court, home, and wisdom school. References to kings and diplomacy (29:12), agricultural imagery (25:13), and parental instruction (3:1–2) imply a variety of settings.

The postexilic period, however, is the likely context for the collection and collation of these sayings. The Babylonians invaded Judah in 586 BCE, destroyed Jerusalem, and deported thousands of Judeans to Babylon. During this period of exile people needed a faith that looked beyond temple, king, and land: wisdom writings offered practical teachings to keep the young from self-destructive behaviors and loss of religious identity. In life around them, the sages discerned patterns of act and consequence, cause and effect, and taught that the path of wisdom leads to positive outcomes while the path of folly leads to self-destruction. This orderly arrangement, in their view, was a gift from God the Creator.

A key element of the historical context of Proverbs to which preachers should attend concerns the radical move to personify Wisdom as a woman in a patriarchal society. The exile brought the destruction of the traditionally male-run institutions of court and temple and the deportation of their leaders. Parental teaching, by mothers as well as fathers, was more crucial than ever. While personified Wisdom honors women's social roles, she did not bring about real women's access to social power in her day, and it is hard to miss the fact that Proverbs also personifies human folly as a woman (chap. 7). That said, the female portrayal of Wisdom has inspired women through the centuries with confidence in their access to divine wisdom. In addition, her identity and activity as described in Proverbs 8 has shaped the depiction of the Word of God in the prologue to the Gospel of John. For both men and women, the message of Proverbs is clear: daily life is the arena for the revelation of a God who still stands at the crossroads and calls us onto the path of wisdom.

LITERARY CONTEXT

Proverbs is by no means a hodgepodge of fortune cookies thrown into a bag. A prologue of nine chapters, most likely written after the exile, introduces the figure of Woman Wisdom (chaps. 1, 8, 9; see also chap. 31) and serves as the literary and theological context for several older proverbial collections that make up chapters 10–30. The title of these first nine chapters, "The proverbs of Solomon," also serves as the banner for the entire book of thirty-one chapters. These chapters depict wisdom as both a divine gift and a human search. They portray Wisdom as active in creating the world (3:19–20; 8:22–31) and now standing at the crossroads of daily life as she summons passersby onto the path of wisdom that leads to life (1:20–33; chap. 2; 3:1–20; chaps. 4–5; 8:1–36). They commend the benefits of the path of wisdom (3:1–18) and warn against the dangers of evil companions (1:8–19), sexual infidelity (5:15–23; 6:23–7:27), and sloth (6:6–11).

Following chapters 1–9 are three other collections of wisdom sayings within Proverbs. Two of these are ascribed to Solomon (10:1–22:16; 25:1–29:27). The third and shorter collection, placed between the two just mentioned, is simply titled, "The words of the wise" (22:17–24:34). Chapter 30 is titled "The Words of Agur," a figure about whom Proverbs reveals next to nothing, and is a series of riddles that commend humility and warn against dishonoring parents, infidelity, jealousy, and arrogance. Within these broad collections are narrower sets of proverbs related to specific themes.

Chapters 10–15 contain sayings that distinguish sharply between wise and foolish behavior and people. For example, 11:3, "The integrity of the upright guides them, but the crookedness of the treacherous destroys them." This is referred to as "antithetical parallelism," which presents a clear choice between desirable and undesirable qualities.

Chapters 16:1–22:16 contain sayings that elaborate on the evils of folly and the benefits of wisdom, such as "Pride goes before destruction, and a haughty spirit before a fall" (16:18). This form, in which the second phrase specifies what is said in the first phrase, is called "synonymous parallelism." The second phrase, by making the first more vivid, increases its impact.

Proverbs 22:17–24:22 shows remarkable similarities to a collection of teachings from Egyptian scribes called The Instruction of Amenemope. Its inclusion witnesses to the fact that wisdom was not an impulse unique to Israel, but a broad impulse across the ancient Near East. The Amenemope collection emphasizes the protection of the poor (cf. Prov. 22:22–23; 23:10–11), the virtues of impulse control (cf. 22:24–25), and the condemnation of unjust gain and reservations about the value of wealth (cf. 23:4–5).

Chapters 25:1–29:27 reveal the sages' genius at discerning analogies between the natural world and human behavior, such as "Like a bad tooth or a lame foot is trust in a faithless person in time of trouble" (25:19).

Proverbs ends with a poem, likely of postexilic origin, for which some modern editions of the Bible add a title, "Ode to a Woman of Worth" (31:10–31). The qualities for which this "capable wife" is praised match those of Woman Wisdom in the preceding thirty chapters. She sheds light on the way of those who follow her (cf. 31:18b to 13:9) and is worth more than precious jewels (cf. 31:10 to 3:15; 8:11; 16:16). She brings prosperity, protection, and honor upon those who trust in her (cf. 31:11–12 to 4:5, 8–9). She honors the poor and trusts in the Lord, hallmarks of the wisdom seekers in Proverbs (1:7; 9:10; 15:33). The woman of worth invites wisdom seekers to become members of her household, where they will be provided with the necessities of life, with purpose and with wisdom.

The literary context of Proverbs consists of the interplay of personification and proverb. Personification draws readers/listeners to Woman Wisdom, heeding her summons to "lay aside immaturity, and live, and walk in the way of insight" (9:6). A proverb propels us out into the world, to discern situations in our daily lives that are an apt fit with the proverb's particular piece of wisdom. It is characterized by vividness, connection to daily life, and the ability to evoke ethical reflection. Proverbs are more like ethical flashlights that light up certain situations than ethical floodlights that bathe the whole landscape of life. Not every proverb fits every situation (e.g., cf. the contrasting advice given in 15:1 and 28:23).

THEOLOGICAL CONTEXT

Israel's religion affirmed two modes of divine revelation: God reveals Godself through decisive historical interventions and through the natural order. While Israel's sages acknowledge the first mode of revelation in God's saving acts of promise, exodus, election, law giving, and wilderness guidance, their focus is on the second mode: nature and human experience as arenas of encounter between God and humankind.

Wisdom is, on the one hand, a divine gift of an order to be discerned in human relationships and the natural world. On the other hand, it is a disciplined, lifelong search for that gift. This is the basic theological paradox of Proverbs, that wisdom is both a gift and a lifelong search (Prov. 2:1–15).

That search begins with "the fear of the LORD." The "fear of the LORD" is the Wisdom literature's code word for faith. It is the prerequisite or beginning of wisdom (1:7), our human response to the transcendence and trustworthiness of God. We tremble before God's transcendence (Exod. 19:18; Isa. 6:1–5) and trust in the faithfulness of God (Deut. 10:20). In Proverbs we rely on none other than God for moral guidance (Prov. 3:5). Proverbs helps us live wisely, not for wealth and self-fulfillment, but to align our lives with God's purposes for the whole community. While Proverbs does affirm that living wisely increases one's chances of health, harmonious relationships, and a degree of material comfort, the goal of the wise person in Proverbs is deeper knowledge of God and the ability to contribute to the harmony and integrity of the community. This is in sharp contrast with so-called prosperity preaching, which shrinks the message of Proverbs down to materialistic individualism.

While Proverbs expresses optimism concerning the quest for wisdom, it also includes what scholars call "limit proverbs," which acknowledge that human life is unpredictable and that God is, to a degree, inscrutable (16:1, 2; 19:21; 20:24; 21:30–31). This minor theme in Proverbs becomes a major theme in Job and Ecclesiastes as they critique confidence expressed in Proverbs: "The highway of the upright avoids evil; those who guard their way preserve their lives" (16:17).

Preaching on an individual proverb or proverbial theme brings to mind a *matryoshka,* a beautiful, brightly painted Russian doll. Whoever opens one of these hollow wooden dolls finds a slightly smaller doll inside, and a slightly smaller one inside that one, and so on down to the smallest doll of all. An individual proverb is the smallest doll. The next one is the historical, literary, and theological context of the book of Proverbs. Then comes the context provided by the Wisdom literature of the Hebrew Scriptures and the New Testament (the parables and sayings of Jesus, the book of James, the opening chapter of 1 Corinthians, and the prologue to the Gospel of John). Then comes the canonical context as a whole, including the genres beyond that of wisdom. At a time when many people are no longer buying the overarching Christian metanarrative of creation, fall, redemption, and new creation, everybody is still living by a wisdom of one sort or another. Proverbs directs us to daily life as an arena in which we can discern practical guidance that is a gift from God, so that our path "is like the light of dawn, which shines brighter and brighter until full day" (Prov. 4:18).

The literary inscription that has preserved proverbs has sacrificed their oral, situational poignancy and punch. We recover their preach-ability by placing them back into specific situations in our own and our congregation's lives.

Ecclesiastes

ALYCE M. MCKENZIE

Some view Ecclesiastes as an unrelievedly pessimistic book and wonder why it is in the canon at all (as seen by the fact the Revised Common Lectionary only draws on two passages from the book). Yet when we place this book in its historical, theological, literary, and homiletical contexts, we begin to appreciate both its shadows and the glimmers of light that shine through its profound, often poetic words and its potential for the pulpit.

HISTORICAL CONTEXT

The author presents himself as King Solomon in 1:1, but the origin of the book is in the later period of Persian rule. Qohelet, the Hebrew name for Ecclesiates, is the name given to a sage, or a group of sages writing in Palestine in the fifth century BCE, the postexilic period of Persian rule. The name Qohelet probably means "gatherer," "compiler," or "assembler," from the Hebrew verb *qahal*, "to assemble." The Persian kings gave land grants or portions (Hebrew *kheleq*) to their favorite subjects, fostering a growing divide between society's haves and have nots. In this competitive environment, common people were at the mercy of landowners and judges. Qohelet's audience was middle-class working people, homesteaders, perfumers (10:1), quarry workers, woodcutters, hunters, and farmers (10:9). Their daily lives

119

include the risk of accident and death. There is a lot about which to be anxious and little about which to be sure.

Qohelet finds the assurances of traditional wisdom to be inadequate and inaccurate. The inscrutability of God, the inequities of daily life, and the imminence of death mean that one can live wisely and still be stung by injustice and tragedy. One can live foolishly yet be favored and prosper. In this period, some prophets and wisdom teachers, giving up on the present, looked to a future intervention by God, a "new thing" (Isa. 43:18–19), or to wisdom as apocalyptic secrets mediated through angelic figures. In contrast, Qohelet does not give up on the present, though he does not always like what he sees here. With a resigned sigh, he states that there is "nothing new under the sun." But in the next breath, he encourages his students to embrace the limited possibilities of human life in the present moment as good, if precarious, gifts from God (2:24; 3:12, 22; 8:15).

THEOLOGICAL CONTEXT

Ecclesiastes contains positive wisdom teachings (7:5, 6; 8:1, 12; 10:2, 8, 9, 10, 12). Alongside them, however, other sayings subvert those upbeat lessons, highlighting the suffering of the wise and the prosperity of fools (8:14), the oppression of the weak by the powerful (4:1, 2), the fragility of wisdom in the face of folly (9:18; 10:1), and the imminence of death for wise as well as fool (2:16–17; 9:2).

Qohelet's theology consists of subversions of each of traditional wisdom's three core beliefs. Traditional wisdom first affirms that wisdom is a gift from God, expressed by means of personified Wisdom. For Qohelet, the gift is not an encompassing understanding of God and life promised by Proverbs. It is our portion (*kheleq*). "It is God's gift that all should eat and drink and take pleasure in all their toil" (3:13). The word meaning "lot" or "portion" can be understood literally as a plot of land or metaphorically as one's lot in life (2:10, 21; 3:22; 5:18; 9:6, 9). Our lot holds both the reality of toil and pain and the possibility of enjoyment. Joy in the midst of toil is the human portion, and it is the gift we receive from God.

The second affirmation made by traditional wisdom is that "the fear of the LORD is the beginning of wisdom" (Prov. 1:7; 9:10; 15:33; 31:30). Qohelet does not use the term "the fear of the LORD." Rather, he advises his students to "fear God." The God of Proverbs reveals. The

God of Ecclesiastes conceals. God's ways are mysterious (3:11). God is far off and unapproachable, determining the timing of events as God sees fit (3:1–8). God causes happiness and calamities and holds in the divine hands power and social institutions (7:13–14). Qohelet does not interpret negative events as divine retribution; they are simply the acts of God. God has instilled in humans a desire to search for order; at the same time, God frustrates that search, "so that all should stand in awe before [God]" (3:14).

The third theological pillar of traditional wisdom is that living by wisdom leads to a certain order of personal and social life. Qohelet, by contrast, characterizes human life as *hebel*, which is often translated as "vanity" but literally means "breath" or "breeze." Qohelet uses *hebel*, not to describe God, but to describe situations in life in which the expectations of traditional wisdom are disappointed. These include the ephemerality of life (6:12; 7:15; 9:9), joy (2:1), human accomplishments (2:11; 4:4), and youth and the prime of life (11:10). Qohelet questions whether wisdom had any advantage over folly, given that misfortune and death afflict the wise person as surely as they do the foolish one (2:14, 16; 6:8, 11). While Qohelet laments injustice (4:1–4), he does not consider substantial social change to be possible.

LITERARY CONTEXT

Ecclesiastes is a parody of the royal inscription genre in which a king boasts of his accomplishments and legacy. This author-king's achievement is to discover that kings, however wise, have no advantage over fools and that their legacies will be forgotten.

Ecclesiastes features a prologue (1:1–11) in which the author introduces himself and opines the futility of both wisdom and self-indulgence. Chapter 3 is a grim description of the set-in-stone nature of life events. Chapter 7 alternately states sunny proverbs and contradicts them. Chapter 12 is an extended metaphor on the frailty of old age, followed by an epilogue by another hand.

Between these chapters are series of sayings that, while their themes differ, serve Qohelet's goal of showing that traditional wisdom is *hebel*, vapor. He employs several literary strategies to vaporize traditional wisdom's solid assurances. One is to offer a positive proverb that sounds like traditional wisdom and then immediately contradict it. Chapter 7 is a whole series of such "set up, let down" sayings. This strategy causes readers to question their existing assumptions about reality.

Another strategy found in the sayings is the use of paradox: "For in much wisdom is much vexation, and those who increase knowledge increase sorrow" (1:18). Similar is the use of questions that have no answer, called impossible questions: "How can the wise die just like fools?" (2:16). These strategies create in the reader an experience of *hebel*, a repeated setup and letdown like Qohelet's own disappointment in traditional wisdom's promises in his context.

HOMILETICAL CONTEXT

In Qohelet's view, we are set free to experience awe, gratitude, and enjoyment of the present by facing facts of life we would prefer to ignore. Ecclesiastes, our honest if sometimes unwelcome friend, offers us several reminders that can be liberating rather than depressing.

The author reminds us of the limitations of our time, energy, life span, control of circumstances, and knowledge of God (3:9–22; 5:1–7; 8:16–17). We are limited because this is the way God has set things up. We stand before God with humility and allow God to be God (3:9–11; 5:7).

Qohelet reminds us that disappointment is a fact of life. This insight frees us from the fantasy that misfortune will come to everyone but us and opens us to the growth that comes from both tragedy and triumph.

Finally, Qohelet reminds us that focusing on the joy we have at hand is far better than underestimating our current blessings while focusing on ambition, endless toil, and the gains we think they will bring us (9:7–10).

One way to help a congregation understand Ecclesiastes is to show how it relates to the other wisdom books in the Hebrew Bible. On the one hand, Qohelet's melancholy vision of a distant God is balanced by Job's angry knocking on heaven's door. On the other, insistence on the limitation of human wisdom in Ecclesiastes needs to be balanced by Proverbs and its confidence that the one who seeks wisdom will find a great deal of joy and insight in life. Ecclesiastes, with its stress on a distant, unknowable God before whom we are to tremble, needs the assurance in Proverbs that when we trust in the Lord with all our heart, we will find wisdom and life. Qohelet needs Proverbs' depiction of the fear of the Lord as a radical reverence that leads, not just to a recognition of the divide between humanity and God, but to a considerable degree of insight about how best to live one's life. Similarly, Ecclesiastes, with its social passivism and resignation, needs the passion for social justice of the Hebrew prophets.

Christian preachers may want to give congregations permission to debate Ecclesiastes's vision of God as distant and as responsible for justice and injustice alike, and disagree that death is the end of life. At the same time, though, they should lead the congregation in showing appreciation for the book's vision of living fully in the present, filled with awe and gratitude to God, committed to the enjoyment of the pleasures of one's lot, made all the more precious because they are precarious.

Song of Songs

LISA WILSON DAVISON

While most Christian Bibles title this book the "Song of Solomon," reflecting the traditional claim for Solomonic authorship, that is only one of its two possible names. In Hebrew, this book is titled *shir hashirim*, which translates as "Song of Songs." Such repetition is the Hebrew way of expressing the superlative; this text is the song that is better than all other songs. The next words in the Hebrew text are *'asher lishlomoh*, "which is of Solomon." Like the many superscriptions in the Psalms (e.g., *ledavid*), this is not meant as a byline but probably indicates that the text is "in honor of" Solomon or "dedicated to" Solomon. Since King Solomon was known for his many wives and concubines, one can see why a book of love poems would come to be associated with him. One tradition suggested that Solomon wrote these poems about his relationship with the queen of Sheba (see 1 Kgs. 10 or 2 Chr. 9), but there is no evidence to support this claim.

Song of Songs is found among the *Ketuvim*, the "Writings," the third portion of the Jewish Bible, which was the last section to be canonized by the Jews (perhaps not until 200 CE). Scholars think that Song of Songs either was written at a late date (after the Babylonian exile, no earlier than the fifth century BCE), or at least was not accepted until late in the canonization process. The subject matter of the book is erotic love that is expressed within a nonmarital context. It contains no expressions of Israelite nationalism or of any explicit religious/ethical values (the word "God" never appears in the book). It is suggested that the book's subject matter almost prevented it from making it into the canon, or it might have been questioned because the female has such a dominant voice: she is in control of her sexuality and not the possession of some male (which was common in many ancient cultures, including Israelite culture). We know that the rabbis debated its inclusion, and some believe that it was included only because of the traditional belief in Solomon's authorship. However, it is equally plausible that Song of Songs was kept in the Jewish canon because the rabbis understood that the Divine is a part of all life, including sexuality. We are indebted to them for this wise decision.

This work is best viewed as a collection of love poems rather than a single poem. These poems (1:2–8, 9–17; 2:1–7, 8–17; 3:1–5, 6–11; 4:1–5:1; 5:2–8; 5:9–6:3; 6:4–13; 7:1–8:4; 8:5–14) are sexual, depicting relationships that are confident and free. The moods range from serious to playful. There is a lack of a unified style in the chapters. The poems do, though, share many of the common characteristics of Hebrew poetry found in other parts of the Bible (e.g., parallelism, refrains, repetition, puns/wordplays, metaphorical language, etc.), and three main poetic forms dominate the book: monologue, soliloquy, and dialogue.

Also, there are two main characters throughout the poems: the woman and her lover. They are joined by a supporting cast that includes the "daughters of Jerusalem" (who act like a chorus) and other members of the city. One of the poems contains words put into the mouths of the woman's "brothers."

Many parallels have been discovered between the poetry in Song of Songs and ancient Near Eastern love poems, well known for their explicit lyrics and outbursts of emotion by the lovers. These extrabiblical materials date to at least a thousand years before the suggested date of composition for Song of Songs. Some of the poems have been identified as a particular form, called a *wasf.* Such poems were sung by the groom to his bride at the wedding, praising her beauty from head to foot. The three parts of a *wasf* include introductory words by the guests, invitation by the bride for the groom to speak of her beauty, and the groom's praise of the bride. A similar form is found in Song of Songs 4:1–7.

The most popular approach to interpreting the Song of Songs, at least since the first century CE, has been to read the book allegorically. This mode of interpretation claims that the words of the text are not about human love; rather, they refer to something else entirely. For

example, some Jewish interpreters claimed that the poems symbolically represented the relationship between God and Israel, expressing
the love shared between the God and the people. Jewish mysticism
saw Song of Songs as describing the relationship between God and the
Shekinah (i.e., the female companion/side of God). In Judaism, the
book has been linked to the Passover Festival since the eighth century
CE, with some communities reciting the poems every Friday evening
Sabbath service.

Within Christian circles, allegorical interpretation of the Song of
Songs was the norm by the third century CE, but their approaches
varied. Some believed the poetry described the relationship between
the church and Christ, others the relationship between God and the
human soul, and still others the relationship between God and Mary,
the mother of Jesus. In Christian liturgy, the Latin text of the book is
included in the Marian festivities.

It was really not until the rise of modern critical-biblical scholarship
in the eighteenth century that this allegorical approach was debunked.
Since then, scholars have read the poems for what they truly are:
erotic poetry about human love. This is especially true in contemporary scholarship. Feminist scholars have focused attention on the Song
of Songs because of its strong female voice, which speaks boldly of
her excitement and passion at the idea of being with her partner, and
because of its apparent equality of the sexes (e.g., both man and woman
can initiate and enjoy sex without constraints). Queer approaches to
the Hebrew Bible—"queer interpretation" has become the accepted
scholarly term for approaches to the Bible that read the text through a
hermeneutic concerned with justice for LGBTQI persons—are interested in the book primarily because some of the poems seem to describe
a prohibited or scandalous relationship due to differences between the
man and woman in economic class, ethnicity, or other divisions created
by humans.

When read for what it is, Song of Songs can be a rich resource for
faith communities, and it is a shame that only one of its passages (2:8–
13) appears in the Revised Common Lectionary. Its very inclusion in
the scriptural canon reminds us that sex, when shared between two
consenting adults, is a gift from God. The poetry teaches us that sex
is intended for pleasure and not just for reproduction. Song of Songs
provides preachers with material and opportunities for talking about
faith and sex in healthy and holistic ways. While it might be easy to see
how Song of Songs could be used for wedding homilies, these ancient

words also could form the basis for preaching about the goodness of human relationships and the need to respect others' bodies, as well as one's own.

The poetry will also serve well in sermons dealing with the enduring power of love. Song of Songs summarizes its view of such love in these powerful words in the final chapter: "Set me as a seal upon your heart, as a seal upon your arm; for love is strong as death, passion fierce as the grave. Its flashes are flashes of fire, a raging flame. Many waters cannot quench love, neither can floods drown it. If one offered for love all the wealth of one's house, it would be utterly scorned" (8:6–7).

Isaiah

PATRICIA K. TULL

Jesus and other New Testament figures cite Isaiah more frequently than any other prophet, and both Jews and Christians through the ages have found much instruction and comfort in this large and complex book. But those wishing to preach from Isaiah encounter three initial hurdles: (1) the contexts in which Isaiah's passages appear in the Revised Common Lectionary; (2) long-held but mistaken assumptions about biblical prophecy; and (3) the book's own complex composition. We will first address these issues briefly, supplying some of the book's continuity in theme and backdrop in Jerusalem's long history, and then proceed to discuss the importance that parts of Isaiah hold for contemporary preaching.

1. Isaiah appears in the Revised Common Lectionary more often than any other Old Testament book besides the Psalms. But it almost never occurs in a context that facilitates reading it on its own merits. Out of some seventy-nine readings in the course of three years, only four occur in Ordinary Time. The others are governed by the cycles of the Christian year and events of Jesus' story—Advent and Christmas, Epiphany, Lent and Easter—or are paired with Gospel readings to complement their content. To preach Isaiah in any continuous way related to the book's own themes requires breaking from the lectionary.

2. Mistaken but long-held assumptions present difficulties that Isaiah shares with other biblical prophets and the Old Testament in

general. New Testament authors, steeped in a developing scriptural tradition, were challenged to show that their gospel was rooted in Israel's past. Thus when Matthew describes Jesus' birth, for example, he does so in terms of passages from Isaiah and other prophets, showing their correspondence. When Paul retells the story of Gentile inclusion in Romans, he likewise interlaces his argument with Scripture to extend welcome to Gentile Christians.

But by the second century, what had started as continuity and inclusion became discontinuity and exclusion. Christians began to detach the great Israelite prophets from their own people and to claim them as precursors, looking forward longingly to Christ. The prophetic books came to be treated differently by Christians than they were evidently intended and differently from how Jews read them: no longer as concerned with events and people of their own day but rather as predicting, usually in code, the details of Jesus' life, death, and resurrection. Even now, as scholarship increasingly aids understanding of the prophets on their own terms, the lectionary continues to read them as predictors of Jesus' advent and passion.

3. Isaiah's complex composition: Copyrights and pride of authorship not being the same in ancient days as today, most biblical books show history of development through the work of multiple authors. Isaiah stands on a level of complexity far exceeding that of most biblical books. The prophet speaks to his contemporaries about circumstances in Jerusalem, but these circumstances span at least two centuries, as if he had lived through the ages, commenting on events during the Assyrian, Babylonian, and Persian dominations of Judah, through several wars, destructions, and international upheavals.

Over the centuries readers have recognized the disparate times being addressed in the book of Isaiah. With the rise of modern historical criticism, rather than supposing the prophet to have lived more than two hundred years or to have divined detailed messages applicable to generations in drastically altered circumstances centuries after his own, scholars have concluded that Isaiah is a composite text, rooted in Isaiah's own prophecies, but extended by other prophets who were likewise concerned with the evolving relationship between God and Jerusalem. Conventional scholarly wisdom now describes First Isaiah (chaps. 1–39) proceeding mostly, but by no means fully, from the time of Kings Ahaz and Hezekiah in late eighth-century Jerusalem; Second Isaiah (chaps. 40–55) relates to the conquest of Babylon by King Cyrus of Persia in the mid-sixth century; and Third Isaiah (chaps. 56–66), which encompasses a variety of writings about Persian-era Jerusalem, at some time after its reconstitution.

Although in some ways the most diverse part of the book, the eleven chapters comprising Third Isaiah function as its glue, alluding to themes and poems from throughout Isaiah 1–55. Because of this complex evolution, interpreters of Isaiah are compelled both to note the position of the passage they are reading in the book as a whole and, in many cases, to accept some uncertainty over circumstances surrounding the author and intended audience.

The thread on which the entire book hangs is the fate of Jerusalem, often called Zion, beginning in the late eighth century, when Isaiah finds it both externally beset and internally fraught. Externally, the Assyrian Empire is growing in power, and Judah is caught between this superpower and two neighboring states that seek to defy it, Israel and Aram to the north. Internally, Jerusalem is failing to live up to prophetic hopes that it be a city of peace with justice. Like other prophets, Isaiah believes that external politics can be entrusted to God, but leaders must enact justice within their own jurisdiction. If they fail, their country will weaken and fall. The first twelve chapters articulate these concerns, accusing both leaders and prominent society members of moral failure most evident in wealth disparities: widows, orphans, and other outsiders are being "legally" robbed by various mechanisms of greed. For Isaiah, this can only eventuate in economic devastation for the wealthy.

FIRST ISAIAH (CHAPS. 1–39)

In the first chapter Isaiah begins with a scathing indictment of worship without justice. Blame is laid at the feet of those who pile up sacrifices and festivals without learning obedience to God's social policies: "Cease to do evil, learn to do good; seek justice, rescue the oppressed, defend the orphan, plead for the widow" (1:16–17). An abrupt new beginning in chapter 2, certainly redacted, foresees a very different day when Jerusalem will become a global center of divine justice, where nations will seek to learn from Israel's God and will then beat their weapons into farm implements to grow rather than destroy life. The rest of chapter 2 offers a dystopic alternative, in which humankind turns increasingly to idolatry and is humiliated. Chapter 3 comprises a scathing indictment of the upper classes, while chapter 4 returns briefly to a more hopeful, chastened, vision.

Chapters 5–10 embody a complex cycle of prophecies and narratives that continue to indict injustice and disobedience. Chapter 5 begins with the "song" of the vineyard, doubtless a precursor of Jesus' parable about the vineyard's tenants in Mark 12. In Isaiah's vision the culprit is the vegetation itself, which is carefully cultivated but yields only rottenness. The chapter's remainder lists direct indictments against acquisitive greed, thoughtless revelry, and defiance, ending with a warning of disaster.

Chapter 6, one of the book's most well-known texts, is set in Jerusalem's temple, where Isaiah relates seeing God enthroned. When God seeks a messenger, the prophet volunteers, but the message he is given is terrifying and frustrating: he is to say, "Keep listening, but do not comprehend; keep looking, but do not understand" (6:9); since that is evidently just what they are doing, the messenger tells them to do so until they are finally destroyed. Yet in the very next chapter, the prophet encourages King Ahaz of Jerusalem in the face of an impending attack by Israel and Aram. The prophecy of "Immanuel" occurs in this context. Unlike its echo in Matthew 1:23, this passage concerns a "young woman" (not a "virgin") who is already with child in Isaiah's time, and who will name the child "God is with us" (Immanu-El), since the present crisis will be resolved during his infancy. Isaiah offers this signal to reassure the wavering king.

Isaiah seems ever ready to hope for better responses in succeeding generations. Chapter 9 conveys expectation or celebration of a new king, one who will establish justice and righteousness. The expectation is most often associated with Ahaz's son Hezekiah; according to 2 Kings and Isaiah, Hezekiah proved to be a better ruler. Matthew 4:16 remembers this prophecy (Isa. 9:2) in relation to the beginning of Jesus' ministry.

The final vision that follows in chapter 11 is not echoed in the New Testament. But in the century before Jesus' lifetime, this passage describing the peaceable kingdom brought by a Davidic ruler had resurfaced as a popular wish among Jews who opposed both the Roman rulers and the homegrown Hasmoneans they had replaced. Scholars debate whether the prophecy, clearly voicing longing for the justice that Isaiah sought in vain, is anchored in hope for any particular ruler. But its vision of universal peace, like that in chapter 2, remains a touchstone for those seeking alternatives to the violent political world of both ancient times and today.

Many succeeding chapters in First Isaiah are not represented in the lectionary, including the oracles about the nations that comprise chapters 13–23 and most of the proto-apocalyptic sayings of chapters 24–27, which despite their position are thought to be among the latest additions to the growing work. Yet some of Isaiah 25 appears twice in the lectionary, once again offering future hope for nations, envisioning God as host at a lavish banquet and as universal healer, swallowing up death forever.

Chapters 28–32, also absent from the lectionary, appear to return to Isaiah's own time and to continue the prophet's indictments against the powerful of his day. This section is followed by three pivot points leading to the prophecies of consolation that begin in chapter 40 (the opening of Second Isaiah): first with chapter 33, once again envisioning restored Jerusalem; then chapters 34–35, which communicate destruction for neighboring Edom paired with Jerusalem's restoration; and finally chapters 36–39, which retell episodes related in 2 Kings 18–20 about Hezekiah, in which Jerusalem is besieged by Assyria but saved, the king is threatened by deadly disease but recovers, and Isaiah warns the complacent king that distant Babylon will one day carry away the temple's treasures and his own descendants, foreseeing conditions over which a later prophet will seek to console Jerusalem.

Chapter 35 so closely resembles the language and themes of chapter 40–55 that some have believed it to have been written by the same person. It probably reflects knowledge of these chapters and is likely placed where it is as a preview of a resolution to the distressing news that follows in the narrative chapters, which original readers would have known all too well.

Preachers seeking to develop sermons from Isaiah 1–39 should seek to understand Isaiah's words within their own contexts. Since both Isaiah and the Gospels communicate concern for the poor and disdain for greed, these are clear themes to highlight, as is hope in God for the world's future, rather than human leadership.

SECOND ISAIAH (CHAPS. 40–55)

Far more lectionary passages are derived from Isaiah's final 27 chapters, focusing on the hopeful poetry of comfort and restoration. Unlike the

book's first 39 chapters, Second Isaiah (chaps. 40–55) is not disparate in time, subject matter, or genre, but flows as a sequence of lyric
poems that develop, through repetition and variation, the claim that
the advent of King Cyrus of Persia as Babylon's conqueror portends the
return of favor to Israel and the invitation to rebuild Jerusalem.

Chapter 40 opens with a divine command to unidentified messengers to "comfort, O comfort my people." This refrain, found frequently throughout Second Isaiah, responds to the repeated complaint
in Lamentations that Jerusalem has no comforter (e.g., 1:17). It sets
the theme of restoration and reconciliation that plays out in various
ways throughout these sixteen chapters. After an eleven-verse introit in
which the message of comfort is passed from one voice to another, a
second overture begins in verse 12, celebrating YHWH's incomparable
might, which is evident both in the world's creation and in the creation
and deliverance of Israel.

Beginning in chapter 41, the prophet primarily speaks in God's
voice, echoing themes introduced in the opening chapter. Israel, also
called Jacob, is identified as God's beloved servant and assured of God's
help, made concrete in the restoration of green habitats in the desert.
Chapters 41–48 primarily address Servant Israel, assuring God's help
and protection despite past ruptures, and asserting YHWH as the only
God capable of acting in the world. In chapter 42 Israel is given a
mission to establish justice in the earth. This poem issues in a refrain
of praise echoing the Psalms. Its doxological themes will be repeated
several times in Second Isaiah.

After a brief remembrance of Israel's past disobedience, chapter 43
opens once again with assurances of divine presence and help no matter
what obstacles are faced. Remembering the exodus and then claiming
that the new events on the horizon will supersede that grand act of salvation, the chapter concludes with reminders of Israel's past unfaithfulness. Although the coming Persian conqueror Cyrus has been broadly
referenced as God's agent of deliverance since chapter 41, he is not
explicitly named until the climatic end of chapter 44 and beginning of
chapter 45. In chapters 46 and 47 the downfall of Babylon is vividly
imagined.

Chapters 49–55 turn to addressing Jerusalem. Here passages about
Israel as servant alternate with passages addressing Jerusalem with comfort. Unsurprisingly, the lectionary dwells primarily on the servant
passages, implying that they refer to Jesus by placing them in Holy
Week. Yet these passages hold an "if the shoe fits, wear it" quality:

Jesus is indeed remembered as a model of faithfulness in Israel, but Isaiah has offered the model for all Israelites, and indeed, all God-fearers. Interspersed with the servant passages in chapters 49, 50, and 53, the passages addressed to Jerusalem reassure of return, repopulation, revitalization, and comfort.

Even though Second Isaiah is historically specific to the early Persian context, its vibrant and multivalent poetry has continued vividly to convey divine faithfulness in many eras of Jewish and Christian history. Preachers can seek analogies between hopes the prophet held for divine presence and action in that critical time and hopes for healing in our own contexts; they can identify traits of faithful leadership described by the poet that are still applicable today.

THIRD ISAIAH (CHAPS. 56–66)

A corner is turned in Isaiah 56, as the prophet rejoins concern for human justice to divine justice. Following upon First Isaiah's worldwide interests, and YHWH's universal rule as asserted by Second Isaiah, Third Isaiah shows increasing interest in the relationship between Israelites and Gentiles, such as the foreigners who are welcomed in Isaiah 56. Chapter 58, like Isaiah's first chapter, focuses on authentic worship not as ritual bereft of justice, but as generosity to the hungry, homeless, and vulnerable. Chapters 60–62, at the center of Third Isaiah, echo and extend Second Isaiah's visions of Jerusalem's restoration. A communal lament that encompasses 63:7–64:12, perhaps dating from Babylonian times, recollects God's past gracious deeds, despite Israel's sin, and pleads for renewed divine attention. The final two chapters, including the vision of restoration in 65:17–25, foresee a day of peace and prosperity for those who serve YHWH faithfully.

Isaiah's historical sweep reveals in something like "real time" the complexity of ancient Judah's project of seeking faithfulness to divine ideals in the face of harsh political realities. Its gap between actuality and aspiration continues to challenge ethical decision making among believers of every era. Such a gap continues today, and preachers can highlight ideals that fuel partially successful endeavors, especially in furthering justice in our communities.

Jeremiah

MARY DONOVAN TURNER

The book of Jeremiah is an extraordinary resource for preachers not only because it provides passages that both challenge and intrigue, but also because Jeremiah spares no words in describing the life of the prophet-preacher. He feels inadequate, sometimes confident, duped, betrayed, vulnerable, isolated, inspired, and on occasion, hopeful. Contemporary preachers may have feelings that mirror Jeremiah's own; they may find in the prophet a kind of kindred spirit as week in and week out they prepare words for the waiting community.

Seemingly destined to be a prophetic voice for God's word, Jeremiah is the subject, and author, of parts of the book by the same name. The book of Jeremiah has fifty-two chapters, chronicling the forty years of the prophet's ministry. Structurally the book is quite complex; it consists of small units of varying genres. Through extended metaphor and parable, poignant first-person narratives and soliloquies, accusations spoken against Israel and other nations, and profound words of hope, the prophet speaks to a nation, bringing contextualized words that are, at a particular time and place, the words people most needed to hear.

As Jeremiah's story begins (1:1–3), he is introduced to and defined for the reader as the son of Hilkiah, a priest of the priests of Anathoth, a city in the land of Benjamin, just north of Jerusalem. We are given the names of the kings of Judah, Josiah, Jehoiakim, and Zedekiah, who ruled during Jeremiah's prophetic career. Those familiar with the history of Judah would know that Jeremiah's career, then, began in a time of hopefulness and optimism when the good king Josiah was leading the people back to their fundamental covenant with Yahweh.

His prophetic career ended, however, when Jerusalem was taken captive. He saw the nation move from prosperity to devastation, from community to exile. The story of Jeremiah is a painful one. He is deeply affected by what he sees, and throughout his years as a prophet, he knows that the end of the good days is possible, at times, he thinks, inevitable. Jeremiah is thrust into a story of national demise.

Scholars have searched for and defined some possible overarching structures or outlines for the book of Jeremiah, but, in the end, these proposals are not wholly helpful for the preacher. The imposed structures can diminish the variegated and complicated nature of the book itself and may skew the preacher's understanding of the intention or meaning of individual units. It is more fruitful for the preacher to engage, in light of the historical contexts defined above, the features of each unit: its genres, rhetorical devices, images, and metaphors to interpret more specifically and carefully what each passage is doing and saying. Engaging each text in this way may provide for the preacher the focus for the sermon.

The lectionary is helpful in exposing us to the many literary genres that are found in the book of Jeremiah: the prophet's call story, prayers, confessions, oracles, laments, biographical narratives, indictments of the nation, and words saturated with hope. The weaving of these is intricate and complex; the placement and patterns of them often have no observable rationale, narrative movement, or trajectory. When interpreting a word of indictment, it is important to recognize that in other places in Jeremiah are also words of hope and forgiveness. And it is important, when preaching from one of Jeremiah's hopeful oracles, to know the realities of Judean living and the accusations of persistent dishonesty and idolatry against which Jeremiah speaks. Not to recognize these realities makes Jeremiah's radical and audacious hope-filled words naive and superficial.

Below are descriptions of the most prominent or important genres found in Jeremiah and some ideas on how the preacher might engage them exegetically and interpretively for specific communities.

CALL NARRATIVE

The stage is set, and abruptly Jeremiah receives a word, a call from Yahweh (1:3–10). We know nothing about him before his call; it is as if what happened before is not important. Simply the word intrudes and, in first-person narration, Jeremiah recounts it for the reader/hearer. The story is the detailing of the conversation between Jeremiah and the One who has called him, has created him, and now consecrates and appoints him. "Before I formed you," the speech begins (1:5). Before he was even conceived, Jeremiah was known and a part of God's plan. The prophet is not yet told where he will go, what he will say, or whom he will address.

The response of the one called is both familiar (as witnessed in the response of other prophets who receive a call from Yahweh) and understandable. He does not feel qualified for the task on the basis of both his inexperience and his youth. The confession of weakness provides the opportunity for divine words of encouragement. Jeremiah is told to go where sent and speak what is commanded, all with the support of Yahweh's continual presence. We are reminded that often in the Hebrew Bible, the divine response to human anxiety is, as here, "Do not be afraid, . . . for I am with you" (1:8). The same God who calls also protects and delivers.

Yahweh reaches out and touches Jeremiah's mouth. As with the prophet Isaiah, whose lips are purified (Isa. 6:5–7), Jeremiah is made ready to speak. There is an intimacy between God and prophet, the message and the messenger. God's words are put into the prophet's mouth. With only the words that he has been given, Jeremiah will be appointed over nations and kingdoms: he will pluck up and pull down nations. Four verbs describe his mission: he will destroy, overthrow, build, and plant (1:10). All this he will do with words—dynamic, vital, life-changing words.

It is through the lens of this opening chapter that we read and understand all that follows in Jeremiah, as formed and fashioned through editors' hands. In his ministry, Jeremiah does not go unopposed, and in 1:18 he, and we, are warned about the overwhelming obstacles he will face and the despair he will feel about his vocation. As he brings indictments to the people, we realize that we also know oppression, violence, destruction, the abuse of power, and the neglect of the vulnerable in the community. We know about idolatry and injustice and the motives from which they both grow. The preacher can use the words of Jeremiah to motivate the community, thereby to pull up and overthrow what is ungodly and help to build and plant the faithful world that God intended for us.

ACCUSATION/INDICTMENT

Jeremiah 2:4–4:4, a series of accusations against the nation, follows the call of Jeremiah, which ends with two visions (the branch of an almond tree and the boiling pot tilted away from the north). The two visions announce God's judgment: the enemy will come to Jerusalem. From the outset, God does not deceive Jeremiah by telling him that the work will be easy or even successful.

A series of accusations begins with a rhetorical question from God: "What wrong did your ancestors find in me that they went far from me, and went after worthless things, and became worthless themselves?" (2:5). Though Yahweh had brought them up out of slavery through barren to fertile land, the people believed that God had not been faithful to them. They then followed "worthless" pursuits (vv. 5, 8, 11). The people exchanged what was valuable for what was not. They became empty and deluded, evil and bitter (v. 19). The people rejected their God, a source of living water, and they have hewn out for themselves cisterns, cracked cisterns, which hold no water. Verses 14–19 describe the tragic consequences, and we are invited to locate ourselves in their choices and priorities. Where and when are we chasing "worthless things"?

PERSONAL LAMENT/CONFESSIONS

Interspersed in the book of Jeremiah is a series of six personal laments (11:18–12:6; 15:10–21; 17:14–18; 18:18–23; 20:7–13, 14–18). These are outpourings from the prophet, who becomes overwhelmed by the responsibility and the consequences of being one of God's spokespersons to Judah. Rarely in prophetic literature is the private struggle of the prophet so accessible to the reader. The reader of Jeremiah is allowed to enter the inner recesses of the prophet's head, mind, and soul. The lectionary uses part of two of these laments (11:18–20; 15:15–21) and one in its entirety (20:7–13). In the call narrative (chap. 1) there is certainly no guarantee from God that Jeremiah's prophetic vocation will be successful. There are hints that there will be verbal and physical resistances to his speaking. And there were.

Jeremiah 11:18–20. "But I was like a gentle lamb led to the slaughter" (11:19). This simile provides a graphic picture of the life of the prophet, who has been betrayed by those around him, those who devised schemes against him and were bent on his destruction. The lamb is innocent and helpless, but around him there is deceit and violence. Jeremiah calls God to visit revenge on his enemies. The humiliated Jeremiah says to Yahweh, "Let me see your retribution upon them, for to you I have committed my cause" (11:20). We may be familiar, but uncomfortable, with his request for revenge.

For forty years Jeremiah tenaciously and faithfully spoke out against the idolatry and injustice and corruption around him, even when he witnessed no change, only continuing evil and consequent demise. As preachers we wonder what sustained him through the challenges and painfulness of the task. In 20:7–13, the last of Jeremiah's confessions, he speaks not only of the agonizing life of a prophet, but also of how the continued compulsion to speak God's word overwhelms the pain of derision, isolation, and betrayal by friends. Jeremiah says that the word becomes something like a "burning fire shut up in my bones; I am weary with holding it in, and I cannot" (20:9). What issues instill such passion in the preacher? What must we preach because the compulsion cannot be stifled? Where will we not compromise? How do we encourage our congregations to continue their work toward justice even when they witness no obvious change?

SYMBOLIC ACT/STORY/PARABLE

Chapter 18:1–12 recounts a symbolic act in the book of Jeremiah, an illustration of an incident in the prophet's life when an ordinary object, task, or event yields new insight and understanding. Yahweh tells Jeremiah to go to a potter's house. He watches the potter working at the wheel; when he has created something that is flawed, the potter reworks the clay until the vessel seems good to him. Is God saying that God has control over the people as the potter over the clay? Or can Yahweh discard the clay that seems resistant to the potter's purpose? Or just as the potter hopes to fashion the useful vessel, does this story show us that Yahweh longs for the people of Israel to listen to Yahweh's voice and turn from evil? At the very least, the potter works and reworks the clay until the appropriate vessel is made. Power is tempered by patience. If the people repent from faithlessness, Yahweh will repent from anger.

The end of the story of the potter, however, is unsettling. Yahweh calls the people to turn from evil ways and amend their doings (18:11). In this final hour, will people know this is their last chance? The people's desire for repentance appears to be gone. And we wonder, do they not know that there is always the possibility for change? Or have they chosen death so long that they do not know how to choose life?

A variation on this genre of symbolic act is found in chapter 32 when the Lord tells Jeremiah to buy a plot of land in Anathoth offered to him by his cousin Hanamel. This story takes place in the tenth year of King Zedekiah of Judah, when Babylon is besieging Jerusalem, and Jeremiah is imprisoned in the palace of the Judean king because he has spoken harshly honest words about the demise of the nation. In buying the property at a time when the community believes it has no future, Jeremiah renders hope visible. How do the preacher and the community make their God-given hope visible?

The story of the land purchase is followed by a prayer, unusual in the book of Jeremiah. It expresses disbelief and belief. Read in the context of Jeremiah's prison cell (32:17–25), the words take on heightened dimensions of courage and faithfulness.

ANNOUNCEMENTS OF RESTORATION

The prophetic word is a contextualized word. When the people have strayed, the prophet brings words of warnings and accusation, calling them back into right relationship with God. And when they have experienced devastation or they believe there is no hope, the prophet brings words of forgiveness. The latter is found in Jeremiah 30–31, the Book of Consolation. The two chapters contain terse imagery, snapshots that enable the reader to visualize the exiled people who have or who will return to the land given to their ancestors. The section is filled with covenant language: once again God will be their God, and they will be God's people. While chapter 30 does not appear in the Revised Common Lectionary, chapter 31 is used with great frequency. Units from this chapter are used on Easter (vv. 1–6), during Pentecost (vv. 7–9 and 27–34), on the second Sunday of Christmas (vv. 7–14), and during Lent (vv. 31–34). Perhaps this wide usage reminds us that during every season of the liturgical year, preachers need to remind congregations of God's power to restore and renew us.

Preachers would do well to immerse themselves in the vivid and provocative imagery of chapter 31. How are the people feeling? How do they rejoice? Who is finally finding their way home? How is their relationship with God being renewed? The list of those being redeemed is vast and inclusive; Yahweh is taking the initiative in this new relationship.

I will make a new covenant with the house of Israel; . . .

I will put my law within them;

I will write it on their hearts;

I will be their God, and they shall be my people. . . .

I will forgive their iniquity, and remember their sin no more. (31:31–34)

The reader of Jeremiah must wrestle theologically with the words of restoration in conjunction with the harsh punishment that has been handed the unfaithful nation and described elsewhere in Jeremiah. The ultimate challenge may be: how does the preacher find words for a God who has high, radical, covenantal expectations for God's people but whose expectations are nested in grace?

Lamentations

MARY DONOVAN TURNER

The book of Lamentations is a series of five laments that name the horrors and devastation of the fall of Jerusalem in 586 BCE. Tradition attributes Lamentations to Jeremiah. It is not difficult to understand why; the prophet is often found lamenting the plight of the people, how they are not living up to the covenant they have made with their God. Jeremiah, though, was carried off to Egypt after the fall of the city and was not present in Jerusalem to witness daily life in the midst of its devastation. Most scholars believe that Lamentations is more likely a collection of poems written by liturgists to memorialize the fall of Jerusalem.

The vocabulary in Lamentations is similar to the lament speeches in the Psalms and the Prophets. Each of the five laments uses artful and provocative imagery, metaphors, and similes. At the same time each is highly structured, with four of the laments crafted as acrostics, each stanza beginning with a different letter of the Hebrew alphabet. The verses are in alphabetical order, using all of the alphabet's twenty-two letters. While there are some variations in how the acrostic is used in each chapter, the form may be an attempt to organize, and perhaps contain, the profound loss and grief. The use of the entire alphabet from *aleph* to *tau* may serve as a device emphasizing the totality of the destruction, or as we would say, the devastation was from A to Z, complete and all-encompassing.

There are four voices in Lamentations: the voice of the poet; the personified Daughter Zion, a widow who has lost both husband and children; an unnamed person who knows suffering; and the collective voice of the community calling to God for restoration. Eighteen times the one who has experienced the calamity is identified as "daughter." Most often she is called Daughter Zion. This personification had been used to represent Jerusalem sporadically in the eighth-century prophets and then is more frequently used in Jeremiah. The authors of Lamentations lend the reader a more developed and personal picture of this woman who knows devastation like no one ever before (see 1:12b). Additionally, unlike the prophets before them, the authors of Lamentations give her voice. She speaks. See, for instance, 1:9c, 11c–16. In the latter she uses twelve masculine-singular verbs to describe the actions that Yahweh has brought against her. Yahweh is the sole source of her pain. Through the voice of the devastated one, we witness theological questionings about why the devastation happened and what kind of God would cause it. Lamentations serves as a microcosm of the varied theologies found in the Hebrew Bible related to suffering; theological questions of theodicy are raised even if not fully answered. Was the city's demise a consequence or God's response to Jerusalem's social, religious, and political sin? Is God one who punishes or extends mercy? Can God be both the arbiter of devastation and redemption? Is suffering ever merited, and is there a time when it is too late to repent because God's patience has "run out"?

Chapters 1, 2, and 4 of Lamentations each begin with the exclamatory "how . . . ," which signals an expression of grief. They are in the form of a funeral dirge, making constant reference to distress. Consistent with ancient funeral dirges, they contrast Jerusalem in her former days of glory to the desolate present; with numerous references to death are mention of mourning rituals being performed.

While the funeral song seems a natural choice for poems that outline the overwhelming devastation of Jerusalem, the authors did not follow the form of the dirge slavishly. Lamentations also includes motifs of the complaint psalm such as cries for help from the suffering, the demand that Yahweh avenge the foe, and expressions of confidence in the steadfastness of God's care. The dirge form used in chapters 1, 2, and 4 suggests that, for Jerusalem, it is over. And yet, there are pleas for help, cries to Yahweh for restoration. It appears to be over, but the words in Lamentations imply that perhaps it is not. There is hope.

The despair in chapter 3 is palpable. A careful and close reading of this psalm of lament reminds readers of similar songs from the Psalter and opens the imagination to countless people who, in our own day, know this kind of affliction and despair, who are in darkness with no light, whose flesh and skin waste away, who know bitterness, who wear heavy chains, who feel that God has shut out their prayers. There are those who are surrounded by taunt songs, filled with bitterness, perhaps homeless, and whose soul is bereft of peace.

As in other psalms of lament, however, the poem shifts radically from despair to hopefulness. In 3:20–23 the lamenter says his soul is bowed down within him, "but this I call to mind, and therefore I have hope: the steadfast love of the LORD never ceases, his mercies never come to an end; they are new every morning; great is your faithfulness." Inspiring poets and hymn writers over the centuries, these words hold great power because of their context; they pour out of a person knowing the worst kinds of despair, a person whose body and spirit are bent and broken but who is speaking words of trust and hopefulness. Significantly, these words come at the center of the collection of poems, the heart of Lamentations.

The final poem in Lamentations is primarily a communal lament. The community voices despair over its current condition. They are oppressed, hungry, and weary. Women are raped. There is no joy or singing, and the people cry out to the Lord asking, "Why have you forgotten us completely? Why have you forsaken us these many days?" (5:20). Still, the community remains convinced that God can restore them, and they cry out, still believing that God is a listening God.

Together the five chapters of Lamentations remind us that there are important intersections between individual and communal grief. As preachers and care providers, we need to recognize and name both. How should preachers and congregations today ritualize grief and outrage for ourselves and for the people of the world whose lives are reflected in the words of suffering found in Lamentations? Daughter Zion in chapter 1, mired in devastation and seeming hopelessness, can find no comforter (1:2, 9, 16, 17, 21). How is the church called to the ministry of comforting those with pain and sorrow?

Moreover, have we in our churches lost our capacity and willingness to lament? Is there something about lament and the naming of suffering that is helpful for individuals and communities, something beyond catharsis, something that promotes healing? Only the positive, hopeful outburst of the individual lamenter in chapter 3 and the opening description of Jerusalem's overwhelming demise in chapter 1 are included in the Revised Common Lectionary. How could the other poems in Lamentations be helpful liturgically and homiletically as we read the words of despair and remember those in our world whose lives are plagued with violence and war, who know hunger and thirst, refugees and migrants who know no rest, no comfort?

Ezekiel

CHARLES L. AARON

Bizarre, shocking, confusing. No adjective seems strong enough to describe the words of Ezekiel. He might not last six months as pastor of a contemporary congregation. Yet, because of his unconventional writing, not in spite of it, the community of faith should take a closer look at the prophet whose name means "God strengthens." He wrote in an attention-grabbing way, but his words offered hope to those whose spirits had been crushed by bitter defeat and humiliation. He wrote in solidarity with dejected, bewildered people and embodied his message in acts as incredible as his words.

The book is an edited collection of oracles, but the whole piece flows well, with a distinct theological message that moves from judgment to restoration, rooted in the prophet's experience of the Babylonian exile, in the first wave of deportees, when he began his ministry around 593 BCE.

JUDGMENT (CHAPS. 1–32)

The first section of the book proclaims the judgment of God against Israel (chaps. 1–24) and the nations (chaps. 25–32) for their unfaithfulness and idolatry. The section concludes with Ezekiel offering a message of hope following the destruction of Jerusalem.

The average person considering a vocation in ministry might

experience Ezekiel's prophetic call in chapters 1–3 as a prompt to seek pastoral counseling rather than admission to seminary. The astonishing appearance of the divine presence pushes the boundaries of imagination. In a sense, the vision, starting in 1:4, stands in contrast to the first three verses. Biblical visions attest to a reality beyond what one can experience in history. The first three verses describe the history of Ezekiel and his nation. The victorious Babylonians have conquered Judah and carried Ezekiel and the others off to exile. The vision, in contrast, portrays a God with power almost beyond description. This tension between what one sees in history and what God reveals to Ezekiel runs throughout the book. Ezekiel's sign actions (e.g., setting up a brick and lying on his side in chap. 4, shaving with a sword in chap. 5) embody his message. Ezekiel accuses the people of idolatry, a charge that can include both physical representations (see 6:3–4) and unfaithfulness to God (see 8:16–18). Ezekiel describes what could be understood only through revelation: the glory of YHWH (YHWH's presence, gravitas) has departed from the city of Jerusalem (11:22–25).

Chapters 1–24 mostly interpret for Israel the reason for the defeat by the Babylonians and the banishment to exile. Ezekiel seeks to counter the argument that God punished the people for the sins of their ancestors (see 18:2) by making clear that the people themselves have sinned. He counters the argument that God has treated the people unjustly (see 18:25) by proclaiming that God has justifiably punished the people for their own sins.

This condemnation of the people leads the prophet to predict Israel's downfall (24:25–27). Even within the material condemning Israel, however, Ezekiel gives indications of the restoration that will come in time (as one example, see 20:33–38). Such promises teach the purposes of the judgment: to purge and to chastise.

The section of judgment against Israel precedes eight chapters (25–32) of oracles against other nations, primarily Israel's enemies, who mocked Judah (see 25:3). These oracles recognize the sovereignty of YHWH beyond Israel and indicate that YHWH judges the sins of others.

RENEWAL (CHAPS. 33–48)

A turning point in the book occurs at 33:21. A messenger who has escaped from the siege of Jerusalem tells Ezekiel that the Babylonians

have taken the city. YHWH has warned Judah (33:1–9) and has punished them in ways that they should recognize as justified (33:17–20).
With the fall of Jerusalem, however, the prophecies of Ezekiel turn
toward offering hope of restoration. Chapter 34 condemns the leaders of Israel/Judah who have failed the people (34:1–10). God will act
directly as the shepherd of the people (34:11–31). This chapter also
contains a messianic promise of a role for leadership from the house of
David (v. 24).

In chapter 37, perhaps the most well-known passage in Ezekiel, the
prophet's vision compares the restoration of the nation to the reanima-
tion of a field full of dead bones. The vision attests to God's ability to
act in even the most desolate of situations. The field of dead bones represents death, humiliation, and despair. The bones obviously contain
no life; no one buried the bodies; and no individual identity remains of
the soldiers who have died. Nevertheless, God's "spirit" brings "breath"
(the same Hebrew word) to the dead bones. The chapter presents a
powerful image of God's ability to bring hope and life.

Ezekiel promises that God will restore Israel after the exile, but also
assures much more. Two important verses that tie together the two
major parts of the book occur in 18:31 and 36:26. The first, 18:31,
exhorts the people of Judah to change from the inside out: "Get yourselves a new heart and a new spirit!" Then 36:26 promises that God will
provide that new heart. The insight of the book of Ezekiel comes in the
recognition that God must act within the people themselves to enable
them to become a true community of faith. A theme that runs throughout the book of Ezekiel is the affirmation that the people will come to
know YHWH. The prophecy of the dry bones in chapter 37 ends with
the affirmation that the people shall know "that I am YHWH" (v. 13
alt.), and that God will put God's "spirit" within them (v. 14).

In what likely represents a later editorial addition to Ezekiel, chapters 38–39 describe a battle against Gog, a cryptic allusion to an enemy
from the north. The battle represents the final, apocalyptic battle before
Judah experiences peace. This passage has suffered disastrous misinterpretation as if it were a prediction of events centuries in the future. In
its original setting, however, it contains a promise to Judah that God
can defeat any enemy. It is meant to refer to God's actions immediately
after the exile to restore Judah to its land and establish it in peace. This
section of Ezekiel ends with a promise of safety and a stable relationship
with YHWH. The exile and restoration will become a learning and
spiritual growth experience for Judah.

Ezekiel's final vision depicts his return to Israel from exile. In the city of Jerusalem stands a new temple (although the vision does not explicitly name Jerusalem). Much of this section describes the dimensions of the imaginary temple. The temple, both the physical temple that existed before its destruction by the Babylonians and this visionary temple, represents the presence of God among the people. Into this restored temple the glory of YHWH, which had left Jerusalem in chapter 11, returns (43:1–4). God has not abandoned the people forever.

Ezekiel was both priest and prophet. His prophetic visions, actions, and oracles communicate between God and the people. His concern for pure worship attests to the priestly message of the book. This last section of the book contains instruction for worship and the role of the priests in the restored temple. Chapters 40–48 likely were edited after the original composition of Ezekiel. In the final form of the book, these chapters interpret the presence of God returned to the people and the proper response of worship to that presence.

Chapter 47 paints a creative picture of a river of life flowing from the temple. The river brings renewal from the temple to the land. The language describing the life within the river alludes to the creation story in Genesis (see Gen. 1:20). The trees that grow along the river offer both food and healing. God's presence flows out from the temple, bringing abundance, as the river expands quickly to a depth that will nurture life (cf. Rev. 22). The vision portrays the postexilic presence of God to the people in an accessible, sustained, and life-giving way. A book that begins with the prophet in exile and proceeds to describe the departure of God's glory from the holy city ends with the affirmation that God will restore the people and the city. God will dwell with the people and enable their obedience and worship.

Although Ezekiel makes only a few appearances in the lectionary, the strange book from the strange prophet contains much material that could serve as the basis for a sermon, as well as material that leads to reflection on what preaching itself means. Chapter 2 interprets Ezekiel's prophecy as the faithful and courageous speaking of the words God gives the prophet. No preacher finds this task easy, but preaching the truth, as much as one understands it, whether the people listen or not, provides a good start for understanding the role of proclamation (2:5).

Moreover, the very structure of the book makes a theological statement that is important for preaching. Chapters 1–32 contain words of warning and judgment. After the judgment falls, described in chapter

33, the book begins words of restoration. Even within the first section, the word of renewal appears (chap. 17), foreshadowing material to come later in the book. Even in the midst of judgment, God shows grace.

The word of judgment itself shows divine concern for the spiritual state of the people. Ezekiel interprets judgment from God as preparatory for God's acts of renewal. Ezekiel's word of judgment in the first part of the book intends to elicit repentance. The word of judgment comes when the people still have a chance to change. Once the judgment has happened, because the Babylonians have conquered the city of Jerusalem, the prophet turns attention to restoration, grace, and renewal. The book recognizes that alienation from God, idolatry, and sin arise both from within the human heart and from poor leadership. In other words, sin is both individual and collective. Ezekiel 18:30–32 exhorts the people to get a new heart and spirit. This is a communal word, but it still places responsibility for sin and idolatry in the heart.

Chapter 34 recognizes the collective dimension of sin: it condemns the leaders of the people for their failure. Ezekiel, as much as any of the prophets, seems to understand that people change from the inside out, and that good leadership enables faithfulness. God will act to restore the people to the land, but will do even more than that. God will act directly to renew the people from within their own hearts, not just change their circumstances (36:26). God's acts of renewal for Judah arise from divine "mercy" (39:25), but God's purpose is to enable the people to know the name of YHWH. God will renew the people, but the people have a mission, to enable knowledge of the name of YHWH (a phrase repeated throughout the book).

The movement of the book from judgment to renewed favor and presence reminds contemporary preachers that judgment is never the last word. The final word of Ezekiel describes God's immutable presence with the people. The book has dealt with the tension between historical reality and the more profound reality of Ezekiel's visions. The final word of that reality is God's presence among a people whom God has changed and who worship God rightly.

Daniel

CHARLES L. AARON

Perhaps the most basic question about the book of Daniel concerns whether it really is a "book." When one reads through its chapters, it seems almost more akin to a collection of individual pieces rather than a coherent book that moves clearly through a plot or an argument. No transitions connect one chapter to another (implying that the book was not written by a single author). Preachers likely will base a sermon on one of the pieces rather than try to treat the whole book. Nevertheless, the preacher should seek to discern points of unity within the book.

NARRATIVE AND VISIONS

Scholars have struggled for centuries with the exasperating curiosities of the book of Daniel. The first half of the book (chaps. 1–6) takes a narrative form, with intriguing court tales in which Daniel and his companions live under the rule of foreign kings after the exile. Chapters 7–12 relate bizarre visions, heavy with symbolism, mythology, and cosmic battles. The authors used Hebrew in part of the book and the related language of Aramaic for other parts of the book. The visions represent apocalyptic themes that reveal hidden meanings to historical events. In apocalyptic literature, such as Revelation in the New

Testament, a dream, vision, or an otherworldly interpreter gives transcendent meaning to what the readers experience. For example, Daniel's vision in chapter 7 discloses the unearthly beasts that represent historical earthly powers. Daniel's vision in chapter 10 discloses a heavenly battle that corresponds to the conflict on earth. In apocalyptic theology, the full experience of God's victory over evil awaits beyond history. How do the two narrative and apocalyptic genres fit together?

Against seeing them as related, the two parts of the book give evidence of having arisen during different circumstances and were likely written about a century apart (although chap. 1 may have been written as an introduction after all of the other chapters were collected). Even though the narratives themselves depict a setting in the sixth century, after the Babylonian exile and the subsequent Persian conquest of Babylonia, textual evidence (such as Greek loanwords) suggests that chapters 2–6 may have been written much later, during the third century BCE, when Diaspora Jews faced the general problems of Hellenization after Alexander the Great. The visions of chapters 7–12, on the other hand, clearly reflect the situation of the second century BCE, when Judeans lived under the brutal reign of Syrian ruler Antiochus IV, who tried to force conformity on his whole empire (see 1–2 Maccabees).

Even though the two sections were likely written under different circumstances, certain consistent motifs do emerge throughout the two halves. One way to look at the relationship between the narratives of chapters 1–6 and the visions of chapters 7–12, then, is to see how the visions develop certain implicit themes from the court tales. These themes include revelation from God, the historical and supernatural rebellion against God, God's reassertion of divine sovereignty, and the ethical response of God's people during the interim until God acts. These four theological foci bring coherence to a complex work and deserve closer examination.

Before we examine each of these individually, however, it is important to notice that one way scholars have discerned these to be the central theological emphases of Daniel is to observe the use of poetic passages throughout the book. Within the court tales, the theological foci emerge out of a comparison of the events narrated in the tales with poetic passages (e.g., either prayer or doxology) uttered by the Judean heroes or the foreign kings. The poetic passages make certain theological affirmations, reinforced by the events of the tale in which the poem is embedded. Similarly, the visions contain theological summaries, often in the form of pronouncements by celestial beings, but also in prayer.

REVELATION FROM GOD

Throughout the Hebrew Bible, God communicates in a variety of ways: God speaks through Torah, the mouths of the prophets, creation, and the events of history, such as the escape from Egypt. Within the narrative world of Daniel, these means of communication have become complicated. For example, Daniel and his companions face the problem of living under two sets of laws: the Torah and the laws of the foreign kings. Moreover, the Judeans are tempted to interpret historical events as meaning that the gods of the Babylonians are stronger than their God.

Thus, within the book of Daniel, God communicates through dreams, mysterious handwriting on a wall, visions, and angelic interpreters. The Hebrew Bible sometimes has affirmed dreams as a means of communication (e.g., Gen. 20), but also has derided those who paid attention to dreams (e.g., Deut. 13:1–5). In Daniel, this ambiguity clears up as God consistently communicates in dreams and visions. These phenomena intrude into reality to reveal God's message. Even the message of the dreams and visions must have interpretation, however. In chapters 1, 2, 4, and 5, Daniel can interpret the dreams of others and mysterious occurrences. Starting in chapter 7, Daniel himself experiences visions that reveal messages not available to one's regular senses. In chapter 7, his dream seems to arise spontaneously. By contrast, in chapter 9, Daniel fasts and prays, hoping for revelation (see also 10:2–3). Chapter 9 contains an interpretation of Jeremiah 25:11–12 and 29:10.

With the failure of Torah, history, and such to make sense of the current situation, the book of Daniel makes sense of the triumph of foreign empires and the persecution by Antiochus through revelation that comes via indirect means, such as dreams and visions. This does not imply there is no continuity with early biblical understandings of God's revelation: Daniel's use of dreams and visions draws on ideas within the Hebrew Bible about mysteries beyond human comprehension (see Deut. 29:29; Eccl. 7:23–24). In Daniel, the suffering of the people under foreign rule falls under this category of mystery. A reality

exists beyond what human senses can detect. Dreams and visions reveal
that reality.

HISTORICAL AND SUPERNATURAL
REBELLION AGAINST GOD

While numerous passages in Daniel (2:20–23, 44; 4:32; 5:21–23;
6:26–27; 7:14) touch on this theological emphasis, two passages, one
from each major part, are exemplary in that they give brief descriptions
of God's will for creation. In the rather strange chapter 4, Nebuchadnezzar has a troubling dream of a tree. The great tree connects heaven
and earth, providing food, shade, and shelter. On one level, the dream
reveals an understanding of the role of earthly leaders: to provide security for all of the subjects under their care. On another, the dream also
suggests that God wills for people to have adequate provision for their
needs. The dream paints a picture of harmony, which the king should
promote. From the second part of the book, in chapter 9, Daniel's
vision reveals the true meaning of a prophecy of Jeremiah 25:11–12;
29:10–14. The prophecy from Jeremiah predicts a seventy-year Babylonian exile. Daniel, writing centuries later, interprets the prophecy to
apply to the persecution at the time of the writing. The time of captivity
will be much longer. Chapter 9 holds out a promise, however. At the
end of Judah's captivity, a time of fulfillment will arrive, "to finish the
transgression, to put an end to sin, and to atone for iniquity, to bring
in everlasting righteousness, and to seal both vision and prophet, and
to anoint a most holy place" (9:24). The vision offers a description of
holiness, forgiveness, restoration, right relationships ("righteousness"),
fulfillment of God's promises, and worship ("a most holy place"). The
everlasting nature of God's reign contrasts to the upheaval of world
events, in which one empire after another rules the Judean people.

Daniel views an assault on God's reign, on the divine will for creation, as coming from two main sources, and at times the book indicates
that the two sources are in cahoots. First, the *foreign kings* throughout
the narrative half of Daniel display weakness, vanity, and arrogance
toward God and God's people. For Daniel, even a foreign king has an
obligation to become God's instrument to provide for security and stability. Chapters 1–4 offer Nebuchadnezzar as an example of such a foreign ruler who fails to acknowledge God's sovereignty and must suffer
punishment. The author presents Nebuchadnezzar as ruling through

fear and intimidation, with even his own security personnel living in terror of making a mistake (1:10). The king displays irrational anger, endangering his own advisers (2:12). He co-opts the arts and delegitimizes persons in lesser authority to command worship of his statue (chap. 3). Similarly, Belshazzar shows no respect for the sacred vessels of God's temple, perhaps feeling threatened by his father's legacy (chap. 5); Darius succumbs to flattery so that his advisers can easily fool him (chap. 6). All of these flawed character traits undermine the ability of the foreign kings to rule in a way that promotes harmony, as God wills.

Second, in the visions the assault on God's reign takes on a *cosmic scope* of disharmony. In Daniel's vision of chapter 7, four beasts arise out of the sea, typically a home for demonic forces. The four-beast vision echoes a schema presented in chapter 2, in which four kingdoms are represented by a statue of different metals (see below). The beasts arising from the sea indicate that the earthly kingdoms are in some sense the tools of evil forces more sinister than the personal failures of the kings themselves. The fourth beast, representing the Greek Empire, manifests a "little horn," representing Antiochus IV. The vision of the four beasts displays complex symbolism that defies easy summarization, but it reveals an evil deeper and more powerful than human arrogance, and that is cosmic in scope.

DIVINE REASSERTION OF SOVEREIGNTY

Over against the rebellion against God's will by foreign kings and cosmic forces, Daniel affirms that God will establish sovereignty within history. Within the court tales of Daniel 1–6, chapter 2 (mentioned above) asserts this most clearly through Nebuchadnezzar's dream of a giant statue of differing materials. This statue represents the empires of Babylon, Media, Persia and Greece. A stone cut out "not by human hands" destroys the statue (2:34). Following the destruction of the statue, the dream asserts that "the God of heaven will set up a kingdom that shall never be destroyed" (v. 44). Because this passage has a poetic quality and takes the form of a dream, it does not describe the precise way in which God will act. Nevertheless, it makes its point clearly enough: the God who has set up the earthly kings will bring down their empires and establish some form of direct rule that will provide stability within history.

Chapter 7, within the visions portion of the book, takes the message

of divine sovereignty of chapter 2 into cosmic and mythological territory. As noted above, in this vision, four beasts arise from the sea, with
each beast representing one of the empires named in chapter 2. Each
empire defeats the previous one, climaxing with the ferocious fourth
empire. God, personified as the "Ancient One," takes the throne and
judges the fourth beast, removing its power and putting it to death. An
enigmatic figure, "one like a human being," comes before the Ancient
One to receive dominion. Although God (the Ancient One) establishes
sovereignty, the one like a human being, who serves as a contrast to
the beasts, exercises dominion as well. Although scholars dispute the
identity of the "holy ones of the Most High" in the vision, they likely
are heavenly beings who exercise dominion in the celestial realm. "The
people of the holy ones of the Most High" (v. 27) are the persecuted
Judeans who participate in the sovereignty of the Most High. Within
the vision, the Most High, the one like a human being, and the holy
ones of the Most High exercise dominion together. They establish harmony and stability in heaven. The one like a human being and the
people of the holy ones of the Most High exercise authority on earth.
Both realms, then, experience God's sovereignty. (Thinking about the
character of "the one like a human being" underwent development
before the writing of the New Testament. This figure, often poorly
translated as the "Son of man," played a role in the interpretation of
the significance of Jesus in the Synoptic Gospels; but Daniel did not
predict the coming of Jesus.)

It is encouraging to notice that, as part of asserting divine sovereignty, Daniel also recognizes God's power over life and death. For
example, in chapters 3 and 6 the loyal Judeans face the threat of death,
and in both cases, God rescues them. Moreover, Daniel 12:2 contains
the only clear reference to resurrection found in the Hebrew Bible. In
part, this affirmation of resurrection answers the question about the
fate of those who died under persecution from Antiochus. In resurrection, God would reveal ultimate sovereignty over Antiochus IV: the
God who rescued the loyal Daniel and his companions would raise
from the dead those who have faithfully endured persecution.

INTERIM ETHICAL RESPONSE OF GOD'S PEOPLE

Daniel stands in contrast to the stance of those involved in the Mac-
cabean revolt. As recounted in 1 Maccabees, a group of Judeans led

by the priest Mattathias and his sons respond in military resistance to the persecution of Antiochus IV. Daniel, however, does not advocate armed resistance. Instead, the book calls on the persecuted Judeans to wait for God's intervention. For Daniel, the important battle takes place not on earth, but in heaven as part of God's ultimate reassertion of divine sovereignty (see 10:12–13).

In the interim, before God brings in this everlasting, divine dominion, the wise among the Judeans practice faithfulness (see 11:35). Within the tales of 1–6, Daniel and his companions model this faithfulness, maintaining their identity, avoiding idolatry, worshiping courageously, and depending upon God. They avoid the king's food, even going beyond what was required by Hebraic food laws and eating only vegetables. The three young men refuse to bow to the king's statue. Daniel worships God, even under threat. They seek ways to exist in a foreign court yet remain loyal Judeans. This theme of faithfulness appears in the second section of the book as well. In chapter 9, Daniel offers a prayer of confession, acknowledging the sins of the people. In chapter 11, the wise instruct others and accept martyrdom, considering it a means of purification. The book of Daniel as a whole encourages trust in God during difficult and dangerous times.

A preacher can use Daniel to affirm that what we experience with our senses does not reveal the full meaning of events. The church faces the dilemma of claiming its identity in the midst of a world that denies God's creation and presence. God's people await the establishment of God's sovereignty in creation. The preacher can proclaim the courage, worship, creativity, and passion of Daniel and his companions. Daniel's understanding of resurrection includes the reminder that this eschatological promise vindicates God, giving the faithful hope amid the temptation to despair.

Hosea

CHARLES L. AARON

Scholars and preachers alike find frustration with the book of Hosea. Academic research in Hosea involves slogging through the unfamiliar northern dialect of Hebrew, making translation treacherous. Social justice pastors might find Amos, Micah, or First Isaiah more useful in thundering from the pulpit about treatment of the poor and marginalized. Conservative pastors might find Hosea's marriage embarrassing. Woman pastors might consider even the reconciliation between Hosea and Gomer too heavy with patriarchal baggage to unpack for the church. Any pastor who accepts the challenge of drawing on Hosea for proclamation must deal carefully, faithfully, and wisely with interpretation and gender issues that have no simple solutions. Despite these real and troubling problems, the oracles preserved in Hosea reveal insights about God and the divine-human relationship that the church needs to hear. Hosea created brilliant, imaginative, and powerful metaphors. Both his artistry and his theological insights have value for the church.

Hosea is composed of three major sections. Chapters 1–3 concern Hosea's marriage. Chapters 4–11 contain oracles against Israel, with chapter 11 providing a poignant understanding of God. Chapters 12–14 conclude the book, with each of the three chapters looking at Israel's situation in a creative way.

Readers of Hosea know little about the historical prophet himself. The narrator identifies him as the son of Beeri and lists four Judean kings along with one Israelite king to mark the timing of his ministry.

He prophesied in the eighth century BCE, during the last days of the northern kingdom. The book leaves no evidence of when his ministry ended.

The final, edited form of the book we have in the canon likely came from about three centuries later. The purpose of the historical Hosea was to call the people of the northern kingdom, Israel, to fidelity to YHWH over against their idolatrous practices. The final edited version became a warning to the southern kingdom, Judah, to avoid the mistakes and fate of Israel, which was destroyed by Assyria. The final form of the book likely took shape around the time of the Babylonian exile, the sixth century BCE.

HOSEA'S MARRIAGE (CHAPS. 1–3)

Hosea's marriage is the most well-known yet controversial and disturbing part of the book. Hosea is commanded by God to "take for yourself a wife of whoredom and have children of whoredom" (1:2). The book does not detail the exact implications of the term "whoredom," and its Hebrew root can mean cultic prostitution (Exod. 34:15–16) or sex outside of marriage (Deut. 22:20–21). The term often symbolizes religious infidelity or idolatry (see 2 Kgs. 9:22). Hosea's wife may have been a cult prostitute, a common prostitute, or a sexually promiscuous wife. The book itself does not explore how, in any of those roles, she was a victim herself, at the mercy of a patriarchal society. Hosea reveals nothing of his internal reaction to the commandment. All three of Hosea's children bear symbolic names: God sows (Jezreel), Not-pitied (Lo-ruhamah), and Not-my-people (Lo-ammi).

Hosea's reality-television family communicates much emotion and provokes reflection on the divine-human relationship. The marriage metaphor of Hosea indicts Israel of its unfaithfulness to God and discloses the pain God feels at the broken relationship. The names of the prophet's children provide a constant reminder of Israel's idolatry, which has led to God's punishment and rejection. This family metaphor communicates Israel's spiritual failings in intimate, graphic, dramatic, but ultimately unsettling ways. Just as Hosea's entire family experiences brokenness, so the relationship between God and the people has suffered damage with spiritual and psychological levels.

Preachers should recognize and name for congregations that the book's use of the marriage metaphor is highly problematic in its initial demeaning characterization of Gomer, followed by the way it puts the blame on the wife, whose perspective and circumstances in a patriarchal society are never given voice. The book objectifies her, using her only as a metaphor for Israel's offense against God and never considering her as a person made in God's image. Readers never hear Gomer's side. They encounter only a male-dominated perspective, in the writing, editing, and canonizing of the passage and book.

Chapter 2 contains a "second honeymoon" scene that becomes a romantic moment. The husband (representing both God and the prophet) promises to "allure" the wife, wooing her back into an intimate relationship (vv. 14–23). God restores the family relationship, calling the children names that reverse their previous shame. Chapter 2 ends well with reconciliation between husband and wife and family, but the verses preceding the reconciliation reflect brutal treatment of the wife. The treatment of the wife sounds like embarrassment, degradation, and hurt. The conflict and possible abuse occur after what seems to be a passage of forgiveness at the end of chapter 1.

After the scene of renewal at the end of chapter 2, chapter 3 begins with Hosea hearing again the command to enter into a broken relationship. Chapter 3 does not make clear whether Hosea marries the same woman again or a different woman. This chapter uses different terms, but the metaphor works on the continuing unfaithfulness of one people (Israel) and one God. An absence of intimacy marks this relationship, signifying the deprivation of the people during their time of defeat.

Scholars will continue to debate the many problems of chapters 1–3. Among the debated issues: do the narratives represent a parable, historical events, two marriages to two women, or a remarriage? On a deeper level, Hosea's relationships generate considerable debate about the use of "a wife of whoredom" (1:2) as a metaphor for the divine-human relationship. One might wish that the text presented a simple, linear progression from a troubled relationship to the reconciliation of 2:14–23. As it stands, though, the text forces the preacher to decide how to extricate a helpful message from a minefield of possible misunderstandings or whether the section should be avoided. The metaphor of marriage speaks to the divine pain caused by human idolatry/infidelity. The preacher cannot ignore either the violence the text itself actually describes, or the potential misunderstandings the use of the metaphor of a "wife of whoredom" might spawn. The theme of intimacy might

serve the preacher well in creating new meaning for contemporary congregations, but the behavior that contemporary readers should consider
abusive to both wife and children must be handled with care. The alter-
nation between seeming reconciliation, renewed intimacy, and a return
to brokenness speaks to the continuing need to rebuild the relationship
between God and individuals or the church. Romantic relationships
and spiritual relationships can break again, even when they seem to
have been restored.

ORACLES OF JUDGMENT (CHAPS. 4–11)

Chapters 4–11 contain oracles of judgment against Israel. With chapter 4 serving as an introduction to this section, the dominant metaphor
switches from marriage and family to the courtroom (4:1). The husband now becomes judge, prosecutor, and complaining victim. The
metaphor of adultery/prostitution appears in this section, but this time
with more balance in the gender roles (4:14). This section of the book
presents comprehensive indictments against the people. Neither priests
nor kings escape blame (5:1). By themselves, oracles of indictment lack
the word of grace that every sermon needs. Nevertheless, the images
and metaphors of sin that fill out these oracles can provide insight into
the human condition, generating theological reflection.

Chapter 6 presents the people as deciding to return to God. They
recognize that their wounds have come as punishment from God, but
they know that only in God can they find healing. God, however,
despairs that their newfound desire for relationship will not endure
because their love is like a cloud or dew that easily dissipates (6:4).
The people desire to return to relationship with God, but the desire is
self-serving and remains superficial. A true return would come from a
deep place within, as suggested by 6:6, a verse Matthew presents Jesus
as quoting (Matt. 9:13; 12:7).

Chapter 11 offers a profound understanding of God. No longer the
jilted spouse or the stern judge, God is here presented as a distraught
parent who knows no strategy to reclaim a wayward child. The memories of Israel's "early childhood" haunt the parent who cannot "reach"
the child. The chapter presents translation difficulties, but the power of
the image remains. The metaphor shifts to a roaring lion, but one who
roars on behalf of Israel. God chooses to remain in relationship with
the people. They do not deserve such loyalty, but God's very nature

includes persistence. The roaring lion will bring them back from exile, like migrating birds. Despite their rejection, God will remain loyal.

CREATIVE APPROACHES TO ISRAEL'S
SITUATION (CHAPS. 12–14)

A careful reader can discern the form of a poetic sermon in chapter 12. The prophet recounts the story of Judah/Jacob, from the birth narrative (Gen. 25:26), to the wrestling match at the Jabbok river (32:22–32), to the dream at Bethel (28:10–17, told out of order in the poem). The poetic sermon exhorts the people to follow the example of Jacob in seeking the presence of God.

The final judgment and sentencing of the trial (see 12:2) comes in chapter 13. This chapter affirms the efforts of God to reestablish the relationship (vv. 4–5). Despite these efforts, the people "forgot" their God (v. 6). Because of their idolatry, sin, and betrayal of the relationship, God will destroy them (see v. 3 for a series of images). God will attack and devour them as a predator does prey (vv. 7–8). God threatens to unleash the very powers of Death and Sheol (v. 14, quoted by Paul in 1 Cor. 15:55, but in a different context).

Despite the ferocity of the images of destruction of chapter 13, the final chapter again promises restoration. With the language of confession and worship, the chapter promises reconciliation. God will heal the sin of the people, enabling them to enter the relationship.

Despite its limitations, Hosea offers the preacher an opportunity to proclaim the pathos of God at the alienation between God and people. The God of Hosea displays a vulnerability that rarely occurs in the Bible. God feels the sting of betrayal and rejection. The interweaving of judgment and grace within the book leads to reflection on how those aspects of God's nature work. Even though chapter 2 describes brutal, abusive treatment of a woman, the book as a whole concludes that punishment does not work to evoke repentance (11:9). Only as God acts in healing can the relationship survive and grow (14:4–7). Preachers face an important decision about Hosea: find value in a troubling book or use Hosea, especially the first three chapters, as an opportunity to preach against the text. Preaching against the text does not repudiate its status as Scripture, but acknowledges that the scenario in the book does not always fit with contemporary experience. Preaching against a text recognizes the tension between sources of authority. In this case,

Hosea stands in tension with the authority of lived experience. A broken marriage, even one marked by the infidelity of the wife, typically reflects a damaged relationship to which both parties contribute. While proclaiming the vulnerability of God, the preacher can use the book of Hosea as a teaching moment about the exploitation and abuse of women. A sermon from Hosea can reveal the pain of God, yet also serve as an opportunity to teach about healthy relationships.

Joel

CHARLES L. AARON

Within the preaching ministry of the church, the enigmatic book of Joel waits silently in the wings most of the time, only showing up three times in the lectionary. It is likely best known for its cameo appearance in Peter's Pentecost sermon in Acts 2:16–21. This is a shame because the book offers some interesting theological reflection and much rhetorical skill besides providing a source for Peter's sermon to the early church.

The book has generated much debate concerning its date and unity. The prophet gives little information about himself or the time period in which he wrote, although the book gives evidence of a date after the Babylonian exile. This essay will treat the final form of the book without speculating on whether the book underwent editing. No conclusive answer to the unity of the book has emerged, and the preacher can observe how the final form makes its statement.

In calling the listeners to attention (1:2–3), the prophet interprets a locust plague that has devastated the crops of the land. Although the plague could serve as a metaphor for an attack by a human army, the book likely refers to an actual insect infestation. The proper response to this plague includes lamentation, at least in part because the people cannot offer worship. Lamentation both ventilates the feelings of the people (1:12b), and connects the people with God (1:14b). Characteristic of Joel's theology, he connects the locust plague to an apocalyptic event, the "day of the LORD." The day of the Lord, mentioned

elsewhere in the Prophets (e.g., Amos 5; Zeph. 1; in Isa. 19 the term
is shortened to "that day"), refers to a day when God will act decisively. This action could be an event of vindication against Israel's
enemies and reward for the people's faithfulness, or a time of judgment and confrontation against Israel. Joel uses both interpretations
of this decisive divine action. In this chapter, Joel interprets the locust
plague as a harbinger of the day of the Lord. The devastation of the
insect pestilence takes on eschatological significance. The destruction of the locusts, which has affected people, animals, and nature,
adumbrates the experience of the day of the Lord. Joel does not spec-
ulate on exactly what might happen on the day of the Lord, but he
wants the plague to focus the attention of the people on the coming of
that day.

From the association of the locust plague with the day of the Lord,
Joel moves in chapter 2 to a call to repentance. The chapter begins
with what sounds like a call to battle. The call to battle comes because
a ferocious invading army has arrived. Instead of battle, the trumpet
and the alarm actually summon to repentance (2:12). This repentance
should arise from within, so that the people "rend . . . hearts and not
. . . clothing" (v. 13). Unlike other prophets, Joel does not name the sin
of the people. Instead, using a traditional statement found throughout
the Old Testament (see Exod. 34:6; Ps. 86:15), Joel couches the call
to repentance in the nature of God. The tone of the chapter changes
at Joel 2:18. God responds to the repentance and blesses the people.
The "army" of locusts is banished (v. 25). The food will be restored.
The land and the animals will enjoy the favor of God. Worship and
relationship with God will mark the new experience (vv. 26–27). An
outpouring of God's spirit will accompany God's response to the repentance. The outpouring of the spirit will result in prophecy, dreams, and
visions (all means of divine-human communication) and will reduce
social boundaries. Just as the day of the Lord as judgment has cosmic
implications (2:10), so the gracious actions of God will involve cosmic
dimensions (2:30–31).

At the end of the book (chap. 3), the day of the Lord moves from a
time of fear, judgment, and deprivation to a time of salvation. Repentance and worship bring salvation. The nations who have fought and
conquered Judah and Jerusalem will experience God's judgment. This
shift in emphasis, from the day of the Lord as a judgment on Judah to
judgment on the nations, has led some interpreters to see the last part

of the book as an editorial addition, but the evidence is not clear. God will declare war on the nations who have oppressed Judah. Micah 4 and Isaiah 2 hold out a vision of peace, when weapons of war will become farming implements to provide life and food. Joel 3 reverses the promise. The nations will need to prepare for war by beating "plowshares into swords and . . . pruning hooks into spears" (v. 10). The judgment of the nations will be fierce (v. 13). The people of Judah, however, find refuge in YHWH (v. 16b). As do other prophets, Joel promises that God will restore Jerusalem and dwell within it, so that God's presence will be available (3:17; cf. Isa. 65:18–19, Zech. 8:3). An abundance of wine, milk, and water will mark this time of restoration (Joel 3:18). The Gospel of John reflects this abundance of wine in the wedding of Cana, narrated in chapter 2 (see Amos 9:13).

Preaching from Joel will require great care. Joel uses the locust plague to invoke an eschatological threat. This eschatological threat should compel the people to repent. The contemporary community of faith hears enough about how a hurricane, a drought, or an epidemic occurs because of divine judgment. Even though Joel does not name the sin of the people, he assumes the locusts constitute God's direct judgment for that sin. The preacher can decide how God acts within natural phenomena. To put too much emphasis on God acting through natural forces—such as storms, infestations, or hurricanes—can make God seem cruel. Those who confidently proclaim God's judgment in the form of a hurricane often seem self-righteous. Despite these misgivings, Joel gives the preacher the opportunity to talk about God's judgment, opens the door to theological reflection on contemporary events, and invites proclamation on lamentation and repentance.

With eloquence Joel describes the restoration brought by God following the repentance of the people. His call for the people to tear their hearts and not rip their clothing can bear much fruit in the contemporary community of faith. The creedal statement in 2:13 occurs elsewhere in the Old Testament, but Joel's use makes it fitting to come after lamentation. To use Joel's affirmation about the outpouring of the spirit at a time other than Pentecost Sunday can put the focus on the egalitarian effect of the work of the Spirit. Not only does the Spirit break down divisions between people, but the prophecy, dreams, and visions describe an abundance of divine presence and accessibility. A preacher might wisely choose to avoid Joel's vindictive pronouncements about the fate of the nations (chap. 3). One can decide one's own theology about judgment, but Joel calls for an all-out war against the nations, with God's people safe.

Joel offers the careful preacher an opportunity to talk about the spiritual dimension of natural disasters, heartfelt repentance, the healing that comes from lamentation, and a gracious God who forgives and blesses with the spirit.

Amos

CHARLES L. AARON

Bold, passionate, uncompromising, and creative are among the adjectives one could use to describe the writings attributed to the prophet Amos. He left scant and cryptic information about himself behind, but his words have endured. His oracles have inspired those who seek justice for the poor and marginalized through the centuries. His insights raise questions about the role of prophecy and the authenticity of the worship of synagogue and church. Amos seems to have initiated the practice of pronouncing judgment against the whole nation of Israel. He embodied the role of a faithful layperson who proclaimed a divinely inspired word.

Amos describes himself as a "herdsman, and a dresser of sycamore trees" (7:14), and rejects the title of prophet. If one can assume that God uses a person's gifts in the act of prophecy, Amos was an educated man, who understood politics and world affairs. If that assessment is accurate, Amos was likely what today would be called an "agribusiness man." He came from the southern kingdom, Judah, in the eighth century BCE to announce divine judgment on the economic injustice and shallow faith of the northern kingdom, Israel. For Amos, that judgment takes the form of the invasion of the Assyrians under Tiglath-Pilaser III.

Scholars think that the evolution of the book of Amos came in stages. The oracles Amos left behind were collected and edited at a later date, likely as a warning for the southern kingdom when it faced the threat of Babylonian invasion. Another final editing took place during the Babylonian exile, and this revision included the promise of restoration. Due to this editorial process, readers find three different messages in the final form of the book: one message of total destruction of Israel (3:12), one of the possibility of repentance (5:4, 6, 14–15), and one of restoration (9:11–15).

DESTRUCTION

Following the superscription, which gives information about Amos, the book opens with a powerful image of an impassioned God (1:2; see Joel 3:16). Displaying an understanding of YHWH with authority beyond Israel itself, the first two chapters of Amos condemn the sins of the nations around Israel (1:2–2:3). These chapters provide material that a preacher can use within a sermon to condemn atrocities. The oracles condemn what one might call human rights violations. They give preachers the warrant to speak out against the violence of war (1:3), abuse of women (1:13), violation of a corpse (2:1), as well as cruelty and torture in general (see 1:11). By themselves, however, these oracles lack any word of grace, and preachers focusing on these texts will need to remind hearers they do not represent God's final word.

Beginning at 2:4, the book turns to Judah and then Israel. The oracle against Judah may represent a later addition to the original collection of the words of Amos. Since Amos preached in the north, the oracle against Judah seems out of place. If this oracle arose later, it speaks to the continuing relevance of the preaching of Amos and to the continuing effort to speak to successive generations.

The oracle in 2:6–16 focuses on the sins of Israel, the primary focus of Amos's ministry. This oracle contains several themes important to the book of Amos: God's deep concern for the treatment of the poor (vv. 6–8), the special relationship between YHWH and Israel because of the divine actions to create Israel as a community (vv. 9–11), and the devastation of divine wrath (vv. 13–16).

These themes continue in chapters 3–4, with skillful rhetorical strategies by the prophet. Following renewed emphasis on the relationship between YHWH and Israel (3:1–2), the prophet asks a series of questions that presuppose the answer "no." These questions lead to the affirmation that the destruction of Israel will happen at divine initiative: "Does disaster befall a city unless YHWH has done it?" (3:6 alt.). Israel will suffer complete devastation (3:12–15) because of the depth of the people's sin (3:10). In chapter 4 the prophet uses sarcasm and mocking to make his point. The rich society women of Bashan are self-indulgent "cows." They will experience humiliation at the time of punishment (4:2–3). The prophet creates a parody of a call to worship in 4:4–5. The oracle calls the people to come to a place of worship to transgress. The rest of chapter 4 details the divine efforts to claim the attention of the people in the form of famine, drought, crop diseases, pestilence, and military defeat, none of which motivated the people to return to God.

REPENTANCE

If the original oracles of Amos were collected and edited, and then reedited again, chapter 5 represents the tension between the first edition and the second edition, or at least the two voices of the majority of the book. Amos 5:2–3 paints a picture of the near-complete destruction of Israel. Israel will have only a tenth left. If the supposition is correct that the original oracles of Amos announced this level of devastation, then the mission of the historical Amos was simply to announce divine judgment on Israel. Because the divine efforts recounted in chapter 4 had not worked, YHWH seemingly had no choice but to destroy Israel as a testament to their recalcitrance. Perhaps the mission of Amos was to interpret why the destruction happened. The contemporary preacher might use these passages in a limited way to proclaim God's power over the church and God's frustration with human sin.

Starting in 5:4, however, the reader finds words calling for repentance. These verses hold out hope that God will relent on the punishment. In the writing and editing of the book, this new emphasis may have represented a new stage. Theologically, this new message speaks to one of the important purposes of announcing God's judgment. Judgment is not an end unto itself. Preachers should interpret biblical expressions of God's judgment as a means for people to understand God's expectations and will in order that they repent and become obedient.

One of the well-known oracles of Amos begins at 5:18. One can surmise that the "day of YHWH" was anticipated by the people of Israel as a day of affirmation and reward. Amos turns the tables, proclaiming the day of YHWH as a confrontation. The oracle proceeds to denounce the worship life of the people. God pays no attention to the worship of the people. Describing multiple senses, the prophet declares the divine disinterest in the worship of the people. YHWH will not "smell" the offerings, will not "see" the offerings, and will not "hear" the songs. The critique of worship ends with a powerful and unforgettable image. The prophet calls for justice to come swiftly, like a sudden shower, and righteousness to continue like a constant stream. Justice refers to fairness, attention to the poor, a responsible judicial system, and recognition of Israel as a community. Disparity between rich and poor is not consistent with justice. The image of the waters calls for justice to come quickly and to last, as a reliable water-delivery system would.

RESTORATION

The last part of the book describes visions given to Amos. The prophet intervenes on behalf of the people in 7:2–3. This intervention indicates the true stance of any prophet. The prophet does not take smug satisfaction in the destruction of the people but seeks mercy on their behalf. An important confrontation occurs starting in 7:10. The priest Amaziah seeks to silence the prophet for the sake of stability and decorum. Amos declares his divine mandate to preach.

In some prophetic books, oracles of judgment are interspersed with oracles of grace and salvation. In Amos, however, the word of restoration and renewal comes only at the end of the book. Likely added to Amos during the exile as a message of assurance, the oracle in 9:11–15 promises the return of the Davidic rule (v. 11) and a time of prosperity and abundance.

The book of Amos gives preachers the mandate to preach about violence, the plight of the poor, shallow worship, and economic stratification in society. According to the prophet, because of God's actions on behalf of the people, God has the right to demand justice and equity within the community. God's anger does not negate God's love and desire for the people to live in peace, even marked by authentic abundance and security. In the final form of the book, all messages of judgment create space for repentance, which leads to restoration. It is interesting to note that the Revised Common Lectionary draws readings only from chapters 5–8, where themes of repentance and restoration are evident. The earlier chapters, though, are worthy of preachers' attention. Regardless of whether a preaching text derives from the first, second, or third theological voice of the book, preachers should bring the whole of Amos's message into play in the sermon.

Obadiah

CHARLES L. AARON

For such an exceedingly small book (only twenty-one verses) dealing with such a narrow topic (condemnation of the nation of Edom), Obadiah has produced many lengthy scholarly and hermeneutical debates. Does an actual prophet named Obadiah stand behind the book, or did editors assign the book this name, which means "servant of YHWH"? Did more than one author or editor contribute to the book? How should the reader evaluate the similarities between Jeremiah 49:7–22 and parts of Obadiah? How accurately does Obadiah reflect actual historical tensions between Israel and Edom? How can the contemporary church proclaim the unrelenting message of judgment against Edom in light of the Bible's overall message of forgiveness and divine love for all people? (The Revised Common Lectionary answers this question by assigning no readings from Obadiah.) In spite of these debates, the book of Obadiah contains both psychological and theological insights that are worth preachers' considerations, if they use care in interpreting this enigmatic book.

ISRAEL AND EDOM: THE BACKSTORY

A complicated history between Israel and Edom lies behind the oracles of the book. Within the narrative world of the Pentateuch, the nations of Israel and Edom trace their lineage back to the brothers Jacob and

Esau (see Gen. 36). Even in the womb, the twins competed for status (25:26). As children and adults, the conflict continued (Gen. 26–33), with acts of forgiveness and reconciliation on occasion (Gen. 33).

The nations of Edom and Israel continued the enmity (see Num. 20:14–21). Second Samuel 8:12–14 relates David's defeat of Edom, a bloody affair, and David's treatment of the Edomites. Later the anger of the prophets against Edom arose from Edom's cooperation with Babylon as the Babylonians invaded and destroyed Jerusalem (2 Kgs. 25; Ezek. 35; Ps. 137:7; see also 1 Esdras 4:45). Other references suggest that the Babylonians also conquered Edom (Jer. 27; Ezek. 32:29). Whatever might have happened in history, the prophet Obadiah, among others, felt bitterness toward the Edomites for their participation in the destruction of Judah.

OBADIAH'S CONDEMNATION

Obadiah opens by painting a picture of the devastating judgment that awaits Edom. Following the briefest of superscriptions (v. 1a), the poem offers a "vision of Obadiah" that moves from the heavenly realm to the earth. The judgment of Edom originates among the heavens, from whence comes a "messenger" who will motivate the nations to begin the punishment. In their pride, the Edomites have assumed that they are secure from attack (v. 3). Despite this arrogance the punishment of the nations will bring them humiliation and degradation. The Edomites cannot find a safe escape from God (v. 4), even in the sky as far up as the stars (cf. Ps. 139).

The poem taunts the enemy. Even thieves would show more mercy by leaving some things intact (v. 5). Farmers would at least leave some scraps around the edges for gleaners to pick up. The Edomites cannot hope even for that. They cannot even count on their friends and allies (v. 7). They will understand the feeling of a sense of betrayal, by someone close. Although the Hebrew of verse 7 is hard to translate, it seems to suggest that the Edomites will feel betrayed by those with whom they have shared a meal. Although some references suggest that Edom enjoyed a reputation for wisdom (see Jer. 49:7), that wisdom will not protect them. It will lose even that advantage (v. 8). Alluding to the firstborn son of Eliphaz (Gen. 36:11), the poem describes the defeat of Edom's soldiers. The flow of the poem suggests that God will act through the nations to punish Edom.

Starting in verse 10, the poem moves to the accusation against Edom and to the expression of the deep hurt felt by the prophet, speaking on behalf of Israel and Judah. The prophet points out the once-close relationship between Edom and Israel, alluding to the family ties between the two nations (v. 10, "brother Jacob"). The poem assumes the accuracy of the accounts of Edom both helping and smacking their lips in glee at the invasion of Jerusalem by the Babylonians. Obadiah accuses the Edomites of participating in the destruction, gloating over it, and even preventing the escape of those who tried to flee from the advancing army. These actions have violated the relationship between "family" members and caused deep emotions of betrayal on the part of Israel (v. 12). Such betrayal means that the Edomites deserve their fate, with military defeat, debasement, and humiliation.

Boldly invoking the "day of YHWH," the poem moves at verse 15 toward judgment against all nations. Obadiah envisions the "day of YHWH" as an event of vindication for Israel/Judah and judgment for those who have humiliated them. Speaking metaphorically of the defeat of Judah as a "cup," the poet predicts that the nations shall drink from the same cup. God's people shall escape the wrath on Mount Zion, and Esau/Edom shall be destroyed. Verse 18 suggests the restoration of both the northern and southern kingdoms, both of whom shall exact judgment on Edom. The territory of both kingdoms shall spread out.

The poem ends with an affirmation of God's sovereignty. The phrase of the poet, "the kingdom shall be YHWH's," refers to a time when God shall exercise dominion on this earth, with Israel/Judah enjoying renewed independence and influence. With the defeat of their enemies, Israel/Judah faces no threat.

Perhaps the most promising direction for preaching from Obadiah is exploration of the experience of betrayal. The words of the prophet describe well the raw emotion of being kicked in the teeth. A sermon that dealt with this feeling could name the anger, hurt, and bitterness of a broken relationship, on many levels. In certain contexts, Obadiah might speak to violence within a community, perhaps between rival factions. Depending on one's pastoral and theological leanings, the sermon could ask the question of whether reconciliation is possible in all situations. In some acts of betrayal, the aggrieved party can forgive yet choose not to reestablish the relationship.

Even though Obadiah talks of the humiliation of the Edomites, other parts of Scripture talk of healing and eventual reconciliation. The material about punishment can give the preacher the opportunity to affirm that God notices acts of betrayal. The affirmation of God's sovereignty at the end of the poem affirms that God acts even in situations of defeat and humiliation.

Jonah

JOHN C. HOLBERT

Jonah is a story sermon, so preaching from it should be straightforward. The preacher need only go where the story leads to discover ways to make this hilarious narrative live. The story is brief (forty-eight verses), the vocabulary limited, and the division into four nearly equal chapters makes following the story easy. An important note: you cannot preach from Jonah (including the two passages included in the Revised Common Lectionary) without knowing and referencing the entire tale.

JONAH ON THE BOAT (CHAP. 1)

"Now the word of YHWH came to Jonah son of Amittai" (1:1; see also 3:1). The book of Joel begins with exactly this formula (Joel 1:1), so we know that Jonah is a prophet. This fact sets up certain expectations for the reader: Jonah has been called to speak for God; other prophets, however reluctantly, have answered God's call. Such calls have often been specifically directed toward certain groups, and that is true for Jonah as well: "Go at once to Nineveh, that great city, and cry out against it; for their wickedness has come up before me" (1:2). Nineveh was the capital city of the Assyrian Empire, byword for evil for centuries in the Middle East. Of course, Jonah would agree that Nineveh is evil, but preaching against it may be a different kettle of fish!

Instead of heading east to Nineveh, Jonah without a word heads west to Tarshish, perhaps Spain, "away from the presence of YHWH" (1:3). He "goes down" to Joppa, finds a ship, pays the fare, and goes with them, "away from the presence of YHWH." Jonah's intention is clear; he wants nothing to do with YHWH and the call to preach to the Ninevites and imagines he can escape both call and God by heading far into the Mediterranean. What is not so clear yet is this: why is he so anxious to get away? That answer will be delightfully delayed in the story.

A huge storm hits the ship, and the ship itself fears breaking up (1:4). The sailors each cry out to their respective gods and lighten the ship by hurling cargo into the sea. Meanwhile, the fleeing prophet has "gone down into the hold of the ship," has lain down, and is fast asleep. The desperate captain finds Jonah asleep and demands, "Get up! Call on your God! Who knows? That God might care for us so that we do not die!" One might have imagined the prophet to think of that, but not this prophet. On deck, the storm worsens, and the sailors wonder whose fault this is. They throw lots (dice) to discover the culprit, and the lot falls right on Jonah. In response to their questions about his identity, Jonah replies, "I am a Hebrew. . . . I worship YHWH, the God of [the sky], who made the sea and the dry land" (1:9). It is an odd sort of confession, since he is running away from the very God who made the sea and is on the very sea that God supposedly made!

The sailors are immediately convinced that Jonah is the problem, but instead of tossing him into the sea to save themselves, they row like mad to save the wretch. But Jonah demands to be thrown into the sea: "It is my problem," he wails. Finally, after a heartfelt prayer to YHWH, asking not to be accused of bloodguilt over Jonah's demise, they chuck him into the sea, and the sea is instantly calm. And now the sailors, in greatest fear, offer a sacrifice to this YHWH and make vows that they intend to keep (1:14–17).

JONAH IN THE FISH (CHAP. 2)

While the smoke of their sacrifice rises into the sky, Jonah drops like a stone into the depths of the sea, where he is swallowed by a passing great fish. From the innards of the fish, he prays, and his prayer (2:2–9) is an amalgam of psalmic fragments and half-truths. He claims, "YHWH threw me into the deep" (cf. v. 3), a false claim. Jonah claims, "I am driven away from your [presence]," a false claim (v. 4). He also claims, "When my life was ebbing away, I remembered YHWH" (v. 7). A sort of fish-belly confession? He further claims, "Those who pay regard to empty idols forsake true loyalty," a false claim, since the former pagan sailors are this instant worshiping YHWH (cf. v. 8). Finally, he says he will sacrifice and make vows, but he does neither. The sailors are doing both. In short, the prayer is pure hypocrisy. Nevertheless, after that prayer, the big fish throws up!

JONAH IN NINEVEH (CHAP. 3)

Jonah is vomited out and realizes he cannot escape God's call that easily, so he goes to Nineveh, an enormous city three walking days in breadth. Jonah heads a third of the way into the city, stands on a street corner, and utters a five-word Hebrew sermon: "Forty days and Nineveh will be *nehpaket*!" *Nehpaket* is intentionally ambiguous in that it can mean either "changed" or "destroyed." The Ninevites believe him, from king to cow, worrying that they will be destroyed! The fear of destruction actually leads to change. They all cry out to YHWH for salvation, the king, like the ship captain, proclaiming, "Who knows! God may yet relent, change the divine mind, turn from fierce wrath so that we do not die" (cf. 3:9)! God does change, and the city is filled with rejoicing down to the cows. One might imagine that the prophet of God would have thought of that, but not this prophet.

JONAH UNDER THE PLANT (CHAP. 4)

The story could end there: "Prophet makes good! World's worst city repents!" But not so fast! We want to know why Jonah left in the first place. And here it comes. "But it was very displeasing to Jonah, and he was furious" (4:1, alt.). And just what is that "it" that displeased Jonah? YHWH's change of heart? Jonah's failed prophecy, since he wanted destruction but effected change instead? His humiliation in the face of hated Ninevites? Maybe a combination of all three?

Whatever he is thinking, he now wishes he were dead: "That is why I fled to Tarshish at the beginning; for I knew that you are a gracious God and merciful, slow to anger, and abounding in steadfast love, and ready to relent from punishing" (4:2). Nearly word for word, he quotes the famous formulation of YHWH's identity found in Exodus 34:6. But in Jonah's mouth the grand celebration of YHWH's grace becomes Jonah's fury that God will not rub out the disgusting Ninevites. Jonah would literally rather be dead than worship with a Ninevite! (Jonah 4:3).

But YHWH is not yet through with this prophet. God makes a plant grow up over Jonah to shade him from the heat (4:6), and Jonah loves the little plant, the only thing he loves in the story besides himself. But God appoints a worm to attack the plant, which withers and dies so that the sun may once again torment Jonah. "It is better for me to die than live," he again whines (v. 8). And God adds the kicker. "You care for a bush, that grew and died in one night! Should I, YHWH, not care for Nineveh, the vast city, where there are more than 120,000 people, unaware of right from wrong, not to mention all those cows?" (cf. 4:10–11). The end! Or rather, a beginning.

The preacher must know this ending where YHWH announces care for the whole world, including Ninevites, if Jonah's bigoted words and actions throughout the tale are to be seen in their rightful divine context.

Micah

MARY DONOVAN TURNER

The book of Micah is the sixth of the twelve Minor Prophets in the Hebrew Bible. Written in the eighth century BCE, it—along with Amos, Hosea, and Isaiah—represents some of the earliest prophetic works included in the canon. Micah's name means "Who is like Yahweh?" He grew up in a small village in Judah, which may have given him extra sensitivity for the sufferings of the poor and powerless. He was deeply troubled by the ways the rich exploit their power (2:1). The three kings mentioned in the superscription—Jotham, Ahaz, and Hezekiah—reigned in 742–686 BCE. Micah's preaching, then, spanned the last years of the divided monarchy and the first years of the existence of Judah alone. Being aware of the devastation of the northern kingdom by the Assyrian Empire, the beginning chapters of Micah are formed and fashioned by this awareness of a powerful empire defeating a much smaller nation.

Like many prophetic books in the canon, Micah is a patchwork of speeches and oracles, sometimes bringing a word of devastation and sometimes bringing a word of hope. These contrasting words, often abruptly juxtaposed to each other, first call people to repent to avoid devastation and then announce hopefulness when the devastation overwhelms them. Oracles in the book of Micah speak against those who believe that Jerusalem is indestructible. The prophet knows and laments that when the people, or a nation, live life contrary to the

185

covenant they have made with God, they will fall. The people will have chosen death rather than life-giving ways.

It is possible to look at the overall structure of Micah in two ways. First, the book can be divided into three sections based on the introductory Hebrew word "Hear" in chapters 1, 3, and 6. Or, just as easily, the book can be divided into four units. Chapters 1–3 bring accusations; chapters 4–5 bring words of restoration; chapter 6 is a covenantal lawsuit, which indicts the people once again; chapter 7 brings pleas for restoration and witness to a God who throughout the ages has not held God's anger forever, but who shows compassion and clemency and forgiveness. Either way, it is important for the preacher to know that the interweaving of oracles of judgment and oracles of forgiveness is present; together they hold the interpretive key to the prophet's words. Bringing both instruction and grace is part of the pastoral role of prophet, pastor, and preacher.

The book of Micah begins with a call to all who live on the earth (1:2); God, as if in a courtroom, is making witness against them. While some prophetic books focus on the northern kingdom or southern kingdom, Micah speaks a word against both Samaria and Jerusalem. The charges are read; the sins and transgressions of both nations are outlined. The idolatry and the malignancies of the northern kingdom have grown and come down to reach Jerusalem. Both the north and the south will be destroyed, and the prophet asks, "Is the LORD's patience exhausted? Are these his doings?" (2:7). Micah's question is ours as well. Does God bring punishment to Samaria and Jerusalem through devastation wrought by the hand of a foreign nation? Or are the devastated peoples simply dealing with the consequences of their own unfaithful living? There are enormous theological implications in the answer we choose. The third chapter of Micah begins with these words: "Listen, you heads of Jacob and rulers of the house of Israel! Should you not know justice?" (3:1). With graphic metaphor, the prophet describes the actions of those who abuse their power and do not know justice: "You who hate the good and love the evil, who tear the skin off my people, and the flesh off their bones; who eat the flesh of my people, flay their skin off them, break their bones in pieces, and chop them up like meat in a kettle, like flesh in a caldron" (3:2–3).

There are virtually no leaders immune to this harsh critique brought by Yahweh and prophet. Governmental rulers, priests, and prophets alike are scrutinized under the prophet's stern gaze. The indictments against each of these is different, but there is a common, underlying theme (3:11): they can all be bought for a price. When their priority becomes gain for self and not justice for or service to the community, they destroy the flesh and bones of the people who depend upon them.

These accusations against the leaders of Israel climactically bring to a close the first three chapters in Micah, which detail the threats directed against both Samaria and Jerusalem. Immediately chapters 4–5 begin a collection of prophecies of Israel's magnificent future in the "days to come." Preachers do well to ask the same type of question: What is our own vision of the world if it is aligned with God's intentions and hopes for us?

Micah 4:2–5 is the center of the two chapters that describe the wonderful and glorious future of Zion. There will be a day when swords will be beaten into plowshares, and spears into pruning hooks, a day when there will be no more war. No one will be afraid (4:4).

Micah 5:2–5a speaks of a time when a new kind of ruler will come forth out of one of the small clans in Judah. It is not surprising that this particular text should find its way into the Revised Common Lectionary on the Fourth Sunday of Advent. It speaks of Bethlehem, of a woman in labor giving birth, of a child who shall eventually stand and feed the flock in the strength of the Lord, of one who will "be great to the ends of the earth, . . . one of peace." The author of these words in Micah was hopeful that a king would be born that could pull the people out of the mire of injustice and violence and bring them peace. The generations following Micah's read these words and found in themselves the same longing for leadership with integrity, leadership that is concerned about us rather than "me." Reading the indictments of the leadership outlined in chapters 1–3, the reader can understand how the longing would be great for something new, different, and faithful.

Certainly the author of the Gospel of Matthew thought that in his day these words could be used to describe the infant Jesus, who had been sent to shepherd Israel (Matt. 2:6). Some believe that these hopeful words were written in a time later than Micah and inserted after the first three chapters, in which devastation and dishonesty and a lack of justice are described in such compelling fashion. But certainly the words about the king coming from the small city of Bethlehem rather than Jerusalem are consistent with what we have come to expect from the Hebrew Bible narratives. God chooses the least likely, the smallest, to accomplish God's purpose. God will choose one from the small village of Bethlehem to bring peace. The one who comes will be like a shepherd. He will bring peace. Do we know other stories about peace and security that have come from insignificant, small, and surprising places?

At the beginning of chapter 6, we experience another abrupt change in tone and genre. Returning to the courtroom we encountered in chapter 1, the Lord's case is brought forward. The Lord has a controversy, a lawsuit, against the people. It begins with impassioned questioning: "O my people, what have I done to you? In what have I wearied you? Answer me!" (v. 3). The disappointed and disillusioned God recounts the story of salvation experienced by their ancestors in Egypt and how Moses and Aaron and Miriam were sent before them, how they were redeemed. The listeners were reminded of the wondrous act of deliverance that occurred as the Israelites were led out from bondage, the courage and despair of the reluctant Moses, the support of his brother Aaron, and the courageous questioning of Miriam, who would at one time sing a glorious song of victory and at another time stand outside the camp stricken with leprosy because she knew in her heart that she, too, could be a spokesperson for Yahweh. (Including her name here, along with Moses and Aaron, is an act of justice. She is no longer isolated from the community and removed from the narrative; her contributions to the Israelite community are acknowledged, named.) "Do you not remember these stories of your ancestors?" God is asking them. "I have been faithful. Why are you not faithful to me?" God is calling the people to remember.

In response, the prophet (or perhaps a worshiper) replies with his own question. "With what shall I come before the LORD, and bow myself before God on high?" (6:6). The worshiper wonders if multitudes of sacrifices and rivers of oil, even a child sacrificed, is what will satisfy God. No. God does not desire elaborate worship and ritual sacrifices. God requires that we act justly, love kindness, and walk humbly with God (v. 8). These make living faithfully sound quite simple. But it is not. The simplicity of the words is deceiving because doing justice, loving kindness, and walking humbly demands radical inclusivity and unconditional love, an understanding that God's love is for every living creature. But as Micah's name implies, "Who lives like Yahweh?" Who can?

In chapter 7 Micah concludes with a resounding affirmation of a forgiving God who passes over transgression, who does not retain anger forever, who delights in showing clemency, who will have compassion and tread our iniquities underfoot, who will cast all our sins into the depths of the sea, and who will show faithfulness to Jacob and loyalty to Abraham. The writer knows this because the writer knows the history of the faith and the stories of the ancestors from days of old. He has remembered what God has asked him to remember. God is faithful. That, in Micah, is the final word.

Nahum

MARY DONOVAN TURNER

Have you ever heard a sermon from the book of Nahum in the Hebrew Bible? Perhaps not. The Revised Common Lectionary does not include any selections from this prophetic book, one of the twelve Minor Prophets. While the three chapters of Nahum are an extended poem filled with provocative imagery, suggestive metaphors, and similes, its contents pose challenging and thorny theological questions, inviting the reader to ask why it holds a place in the canon at all. Is there anything redemptive in its contents? Is there anything worth the work of its excavation? Some say no, arguing that the display of nationalism by the prophet and its violence are too strong, and it is difficult to justify preaching from it.

We know little about the prophet, only that he is Nahum from Elkosh. Even that, however, is delightfully ambiguous because the exact location of Elkosh is in dispute. This Minor Prophet's name means "comfort," and as we read its inflammatory rhetoric, we wonder: comfort for whom? That question, perhaps, is the key to the poem's power.

The book of Nahum recounts the demise of the Assyrian city of Nineveh, written most likely just before or after its devastation in 612 BCE. Nineveh was a vast city; Nahum 3:1 describes it as a "bloody city, filled with lies and robbery" (my trans.). It had strong military campaigns and frequently demanded tribute and plunder from conquered cities. The Babylonian chronicle of the fall of Nineveh tells the story of its destruction. Babylonia joined forces with the Medes and laid siege

191

to the city for three months. After the loss of its fortresses, the Assyrian Empire lasted only a few more years, until about 609 BCE.

One way to open interpretive possibilities and quandaries in this difficult book is to read Nahum as resistance poetry. Nineveh is the capital city of the Assyrian Empire, known for its oppressive, brutal tendencies, and Nahum describes a God who will come to destroy this most egregious of oppressors. God has been slow to anger but will act. In Nahum 1 the prophet convinces the reader/hearer that God is capable of deliverance by describing the might and power of God. Chapters 2 and 3 convince us that not only *can* God deliver, God *will*. Nahum describes the fall of the city: the city is under siege, and the invaders come full force. Like other songs and poetry and art written and created during times of oppression, this poem asks the citizens to imagine a time when their oppressor will be overthrown, the empire will be completely devastated, and the oppressed will be free. God is powerful enough and desirous of the people's liberation. Like Jonah before and Zephaniah after, the prophetic word nods to the devastation of an empire that is flourishing. Nineveh's demise is Judah's comfort. Thus the book of Nahum is not just a description of the defeat of the empire, but a celebration of that defeat. Those who had experienced the cruelty of Assyria find their freedom in its fall.

In the first section of Nahum 1 (vv. 2–5), God is described as jealous, avenging, wrathful, great in power, and slow to anger. The theological questions raised for the preacher are immense. What do these three short chapters tell us about the nature of God? How do the descriptions of the ways God participates in our living align with our thinking about God's activity in human affairs today? Were the Judean experiences of oppression simply consequences for the choices and decisions they had made, or were they experiencing punishment from God? What does our own life experience tell us?

There are many places in Nahum where the preacher's interest, imagination, and creativity are piqued through a careful reading of the text. Four of these are discussed below.

First, the movement between Nahum 1:6 and 1:7 is jarring. The descriptions of the jealous and avenging God are followed by the affirmation "The LORD is good," and God is then described as stronghold and refuge. What is the assurance/comfort offered to the Judeans? It is this: the Assyrian army is strong and large, but they will be stopped. The burdensome yoke of oppression will be broken. How are we to reconcile God's goodness and God's vengeance as depicted in Nahum, particularly as we think about the oppressed and the oppressor? Can the former be delivered without violence or vengeance toward the latter?

Second, in the graphic description of the demise of Nineveh, the author uses the metaphor of the ravaged and distressed woman to represent Nineveh (3:5–7). The woman is alluring and is a mistress of sorcery who enslaves nations. "I . . . will lift up your skirts over your face; and I will let nations look on your nakedness. . . . I will throw filth at you and treat you with contempt, and make you a spectacle." The use of female imagery to describe the wicked city fits into a recurring pattern in the prophetic material of the Hebrew Bible in which the unfaithful one is symbolized as a woman. This is just one of the disturbing symptoms of the ways that patriarchy and misogyny inform the biblical text. The echoes of these images and understandings of women continue to make a disturbing impact on today's world, and these trends can be acknowledged and named by today's preacher.

Third, while in Nahum it is clear who is oppressor and who is the oppressed, it is not always so clear in our contemporary context. Readers of this book may be addressing congregations that experience privilege, who do not know oppression from the underside, and who do not think of themselves as oppressors. We like to cast aspersion on other oppressors, but one of the uses of sacred text is to allow it to function as mirror. Who is oppressed in our world, in our communities? Who are *we* oppressing by the way we live?

Finally, Nahum is an extended poem, which weaves together, like a tapestry, the words of warning to the city of Nineveh, and the words of comfort and calls to rejoicing for the inhabitants of Judah. Nahum's words are compelling. Like many other Hebrew Bible prophets, he makes the words come alive and gives listeners or readers something to see, hear, taste, and feel through exquisite use of metaphors and simile. In the end, the vivid and provocative language serves as an announcement of celebration. In relation to Nineveh's downfall, the prophet says: "All who hear the news about you clap their hands over you. For who has ever escaped your endless cruelty?" (3:19). How do we as a people called to love our enemies come to terms with a canonical text celebrating the enemy's demise? Does violence become acceptable, even desirable, when the enemy is a brutal oppressor, when those living under the enemy's cruel, self-serving practices are seeking, and then find, freedom and liberation? Additionally, how do we as preachers best work to disrupt the systems that oppress and diminish those with whom we share the world, particularly those systems we support and with which we knowingly or unknowingly cooperate?

The contextual nature of preaching raises interesting questions when the sermon's foundational text addresses oppression. What does the sermon "sound like" when the listening community knows itself to be a collective of oppressed persons desiring freedom?

Habakkuk

MARY DONOVAN TURNER

We have no information about the author of the book of Habakkuk, one of the twelve Minor Prophets in the Hebrew Bible. The name Habakkuk is not mentioned in Scripture anywhere other than in the first and third chapters of this book. In other prophetic books we are given the lineage of the prophet, at least the name of the prophet's father, and sometimes the town and region in which the prophet lives, but not so here. "The oracle that the prophet Habakkuk saw" is all we are given as the book begins (1:1). The words of the book are, in that sense, disembodied. When and where they were written and what situation(s), in particular, prompted these oracles are left unknown to us except for clues in the content of the oracles that implicitly point us to some uncertain conclusions. In the end, however, this ignorance is not so troubling because the questions raised by the prophet are timeless and are raised in every generation.

Habakkuk addresses the questions of unjust suffering and evil by presenting the prophet's questions together with God's answers. Habakkuk helps define one of the important roles of the prophet, that of questioner. Prophets ask questions of God; prophets ask questions of the people. And the prophet facilitates dialogue between them. The questions Habakkuk asks of God and God's answers are remembered in the Revised Common Lectionary (1:1–4; 2:1–4), yet other parts of Habakkuk are worthy of the preacher's consideration as well.

In 1:2–3, the prophet asks, "O LORD, how long shall I cry for help,

195

and you will not listen? Or cry to you, 'Violence!' and you will not save? Why do you make me see wrongdoing and look at trouble?" In 1:13, the prophet questions again. "Why do you look on the treacherous, and are silent when the wicked swallow those more righteous than they?" Such questions of theodicy are echoed in other biblical texts (e.g., Psalms and Job) and by contemporary theologians, preachers, and scholars as well: How long will we suffer? Why do you allow suffering if you are an all-powerful God? Where can we find you in our suffering? Did you bring it to pass? Are you capable and powerful enough to prevent it? And if you are, why don't you? God can seem absent in our suffering: how do we wrestle theologically with what may seem like God's indifference?

The complexity in Habakkuk is compounded by the thought expressed in 1:5–11 that God not only allows suffering but also brings it about. God has brought calamity on the Judeans. How do we think theologically about this claim? We may think that

— God judges or punishes by bringing about suffering,
— the suffering we experience is a consequence of our unfaithful living, or
— suffering is random and not caused by God or human.

It is good for the preacher to help the community think about these questions/alternatives *before* they encounter suffering, so that they have a belief system, a foundation, on which to stand when suffering arises.

We think of prophets as ones who boldly go about truth-telling no matter the consequences. And so they do at times. But prophets are also ones who wait and watch. The second chapter of Habakkuk begins with the prophet taking a stand at the watchtower; he will keep watch for God's message, the vision, the answers to Habakkuk's questions. God speaks to the prophet and tells him to write down the vision and write it plainly, large, so that even someone running by can read it. God tells Habakkuk to wait for the vision that inevitably will come. Preachers might ask today: Who is watching for us? In our local communities, our nation, and the world, who is watching for the vision of God and speaking it clearly to the people?

What have the people done that has been displeasing to God? Habakkuk 2:5 issues a strong indictment that is followed by five woes ("alas," 2:6, 9, 12, 15, 19). All of the condemned behaviors and attitudes stem from the first declaration that "wealth is treacherous" (2:5).

Condemned are those who use violence and plunder others to pile up goods, to pile up what is not rightfully their own. How do wealth and power skew our perspectives and priorities? How does "never having enough" (2:5 alt.) form and fashion the ways we use our time and talents both as individuals and as congregations?

Chapter 3 begins with a prayer of petition by the prophet, followed by a liturgical psalm in which God answers the prophet's petition with an imaginative portrayal of God's defeat of the wicked. Prophetic prayer can be as powerful and helpful/challenging to a community as a prophetic sermon. In 3:2, Habakkuk praises God for God's activity in the past. The prophet wants God's work "revived" to address the suffering of his own time. Because the prophet knows of the faithless living of the people, he also asks God for mercy.

The liturgical reading beginning in 3:3 depicts the majesty and the power of God, who can crush the oppressive enemy. Notice the imagery the prophet uses to describe God's power: "the eternal mountains were shattered"; "everlasting hills sank low"; the earth was split with rivers; "the deep gave forth its voice; the sun raised high its hands; the moon stood still in its exalted place." All this came to pass as God came forth to save God's people; the ramifications of God's redemptive power are individual, communal, global, and as we see here, even cosmic.

Habakkuk 3:16–19 gives witness to the prophet, who is waiting for deliverance for the people. These are words that come from a person who knows despair: "Though the fig tree does not blossom . . ." (3:17). "Yet," the prophet says, "I will rejoice in the LORD; I will exult in the God of my salvation. GOD, the LORD, is my strength; he makes my feet like the feet of a deer, and makes me tread upon the heights" (3:18–19). The prophet stands with the people and knows their sufferings, but still proclaims that God is a listening God, who hears their cries and who will deliver them. Even in times of divine absence or indifference, the prophet remains sure.

The book of Habakkuk has played important roles in Judaism and in Christianity. In the Dead Sea Scrolls is a commentary on Habakkuk 1–2. Paul cites 2:4 in support of his understanding of justification by faith (Rom. 1:17; Gal. 3:11). Rabbi Sinbar cites 2:4 as a summary of all the 613 commandments in Torah: "Look at the proud! Their spirit is not right in them, but the righteous live by their faith." What importance can it hold for the preacher's community today?

In lament, in prayer, in liturgy, Habakkuk struggles with concerns about violence, the lack of justice in the world, and the saving power of Yahweh. As we read these chapters, we cannot completely relinquish the haunting realities of Habakkuk's life and our own and the agonizing questions that life leads us to ask. Preachers are drawn to this book of the Hebrew Bible, not because it gives us answers, but because it asks our questions and gives congregants permission to ask the questions they have never felt comfortable or safe in asking before. There is something wonderfully freeing, even redemptive, about being allowed to voice our own questions before God.

Zephaniah

MARY DONOVAN TURNER

The book of Zephaniah, one of the twelve Minor Prophets of the Hebrew Bible, tells us that the prophet was active during the reign of Josiah over Judah. Josiah was a good king who came to the throne when he was eight years old. This prophet may have prophesied early in Josiah's career, before he began his massive reforms, although some parts of the book seem to come from a later time, when the kingdom of Judah had fallen.

The superscription for the book traces Zephaniah's lineage: he was the "son of Cushi son of Gedaliah son of Amariah son of Hezekiah, in the days of King Josiah son of Amon of Judah" (1:1). The name Cushi, Zephaniah's father, means Cushite or Ethiopian. Some have concluded from this that Zephaniah was from Africa, though others take Cushi as a personal name rather than an indicator of nationality. Regardless, this is all we know about the prophet. As with some of the other prophets, there is no evidence from nonbiblical sources about the person of Zephaniah.

Zephaniah is concerned about the corruption and injustice that appear to be rampant in Judah. God's creation, once pronounced good, is now being undone; God will destroy, sweep away everything on the "face of the earth." To reinforce the totality of what will be swept away, the prophet uses repetition. "I will utterly sweep away everything from the face of the earth, says the LORD. I will sweep away humans and animals; I will sweep away the birds of the air and the fish of the

199

sea" (1:2–3). It is good for preachers to notice repetitions in the text as indicators of things the biblical writer wishes to emphasize. Here, three times, God will "sweep away," indicating that God's anger is deep and wide.

Most of the prophetic books in the Hebrew Bible invite preachers to help congregations think about their comfort or discomfort with the notion of God's anger. Is there room for divine anger in our theologies? Do we believe or even hope that God gets angry at injustices and oppression, things contrary to the realm of God?

Verses 1:12–18 describe those for whom Yahweh will be looking on the dreaded day when what is on the earth will be swept away. Those who are indicted here are not the evildoers, but those who are complacent, those who are apathetic and who say that the Lord will do nothing, and those who think there is no consequence for the ways people are living. How important is naming complacency or apathy in our preaching?

Like other prophets, Joel for instance, Zephaniah emphasizes the "day of the LORD" (1:7–10, 14–16, 18; 2:2–3; 3:8, 11, 16). This is a repetitive and formative feature of his writings. What does the day of the Lord mean to the people who have been unfaithful and have worshiped idols? The prophet's message is in part a warning to the people of Judah that the final days are near and inevitable. There is an urgency that leaves no time for niceties or conditional speech. Time is up! And yet, the prophet also calls the people forth to live out their relationships with God more faithfully. So, was it too late for change? Or not too late? In threefold repetition Zephaniah calls out to the people (2:3):

> Seek the LORD, all you humble of the land; . . .
> seek righteousness,
> seek humility.

These life-giving attributes for those in covenant with God are similar to the prescriptions outlined in Micah 6:8. If you do these things, perhaps you "may be hidden on the day of the LORD's wrath" (Zeph. 2:3). Zephaniah is urgently calling the people to save themselves. When have we seen contemporary prophets speak with the same kind of intensity?

In chapter 3, through the use of repetition and parallelism, Zephaniah paints the picture of comprehensive and total faithlessness in the city of Jerusalem (3:3–4).

The [government] officials . . . are roaring lions;
its judges are evening wolves that leave nothing until the
    morning.
Its prophets are reckless, faithless persons;
its priests have profaned what is sacred, they have done
    violence to the law.

The corruption of leadership knows no bounds—no one in power has trusted or inquired of God. These unjust officials, civil and religious alike, know no shame. They are not repentant, and they do not understand the need for change. It is often easy to recognize the need for change more easily in others than in ourselves, but here all leaders are called to accountability.

Zephaniah gives voice to God's accusations, but the word is not devoid of hope (3:14–20). This is not a naive hope that fails to recognize the realities of people's living. It is a hope that can see through those realities to a better day. In the end, while Zephaniah brings words of total devastation to the earth to Judah and other nations as well (2:4–15), hope is how the book comes to closure; hope is the final word. While it is often difficult for preachers to make the words of hope and comfort, the good news, as compelling as the bad present realities, this is not so in the book of Zephaniah. The words of hope are as powerful as the words of indictment and are recited in the Revised Common Lectionary in years A, B, and C at the Easter Vigil and during Advent in year C. In both seasons, the words of Zephaniah call the community to rejoice because good things, even if they cannot yet be seen, are coming. In Zephaniah, the reason for the good news is that the day of the Lord, the judgment, will leave behind a remnant to carry on. The remnant will be purified, will have good and rightful priorities, and will call upon God as they go about their daily living.

Many theological questions arise out of the book of Zephaniah, prompting the preacher to take a careful and sustained look at our own living. How would we fare if Zephaniah were speaking out about the governmental and religious officials of our day? Are they just, honest? Are their priorities faithful? And what would we need to do to create a world that fulfills the vision of God, the realm of God, in our midst? Are there things we need to sweep away? What are they?

More generally, the entirety of the book of Zephaniah raises questions about the interplay between the political and the religious. Where do they meet? Zephaniah is a religious leader who is acutely aware of and engages the government and its national treaties and alliances, the ways government and religious leaders do or do not promote justice and equality among the residents of Judah. In your own context, how do you see this relationship? Does the church critique what is happening in the world? How do the preacher's sermons engage reflections about the nation, its social challenges and systemic evils, and its leaders?

Haggai

JOHN C. HOLBERT

The name of the prophet Haggai, active in rebuilding Jerusalem, in the province of Yehud in the Persian Empire, precisely from August 29 to December 18, 520 BCE, literally means "Pilgrimage Feasts." His name is indicative of his specific and sharply focused concern with the rebuilding of the temple in Jerusalem. Around that necessary activity, Haggai's oracles continually circle.

After the destruction of the city of Jerusalem and the temple of YHWH by the Babylonians in 587–586, the leaders of Israel were carted off to Babylon and remained in exile there until the Persian overthrow of the Babylonians in 539. As Cyrus, the Persian monarch, assumed power in Babylon, he allowed all those foreigners who had been exiled there to return to their homes, even offering them resources for the journey. In addition, he urged them to rebuild their former lives, albeit under the clear control of a Persian hegemony. In the case of the returnees to Jerusalem, Zerubbabel, a man with Davidic ancestry, was named governor, while Joshua, also a man with deep roots in Israel's past, was named high priest. It was made certain to all that Zerubbabel was no king; the only king was to be found in Ecbatana, capital of Persia.

When the exiles returned to the ruined city, the mandate to rebuild the temple was clear, and work began almost immediately in 538. The book of Ezra tells the tale of how that rebuilding project was thwarted by the people who remained in the land during the exile, mainly in the northern city of Samaria (Ezra 3:6–4:24). These "people of the land" wrote a letter to the Persian court, warning them about the rebellious history of Jerusalem, saying that if the temple were rebuilt, the province of Yehud would soon cause no end of trouble for the Persians. The Persians soon put a stop to the project.

Some eighteen years passed, and the temple continued to lie in disrepair. When Haggai appears in the city in the late summer of 520, he chides the inhabitants of the city, made up mostly of newly returned exiles, by accusing them of living in "paneled houses," obviously comfortable homes, "while this house lies in ruins" (1:4). He then makes the accusation that the desperate state of the struggling economy is the direct result of the sorry state of the ruined temple, once a symbol of YHWH's powerful presence in the land and now reduced to a heap of stones. "You have sown much," he cries, "and harvested little; you eat, but you never have enough; you drink, but you never have your fill" (1:6). "These people say that the time has not yet come to rebuild YHWH's house" (1:2), but Haggai says that it is far past time to rebuild, and further, it is in that rebuilding that the people will find their hope and future.

Here the preacher must tread carefully. It will hardly do to suggest that proper worship in a grand edifice will automatically lead to prosperity and the favor of God. A thoughtful preacher might rather want to conclude from Haggai's oracle that a project focusing the energy and commitments of any community may well serve as a galvanizing event that causes new vitality and joy to spring forth among the people. Such renewed excitement could well lead to fresh hope and newly burgeoning prosperity, both spiritual and physical.

And preachers can further take heart from the very fact of Haggai's effectiveness as a preacher. He begins his ministry in the summer, and within about a month's time, work on the temple has begun in earnest. Haggai 1:15 occurs on September 21, fewer than four weeks after Haggai's original oracle, yet "YHWH stirred up the spirit of Zerubbabel . . . and Joshua, . . . and the spirit of all the remnant of the people; and they came and worked on the house of YHWH, their God" (1:14). Jonah converted the world's most wicked city with a five-word sermon on one street corner of the city that surely may be the most effective sermon in history (Jonah 3:4, counting Hebrew words). But Haggai's four-week preaching series, leading all Judeans to work on the temple with a will, may not be far behind.

A preacher may also learn from the astonishingly precise dates found in this book, a dating precision found nowhere else in the Bible. Jeremiah had predicted a period of desolation that would begin in the exile and end some seventy years later (see Jer. 25:11–12; 29:10). If that period began in 587–86, the great exile of Jerusalem to Babylon, seventy years would lead to 517–16 BCE and would signal a new era for Judah. Indeed, though Haggai does not see the completion of the rebuilt temple, the temple is rededicated in 515. This attention to chronological accuracy emphasizes Haggai's conviction that YHWH has control over the actions of human history. Of course, again, the preacher must use such information carefully. Certain preachers have taken the idea of God's control of history to such extremes as to suggest that every human activity may be predicted by precise calculation from the pages of the Bible. This is absurd on its face. If it were so, all who read the Bible could agree about what is about to happen next! The fact that each biblical reader who makes such claims has different answers to the date of the next important historical happening makes it all too plain that that specificity is not what we must learn from Haggai. What the prophet suggests is that God must always stand in the center of our historical calculations, guiding us to follow God's will rather than our own.

And that leads to one other idea preachers may glean from Haggai. The crucial rebuilding of the temple means the reestablishment of the rule of YHWH, not the reestablishment of a kingship for Israel. What Yehud lacks is not only a physical structure called temple; its lack of temple suggests a lack of the presence of YHWH in its midst. Haggai emphasizes this lack in his final oracle of a future hope (2:20–23). He promises that once again in Israel's future a political ruler will appear, but there will be a crucial difference in this new ruler. Before this new leader shows up, it will be YHWH who will overthrow all foreign kingdoms, and not the human leader. The Davidic model of warrior-king is missing here. Only divine intervention will bring about a universal rule of YHWH. The fact that Haggai mentions the name of the governor of Yehud, Zerubbabel, as a part of the future scene does not imply that he imagines the governor as somehow becoming a future king. On the contrary, by employing a living figure in the future vision, Haggai bridges present and future. A rebuilt temple will bring with it a new place for the rule of YHWH, and priest, prophet, and governor will play important roles in any future organization of the people of Israel. Still, the focus is on YHWH as ruler, beyond any earthly monarch.

Zechariah

JOHN C. HOLBERT

Written later in Israel's history, the prophetic books have been little used in the pulpit, but they contain many valuable insights. This fourteen-chapter book, one of the twelve Minor Prophets, is in effect two books. The former, chapters 1–8, offers oracles closely related to those from Haggai. The second part, chapters 9–14, consists of two long oracles: the first, 9–11, comprises poems against foreign nations, while 12–14 focuses on Israel itself. We will address these two sections of Zechariah separately.

CHAPTERS 1–8

This first section of Zechariah may be divided into three main parts: part 1 (1:1–6) is a short introduction connecting the prophecy of Haggai with Zechariah; part 2 (1:7–6:15) offers a sequence of seven visions and one prophetic vision; part 3 comprises an opening section (7:1–7), a speech to a particular delegation of visitors (7:8–14), and two concluding oracles (8:1–17 and 18–23).

Part 1. Zechariah 1:1–6 shows clearly that Haggai and chapters 1–8 should be seen as a composite work. This is true both thematically and chronologically. Both prophets deal with the structure of national life and institutions in the period of Israelite restoration, and the carefully dated prophecies of both occur during the same time frame: August

29, 520, to December 7, 518 BCE. Moreover, the human characters of each prophecy are in the main identical: high priest Joshua, governor Zerubbabel, various priests, and the citizens of Yehud (Judah), the reconstituted community of recently returned exiles from Babylon. The two prophets are speaking into the same ears and are concerned with the same issues. As we should expect, however, they do not say identical things, but rather speak complementary words as they offer guidance to the community that seeks leadership from their God.

Haggai's words help to begin, or perhaps restart, work on the ruined temple in Jerusalem in 520 as he focuses his attention on the ceremony that will celebrate the reformation of that crucial building as the locus of the new community. That event of reformation relates to Zechariah's visions, discussed below. The detailed chronology of Haggai and Zechariah comprises a span of only two and one-half years, suggesting that the compilation of Haggai-Zechariah could have occurred no later than December 7, 518 BCE.

What more precisely does Zechariah provide by way of guidance to the emerging community of Yehud? It must be remembered that both Haggai and Zechariah are preaching in a world dominated by the rule of the Persian Darius I. Yehud, like all Persian provinces, exists only by the sufferance of that great monarch. Hence, any thought that Yehud might return to the former Davidic kingship model, that of one monarch directly descended from the great David ruling the land, a model that existed for over four hundred years before the Babylonian exile, is fatuous. New models are needed for a new community. Both Haggai and Zechariah are pragmatists in this new Persian world, trying to assist the people into a situation that must be for them "the new normal." That new normal will consist of a newly designed dual leadership model, the two prongs of power being governor and high priest. This new design was probably not an easy sell to people who fondly remembered David and his successors who ruled Israel in its halcyon days. Still, this dual pattern has the advantage of providing a traditional authority both secular and religious in nature while not threatening the Persian overlord with a potentially powerful, singular monarch. Joshua and Zerubbabel, the latter actually sent by the Persians, form a safe and reliable governing authority that recalls the past but points also to a fresh and potentially hopeful future.

Because Zechariah's prophecy extends several months after the rebuilding of the temple has begun under Haggai's demands, he can address the meaning and symbolism of that temple as an expression of this new dual leadership model. Zechariah is primarily concerned with the question: can the new community be comfortable with a temple yet without a king? It is a radically new concept, and Zechariah sets out to make it plausible.

In chapter 3 he presents a portrait of a high priest with expanded power, given to him by YHWH. After YHWH's rebuke of the satan (as in the book of Job, a figure not Mephistopheles of horns and tail, but rather a potent manifestation of unknown origin who stands in the way of the emerging power of the high priest), YHWH commands that the high priest take off his filthy rags and be dressed "in festal apparel," with a clean turban on his head. Then the high priest is charged by YHWH: "If you will walk in my ways and keep my requirements, then you shall rule my house and have charge of my courts, and I will give you the right of access among those who are standing here" (3:1–7). In other words, YHWH, the God of Yehud and the whole world, has personally selected and clothed the high priest and has given to him "rule" over the temple and responsibility for "guarding" or "keeping" or "protecting" (the Hebrew verb can mean all of these things) God's holy places outside of the temple. It is this priest who will have charge of the seven-faceted stone that will "remove the guilt of this land in a single day" (3:9). After that glorious day of YHWH's forgiveness, Joshua will "invite each other to come under your vine and fig tree" (3:10), a familiar prophetic symbol of safety and freedom (see Mic. 4:4; Hab. 3:17; and others). This high priest will have great power!

Part 2. Zechariah 1:7–6:8 shows Zechariah's special concern with the temple, as demonstrated in his seven visions that comprise part 2 of his work. The seven visions may be seen as a group of ever-decreasing circles of interest, the center circle being the subject of the temple itself in chapter 4. The other six visions are concerned with YHWH's word (1:7–17, 18–21), Yehud and Persia (2:6; 5:11), Jerusalem the city and Yehud (3:5; 6:15). But chapter 4 represents the prophet's central interest. In his vision of the temple, he finds two branches of the olive tree that pour out oil through two golden pipes (4:12), an image the prophet cannot at first understand. YHWH reveals that "these are the two anointed ones who stand by the Lord of the whole earth" (4:14). In other words, in the Jerusalem temple, about to be rebuilt and consecrated, one finds the twin leaders, governor and high priest, who will guide the new community into a glorious future with YHWH. The rich imagery of the visions may be understood as statements of

Zechariah's concern with YHWH's selection of high priest and governor, ensconced in the temple as rulers over the community.

Part 3. Zechariah 7–8, the third part of the first half of the book, consists of diverse kinds of prophetic and oracular material, shaped by a certain event described in 7:1–3. A delegation from people living in Bethel, the old central sanctuary of northern Israel, comes to Jerusalem "in the fourth year of King Darius," two years after the oracles of chapters 1–6. The people of Bethel ask a question about fasting, but the question soon turns into a vision that concerns the future of Israel and all the nations. One might say that Zechariah in these two chapters expands his demographic interests from Jerusalem and its temple to the community of Yehud, to the neighbors of Bethel, and finally to the entire universe. "In those days ten men from nations of every language shall take hold of a Jew, grasping his garment and saying, 'Let us go with you, for we have heard that God is with you'" (8:23). Thus, Zechariah 1–8 ends with all streaming to Zion, a reiteration of Isaiah's ancient prophecy several centuries earlier (Isa. 2:3).

CHAPTERS 9–14

Scholarly work on Zechariah 9–14 has been extremely contentious, but a kind of consensus may be summarized: chapters 9–11 consist of diverse material, some even preexilic, finding a final form in the Persian period, while chapters 12–14 come from the Hellenistic period (perhaps the late fourth century BCE). Though the connections between the two parts of Zechariah appear tenuous, these later oracles offer a glimpse of what has occurred in the city of Jerusalem and to the community of Judah, both bad and good.

Four themes of this section may be highlighted: (1) Especially in chapters 9–11 we see YHWH portrayed as a warrior, particularly against foreign nations. The oracles against foreign nations are reminiscent of earlier poems in Amos 1–2. (2) Stark criticism is given to community leaders, both foreign and domestic. Such criticism suggests that the dual leadership model, emphasized both by Haggai and Zechariah 1–8, may not always have been successful in practice, however much it was a gift of God to the people. (3) There will still be a bright and peaceful future for Jerusalem (chap. 14). (4) That future may be good, but it will not be any sort of utopia. Zechariah 14:17–19 demonstrates that the people will not always follow the demands of their God. If they do not go to Jerusalem to worship the King, YHWH of Hosts, the result will be drought. If residents of Egypt refuse to celebrate the Feast of Booths (Succoth), they will be plagued as their ancient ancestors were plagued at the command of Moses. Indeed, the oracle proclaims, anyone who refuses to celebrate Succoth in Jerusalem will suffer the plagues of Egypt.

Because the entire book of Zechariah comprises perhaps as much as two hundred years of prophetic reflection, one might see these later words of chapters 9–14 as a commentary on the late sixth-century prophet's attempts to shape a new Jerusalem now under the might of the Persian Empire. That attempt may have been successful in the main, but as the years went on, and as the Persian Empire collapsed under the power of the emergent Greeks, the city of Jerusalem and its struggling inhabitants made numerous attempts to survive as a tiny community in the ever-shifting scene of great empires. They still saw YHWH as warrior, fighting on their behalf against much stronger foreign powers. Their dual leadership model may have needed changes over the years to continue to be a valuable way to order the community: criticisms of the system appeared again and again. They continued to hope for a bright future for their city and their temple, yet regularly saw difficulties, both in terms of cultic practice and in terms of weak secular leadership.

In short, Zechariah's prophecy, encompassing two centuries of struggle and reflection, continued to raise many of the issues that had bedeviled the chosen people from the beginning of their relationship to their God. How can they remain faithful to that God in a constantly changing world? It remains our question to this day. A preacher needs to be attentive to this central concern of Zechariah that flexibility in changing ecclesial and cultural conditions calls for flexible responses to those changes. The prophet makes clear the fact that old reactions to change are not always the most helpful. New realities make new duties.

Malachi

JOHN C. HOLBERT

This last book in the Hebrew canon, and one of the twelve Minor Prophets, looks back to the preexilic prophets and also forward to fulfillment of YHWH's covenant promises. It is a well-integrated whole, consisting of several sharply pointed disputations between YHWH and the chosen people. Much scholarly attention has been given to the time of the writing, and a certain consensus has formed that places the book in the years after the rebuilding of the temple in Jerusalem in 516/515 BCE. The period between the reconstruction of the temple and the appearance of Ezra and Nehemiah (mid-fifth century) presents the likely backdrop of Malachi's work. This time frame is often called the "pre-Ezra decline," during which the hopes of Ezekiel, Haggai, and Zechariah for a renewed YHWH community have not been fulfilled. Commitment to the covenant of YHWH is weak, and Malachi directs focused attention on those weaknesses.

Before he begins his pointed questions for Judah, the prophet restates the absolute certainty of YHWH's unbreakable love for Judah. "I have loved you, says YHWH. But you say, 'How have you loved us?' Is not Esau Jacob's brother? says YHWH. Yet I have loved Jacob but I have hated Esau; I have made his hill country a desolation and his heritage a desert for jackals" (1:2–3). In other words, YHWH's love for Jacob/Judah is ongoing, while the heirs of Esau, especially the tribes in the north, are not uniquely loved by YHWH. Malachi's prophecies are written particularly for the chosen people of Judah. Malachi feels that he must first ground his sharp questions for the Judeans in the certainty of YHWH's unquestioned love for them.

Then Malachi turns to a series of disputations, attempting to uncover why the community has fallen away from YHWH's covenant and has therefore suffered the pain of a broken society.

At 1:8–2:9 he claims that the priests are corrupt and slack in their attention to their required work. He accuses them first of polluting YHWH's altar by offering foul food there, blind, sick, or lame animals (1:8), rather than the finest as required in the Levitical law (Lev. 22:20–22; Deut. 15:21). He further indicts the priests for their lack of moral leadership for a people in desperate need of it. "For the lips of a priest should protect knowledge; people should seek Torah from his mouth, for he is the messenger of YHWH of Hosts. But you have turned aside from the way; you have caused many to stumble through your (so-called) Torah" (2:7–8, my trans.). Malachi would rather the doors of the temple be shut (1:10) than have these priests continue their evil activities.

But the priests are hardly the only problem in the land; the Judean laypeople are equally guilty of faithlessness to their God (2:10–16). "Judah has been faithless, and abomination has been committed in Israel and in Jerusalem; for Judah has profaned the sanctuary of YHWH, which [YHWH] loves, and has married the daughter of a foreign god" (2:11). As one finds in nearly all of the preexilic prophets, idolatry is said to be a hallmark of faithlessness among the people. When YHWH is no longer worshiped, some other god will be substituted. And with idolatry comes a similar faithlessness in the intimate lives of the people as they divorce their Judean wives and marry foreign women (2:14–16). Such censure against easy and precipitous divorce anticipates the language of Jesus and Paul (Matt. 19:1–11; Mark 10:1–10; 1 Cor. 7:1–16; in contrast to Deut. 24:1–4). Ezra will later see these relaxed marital practices as a sign of Judean failures and will demand that all foreign wives be put away as a clear sign of covenant faithfulness.

In 2:17–3:7 Malachi then turns to a further indication of Judean unfaithfulness: they even speak falsely about YHWH by their accusation that YHWH rewards evil and is basically unjust. "All who do evil in YHWH's eyes are good; YHWH delights in them. Where is the God of justice?" (2:17, my trans.). Such outright blasphemy leads to a variety of moral and social abuses in the community. "Then I will draw near to you for judgment: I will be quick to bear witness against the sorcerers, against the adulterers, against those who swear falsely,

against those who oppress the hired workers in their wages, the widow
and the orphan, against those who shove aside the immigrant, and do
not fear me, says YHWH of Hosts" (3:5 alt.). Amos could easily have
uttered those lines, and Malachi conjures his ancient forebear in his
righteous fury.

Despite the foolish claims of the Judeans, Malachi avers that YHWH
has been just and fully consistent to the one YHWH has always been.
"I, YHWH, do not change; that is why, O children of Jacob, you have
not perished. Ever since the days of your ancestors you have rejected
my statutes and have not kept them" (3:6–7, my trans.). Even though
the Judeans of Malachi's day are no different and no better than their
ancestors who have preceded them—consistent idolaters and rejecters
of YHWH's demands—the very fact that they are still alive in the land
is the clearest sign of all that YHWH still loves them!

Malachi offers one more sign of their spiritual bankruptcy at 3:8–
12: their refusal to bring a genuine tithe to the temple. The tithe was an
important element of Israelite religion (Lev. 27:30; Num. 18:26–28),
but after the prophet's attacks on basic social evils like oppression of
the poor, surely Malachi is not implying that a full tithe will satisfy
YHWH and cause blessings to flow once again. The tithing problem
must rather be simply another sign of their spiritual emptiness. Along
with the other deep problems identified by the prophet, the stinginess
of the people is just one more indication that the community is bereft
of genuine piety and badly in need of reformation in too many ways
to number.

Malachi concludes his disputations against Judah at 3:13–15 with
their belief that YHWH has allowed wickedness to triumph over righteousness and has been loath to judge sin at all. "You have said, 'It is
useless to worship God! What do we profit by keeping God's command? . . . We count the arrogant happy; evildoers not only prosper,
but when they test God, they get away with it" (3:14–15, my trans.)!
Following YHWH gets us nothing, cry the Judeans, and YHWH cares
not at all. But Malachi answers them by announcing the coming day of
YHWH, when God's justice will be vindicated and the wicked will be
separated from the righteous in the divine judgment (3:18).

The book ends (4:1–6) with a vivid scene of YHWH's judgment
on the Judeans and indeed on the whole world. "For you who revere
my name the sun of righteousness shall rise, with healing in its wings.
You shall go out leaping like calves from the stall" (4:2)! No one should
accuse this prophet of being concerned only with cultic and priestly

details. In many ways, his work is a summation of the prophetic work of the Hebrew Bible, concerned with proper worship and reverence for YHWH, a reverence that leads to proper human activity in the world. And in the end the promise is that God will offer "healing in [God's] wings" for those who follow God's will and way. It is a fitting promise to close the canon of the Hebrew Scriptures.

A preacher will want to take special care not to reduce Malachi to a "do this/receive this" sort of theology. YHWH's gifts to the people of grace and hope are not ultimately based on a tit-for-tat relationship of our acts and God's response, but rather on God's free gift of grace, which makes possible any human actions.

New Testament

Matthew

O. WESLEY ALLEN, JR.

The Gospel of Matthew is the first Gospel in the New Testament canon and was the most popular of the Gospels in the ancient church (reflected in the contemporary church in the fact that it serves as the anchor for Year A of the Revised Common Lectionary). Scholars agree, however, that Matthew was written after Mark (probably around 80 CE) and used Mark as its primary source. The Gospel is anonymous but was traditionally (and incorrectly) attributed to the apostle Matthew, probably due to the Gospel's reference to Jesus calling Matthew the tax collector to follow him (9:9), while Mark and Luke refer to the tax collector as Levi (see Mark 2:14; Luke 5:27). (Scholars continue to refer to the author as "Matthew" for the sake of convenience.)

The fact that Matthew used Mark as his primary source means that preachers can benefit from noting ways Matthew changed Mark in shaping his own narrative. The ways in which Matthew follows Mark closely show how much the author appreciated the earlier Gospel. The ways in which he changed Mark, however, are clues to ways he critiqued Mark and shaped the story of the Christ event with his unique theological emphases. In similar but not quite as clear a way, preachers can also compare Matthean passages to Lukan ones when there are parallels. Most scholars generally assume that in addition to Mark, both Matthew and Luke used another source (or collection of sources, generally referred to as "Q") but without knowledge of the other. This independent usage allows for comparison and contrast but does not

219

as easily lead to conclusions about authorial intent. Importantly, the common features between the three "Synoptic" (similar look) Gospels should not tempt preachers to harmonize Matthew, Mark, and Luke, but instead the differences between them allow for exploration of different theological perspectives on Jesus as the Christ.

MATTHEW'S CIRCUMSTANCES

Matthew's unique theological perspective is informed in part by being written in different circumstances than that of Mark. Mark was written around 70 CE and was attempting to deal with the crisis of faith that the defeat of the Jewish Revolt by the Romans and the fall of the temple caused for those who emphasized resurrection, a victorious theology. Matthew's Gospel appears to have been written after that crisis had passed. A major concern that lies behind Matthew's narrative, then, was the need for a version of the story of Jesus that served the ongoing life and faith development of the community of faith in contrast to a crisis-oriented narrative. This concern plays out in a number of ways.

First, Matthew's narrative tries to legitimize the church by demonstrating the Christian faith to be a rightful heir to Israel's traditions and practices. This is seen most obviously in Matthew's obsession with showing that Jesus was a fulfillment of Hebrew Scripture and prophecy (e.g., 1:22; 2:5–6, 15, 17–18, 23; 4:15–16; 8:17; 12:17–21; 13:14, 35; 21:4; 27:9–10).

Matthew's emphasis is complicated, however, by the fact that the church was not alone in vying for such legitimacy. After the fall of the temple, many Jewish sects (such as the Sadducees, Essenes, and Zealots) disappeared because their identity and purpose were centered on control of practices at the temple. That left two Jewish groups competing to be the legitimate heirs to Israel's traditions and practices: the Pharisees (synagogue) and the Christians (church). Regrettably, part of claiming such legitimacy included vying against the claims of the sibling group. Matthew imports this conflict from the final decades of the first century back into his narrative in the form of the Jewish religious authorities in conflict with Jesus and the disciples. It is important for preachers to recognize that this sibling rivalry lies behind much of Matthew's portrayal of the Jewish authorities in order to avoid making anti-Jewish and anti-Semitic claims in contemporary sermons that have been a shameful part of the history of the church. When dealing with passages that involve such conflict, preachers should focus on the positive claim Matthew is making about the church without demonizing Judaism.

Second, Matthew's long-term interests show up in his emphasis on Jesus' teachings. Whereas Mark spoke about Jesus as a teacher but provided only a little of his actual teaching, Matthew expands Mark's outline by including great amounts of Jesus' sayings as passed down by the church. Matthew expands Mark's parables (Mark 4) and eschatological discourses (Mark 13) into five longer discourses. They are the Ethical Discourse (Sermon on the Mount, chaps. 5–7), Missionary Discourse (chap. 10), Parables Discourse (chap. 13), Ecclesial Discourse (chap. 18), and Eschatological Discourse (chaps. 24–25). That Matthew wants readers to see these discourses as a compendium of Jesus' teaching instead of unrelated sermons can be seen in the formulaic ending he uses for each one: "When Jesus had finished saying these things . . ." (7:28; 11:1; 13:53; 19:1; and note the change in 26:1).

A third way Matthew demonstrates his concern for the ongoing faith and life of the community is the way he redeems the role of the disciples compared with their portrayal in Mark. Mark presents the disciples as near-buffoons, understanding little about the Messiah they were following to serve as representatives of the readers and their christological misunderstanding. While Matthew does not turn them into all-knowing saints, he clearly foreshadows their role in establishing the church of which Matthew's late first-century community is beneficiary. Consider, for example, the scene in which Peter professes Jesus to be the Christ in Mark 8:27–33. Mark presents Peter as using the right word but clearly misunderstanding because Jesus silences him and then has to rebuke him, calling him Satan. Matthew 16:13–23 expands the story. While Jesus still instructs the disciples to tell no one and rebukes Peter, the chastisement is softened by the fact that Jesus praises Peter for correctly identifying who Jesus is, claiming the knowledge to be that of revelation, and promising Peter the keys to the reign of heaven.

Fourth, Matthew demonstrates his interest in grounding the ongoing life of the church in Jesus' story by expanding Mark's version of the story. We have already noted that Matthew added teaching materials to Mark's narrative, but the author also added narrative materials not found in Mark's story, particularly at the beginning and end of the narrative. Mark's Gospel started with the ministry of John the Baptist (Mark 1:2), but Matthew backs up to Jesus' birth (chaps. 1–2). One can easily imagine that as years passed, members of the church had an increasing interest in biographical details of Jesus. These opening chapters help fill in such details as well as claim that Jesus was not adopted as God's Son at his baptism but was born the Son of God.

Similarly, Matthew expands Mark's ending. Even though Mark had foreshadowed the resurrection in his narrative, after the crucifixion and burial the story ends abruptly without the risen Jesus appearing and the women telling no one of the empty tomb (Mark 16:1–8). This was part of Mark's parabolic approach to correct his community's Christology following the fall of the temple. For Matthew, such an ending was not appropriate for the ongoing life of the church. In his version he deals apologetically with claims that disciples stole Jesus' body and has Jesus meet the disciples in Galilee (with language implying that it is on the same mountain as the Sermon on the Mount), giving them advice for advancing the church (27:62–28:20).

Fifth, Matthew demonstrates his interest in shaping the continuing faith of the church some fifty years after Jesus' crucifixion by emphasizing the eschatological dimension of Jesus' teaching and of the Christian life. Concern about the delay of the Parousia (Jesus' return) is a theme that shows up in several places in the New Testament. It is easy to imagine that by Matthew's day, there would have been people in his community who claimed that Jesus had not returned (as promised in Mark 13) and that it was never going to happen. Instead of conceding the point to such a view, Matthew doubles down on eschatology. For example, Matthew names in strong terms the judgment that is part of the Parousia by adding parables to the Eschatological Discourse that warn of what happens to those not prepared for Christ's return (24:37–25:46).

Matthew's eschatology is best understood in the context of Matthew's broad picture of salvation history. Although Matthew's plot extends from the conception to the resurrection of Jesus, his story world extends from Abraham (1:1) to the end of time (28:20). Put differently, at all times in his narrative, Matthew has in view both Israel's past and the church's future, and the story of Jesus serves as the hinge between the two. Jesus leans toward the future of the church (and indeed of the cosmos) in that even the death and resurrection narrated within the story line is not the end of his work: the Parousia is.

Matthew, however, nuances his understanding of the Parousia to fit the late first century. The cosmic description of eschatological expectations in 24:29 shows that while Matthew is clearly persuaded that a literal salvific judgment is in the future and wants to persuade his readers of such, he is more concerned with his readers living eschatologically in the present. As long as the sky is the same way it was yesterday, you need to keep living toward God's future.

This is the "already/not-yet" of eschatological existence. God's salvation and judgment have *already* arrived in Christ (as seen in the existence of the church), but they are *not yet* fully consummated (as seen in continuing evil in the world). For Matthew, it is incorrect to view the first coming of Jesus as historical and the second as eschatological. The birth, teachings, healings/exorcisms, death, and resurrection of Jesus as a whole mark the incursion of the end of the ages, in which we currently live and which we wait to see fulfilled. In Matthew's view, you cannot be a Christian and not experience existence eschatologically.

GEOGRAPHICAL STRUCTURE

In addition to preachers contextualizing passages from Matthew in relation to the various situational and thematic concerns listed above, it is important to recognize also how a passage relates to its literary context. Not only the content, concepts, vocabulary, and images in the Gospel, but the very flow of the story of Jesus' birth, ministry, teachings, passion, and resurrection is theological. Highlighting where a passage is embedded in this flow can be especially helpful for preachers to share repeatedly with congregations following the Revised Common Lectionary, since the Gospel lections chosen (at least from Advent through Pentecost) follow liturgical themes and structures more than the unfolding of Matthew's story.

The problem is that there is no clear scholarly consensus concerning Matthew's structure. Preachers should remember, however, that outlining an ancient narrative is as much a heuristic device helping us get a handle on a literary work as a whole as it is discovering what the author actually planned. Thus in the long run, for a preacher, it is more important to recognize key narrative connections and transitions in the Gospel that help put any individual pericope in an insightful narrative and theological context in the aid of proclamation than it is to determine precise and detailed narrative divisions that are argued for in different scholarly commentaries.

In the past many argued for viewing the five discourses mentioned above as also functioning structurally so that the text alternates between narrative and discourse. Such a view can be helpful, but often the narrative between discourses is not as tightly connected as the material in the discourses. Moreover, this outline provides little sense of a developing plot.

Some scholars have adopted a trifold division of Matthew (1:1–4:6; 4:17–16:20; 16:21–28:20), divided by the phrase "From that time Jesus began to . . ." in 4:17 and 16:21. The first section involves the establishment of Jesus' identity through his birth, baptism, and temptation. The second is initiated by public proclamation of the reign of heaven. The third is initiated by private instruction about the passion and resurrection and what leads to that. While this outline is better than the first in helping preachers see Matthew as a story that unfolds, the outline is not without problems. The phrase argued to be transitional is simply not prominent enough in the Greek to be the kind of marker proposed. (Moreover, part of the phrase "from that time" appears also in 26:16 in reference to Judas.)

Another proposal is simply to view the structure of the First Gospel in relation to the geographical setting/movements of different sections of the narrative. The main divisions of Matthew in this outline are as follows:

Beginning: From Bethlehem to Nazareth (1:1–4:11)
Capernaum-based Ministry (4:12–18:35)
Traveling to Jerusalem (19:1–20:34)
Conflicts, Passion, and Resurrection in/around Jerusalem
    (21:1–28:15)
Beginning Again: In Galilee (28:16–20)

One of the most striking things to notice from this arrangement of Matthew's material is that four out of the five discourses fall within the narration of Jesus' Capernaum-based ministry. For all of the space Matthew gives to the discourses, they do not drive the narrative as a whole. The overarching story, instead, is moved along by *growing conflict* between Jesus and the disciples on the one side and the demonic powers and religiopolitical authorities on the other. Understanding where any individual passage is located in relation to this evolving conflict in Matthew will help the preacher name appropriately what is at stake in the scene.

In the Beginning section, Herod (along with religious authorities summoned and supported by him) seeks to kill Jesus, but through divine providence Jesus is rescued. This conflict, which leads Jesus from Judea to Egypt then to Galilee, serves as a pattern for the traveling conflict that defines the rest of the story.

In the Capernaum-based ministry (on Jesus setting up headquarters in Capernaum, see 4:12–25), Jesus begins critiquing religious authorities in the Ethical Discourse by calling his followers to a higher righteousness than the religious leaders practice. After the discourse, Jesus begins healing and casting out demons, and the religious authorities begin challenging his works, practices, and teaching even to the point of accusing him of using the power of Satan in performing exorcisms (9:34; 12:24) and ultimately scheming to destroy him (12:14).

In the section in which he and the disciples travel to Jerusalem, the religious authorities increase their testing of Jesus (e.g., 19:3–9).

Jesus' public and symbolically loaded entry into Jerusalem and his attack on the temple intensifies the conflict in the opening of the final major section of the narrative. The religious authorities respond by challenging Jesus on numerous issues while he teaches in the temple, but Matthew gives Jesus the last word with the strident condemnation of the religious authorities as powerful and oppressive hypocrites (chap. 23). The religious authorities (in cooperation with the political powers), however, have the last act: they arrest, try, brutalize, and kill Jesus. Yet Jesus' death is not the end of the conflict. The religiopolitical powers carry the conflict to the tomb by placing guards there. God, however, trumps all in the end by raising Jesus from the dead, reducing their power to naught.

In the final and shortest section of the narrative, in which Jesus and the disciples meet once again in Galilee, Jesus claims to have been given all authority in heaven and on earth in a word that declares the conflict ended and won (28:18).

Mark

O. WESLEY ALLEN, JR.

Mark is the second Gospel in the New Testament (and the anchor of Year B in the Revised Common Lectionary). Most scholars argue, however, that Mark was the first of the Gospels to be written and was composed around 70 CE, the year in which the Jerusalem temple was destroyed as the Romans squashed the Jewish Revolt (66–73). This date of composition is signaled in the eschatological discourse in chapter 13, when Jesus predicts the fall of the temple (vv. 1–2) and when the narrator signifies the importance of this event for understanding the narrative with the only instance in the entire narrative of injecting his own voice into Jesus' speech to speak directly to the reader: "But when you see the desolating sacrilege set up where it ought not to be (*let the reader understand*), then those in Judea must flee to the mountains" (v. 14, emphasis added).

MARK'S PURPOSE

Mark—even though the author is anonymous, scholars continue to follow tradition in calling him "Mark" for the sake of convenience—then does not write his Gospel to create a historical biography of Jesus in some general sense, but to deal with this specific situation. The fall of the temple would have created an existential crisis for the church since it represented the dashed hopes of freedom from Rome, the loss of the

227

central symbol of God's presence, and questions about why the resurrected Christ did not return to bring victory to the Jewish Revolt. In other words, one of the driving forces behind the narrative is for Mark to answer a key question for his community of faith: What good news is there for the church in the shadow of the destruction of the temple?

The way Mark answers this question is to take the story of the Christ event that was already known to his readers and put a new spin on it so that they could hear it in a radically new way. (An analogy might be all of the movies that take a classic story like Cinderella and try to find a new way to tell it, even to the point of recharacterizing Cinderella so that the story has a feminist bent. With Mark, however, the purpose of telling the story through a new lens is not related to entertainment but to help the original Christian readers keep and renew their faith in Jesus Christ, the Son of God.)

MARK AS PARABLE

This literary and theological strategy is most evident in the strange ending to the narrative (16:1–8), in which the tomb is empty, but the resurrected Jesus makes no appearance, and the women tell no one what they have seen even though they were instructed to do so. (While translations have possible endings to Mark that extend past 16:8, scholars generally agree that these were later scribal additions and not part of Mark's original narrative.) The lack of a resurrection appearance does not mean that Mark does not affirm the resurrection: after all, the tomb *is* empty, and Jesus predicts being raised numerous times (8:31; 9:9, 31; 10:34). Moreover, this open ending is foreshadowed from the very beginning when the narrator titles the work "The *beginning* of the good news of Jesus Christ, the Son of God" (1:1, emphasis added) as opposed to simply titling it "The good news of Jesus Christ, Son of God." Still, even with the foreshadowing, the reader is left to puzzle over why the author chooses to end the story in this particular way.

Since Mark leaves the ending without a resurrection appearance even though his hearers would have likely been familiar with the story of Jesus appearing to the women and/or the disciples, he only claims to tell the beginning of the story of Christ; and since he is writing this story for his specific community of faith, that to which preachers need to attend most are the ways Mark reconfigures the story to offer his hearers a new hearing of who Jesus is. One way of doing this is to read the entire Gospel as a parable. This long story is a parable *about* Jesus modeled on the short parables taught *by* Jesus in the narrative.

In chapter 4, Mark includes Jesus' parables discourse. After the opening parable of the sower (vv. 3–9), Mark includes the following exchange concerning the purpose of parables:

> When [Jesus] was alone, those who were around him along with the twelve asked him about the parables. And he said to them, "To you has been given the secret of the kingdom of God, but for those outside, everything comes in parables; in order that
> 'they may indeed look, but not perceive,
> and may indeed listen, but not understand;
> so that they may not turn again and be forgiven.'" (4:10–12)

For Mark, parables are not like modern sermon illustrations, which make complex theological ideas concrete and simple. Instead, they draw a line between insiders and outsiders. And they do this by the oddness of what they portray. For example, everyone in the ancient world knew that the mustard plant was not the largest of all shrubs (4:32) and would have pondered what Jesus' hyperbole was meant to convey. Similarly, Mark twists the story of Jesus that they already knew (e.g., the story of the resurrection) in ways that would lead them to similar sorts of theological reflections. To help his original audience hear the story of Jesus with new ears, Mark takes their status as insiders in the faith— insiders in the reign of God—and turns it upside down so that they question not only their status as insiders but also their very understanding of Christ.

THE ROLE OF THE DISCIPLES
IN THE MARKAN PARABLE

This challenging of the readers' status as insiders is done primarily through the characterization of the disciples, with whom the original readers naturally identified. The readers, after all, already knew of and revered the disciples as the pillars of the very church of which they were a part. In their first appearance in the story, Jesus calls the four fishermen to follow him (1:16–20). Without having heard him preach or teach and without having seen him perform a miracle, these respond obediently, leaving livelihood and family behind. That is the paradigmatic Christian response. Of course, the readers would identify with them.

Having established this positive identification, the author slowly deconstructs it. First, the author narrates scenes in which various outsider groups show up: groups that do not fully understand, fear, or even resist Jesus. These groups include demons, crowds, religious leaders, Jesus' hometown, Roman military rule, and even his family. In contrast, the disciples are very attractive to the readers as points of identification, as models of Christian faith, . . . until the parables discourse in chapter 4 mentioned above. These supposed insiders suddenly do not understand the parables and need Jesus to explain to them the very stories intended for insiders (see 4:13, 33–34). Then at the end of the chapter, Mark narrates the scene in which Jesus and the disciples are in a boat together when a storm arises. When Jesus calms the storm, the disciples explicitly ask, "Who then is this, that even the wind and the sea obey him?" (v. 41). The disciples do not know the very person they are following!

This ignorance becomes more and more evident throughout the Gospel. When Jesus asks the disciples who people say he is, the answers show that the masses are clearly confused (8:28). When Peter answers for the disciples, however, the reader might think that he finally gets the answer correct: "You are the Messiah" (v. 29). The problem is that Jesus immediately silences him (v. 30), implying that the answer is not correct, or better, that Peter does not understand the answer he has given. Jesus then describes his coming passion in terms of the "son of the human" instead of "Messiah," only to have Peter try to rebuke him, showing the depth of his misunderstanding of Jesus and his mission (vv. 31–32, my trans.). Jesus adds an exclamation point to highlighting Peter's misunderstanding by calling Peter "Satan" (v. 33), the ruler of all outsiders, the "strong man" whom Jesus binds (3:27). There is no worse insult that Mark's Jesus could have delivered, and it is intended to be pointed not only at Peter but also at those readers who were led to identify with the disciples, of which Peter is the chief representative.

The disciples' status as outsiders is deepened throughout the rest of the narrative even to the point at which Judas betrays Jesus (14:44–45), all of the disciples abandon him in Gethsemane (v. 50), and Peter denies him three times (vv. 66–72). Peter thinks he is lying when, in his third denial, he says, "I do not know this man you are talking about" (v. 71), but he ironically (and parabolically) speaks the truth. And Mark wants his readers to recognize that Peter speaks for them as well. *We* do not know who Jesus is, at least not fully.

The thoroughness of misunderstanding that Mark wants readers to experience by engaging his narrative parable is seen in the fact that throughout Jesus' ministry in Galilee, he repeatedly tells those he heals, demons he confronts, and his disciples to tell no one about his acts of power (e.g., 1:43–44; 3:11–12; 5:43; 9:9). Scholars call this Markan literary device the "Messianic Secret." Mark seems to be arguing that Jesus' acts of power cannot be understood fully until the climax of the narrative.

Over against a misunderstanding of Christ that emphasizes the resurrection and acts of power and thus might expect the risen one to return to bring a military victory over the Roman Empire, Mark emphasizes the lowly, abandoned death on a cross as the climax of the Christ event. It is at the point of his death that the most outside of outsiders—a Roman centurion responsible for the actual act of crucifying Jesus, the symbol of military oppression of the Jews and persecution of the Christians—becomes the only human in Mark's story to recognize Jesus as "God's Son" (15:39). Instead of primarily understanding Jesus as the Messiah through the lens of the resurrection (and the Jewish Revolt against Rome), Mark urges his original readers to re-view Jesus' identity and significance through the lens of the crucifixion.

According to Mark, at the moment that Jesus dies, the curtain of the temple, at the opening of the Holy of Holies, is torn in two (15:37–38). While some scholars have argued that this notice symbolizes the inclusion of Gentiles (certainly a concern of Mark's), it can also be viewed as symbolizing the departure of God. Interpreted in this fashion, Mark does not intend the divine departure as a critique of Jewish worship at the temple but as a sign that when the Romans destroyed the temple in 70, they did not (could not!) rob the people of God's presence. God is found elsewhere.

The open ending at the empty tomb after the crucifixion and tearing of the temple curtain puts the readers in a position to speak to the world what the women left the tomb too afraid to say to the disciples (16:8): Christ has gone before you into Galilee, and you will see him there, in the midst of disease, religious tensions, imperial rule, demon possessions, and a bumbling group of Jesus-followers. That is where the crucified Messiah, the Son of God, is found. That is where God is found.

While there are many different theological elements at play in the Gospel of Mark, preachers will do well to look for this corrective Christology as a backdrop to most passages in the narrative. Christians today, just like Christians of the first century, are more than willing to remake Jesus in our own image and to our own liking. By asking congregations to identify with the disciples (and others throughout the narrative) who misunderstand Jesus in Mark's story, preachers offer them an opportunity to expand their understanding of Christ in significant ways and thus to be a different sort of church.

MARK'S STRUCTURE

In addition to attending to this central christological theme in relation to specific passages, preachers should also note where in the development of this theme, in the progression of Mark's plot line, the passage falls.

Unlike Matthew and Luke, Mark has no infancy narrative in which Jesus is born as God's Son. Instead, following the title in 1:1, Mark immediately starts with John the Baptist as the precursor to Jesus and with Jesus' baptism (which serves as the point at which Jesus is adopted as God's Son), and Jesus' testing in the wilderness (1:2–13).

The next major section of Mark's narrative introduces Jesus' preaching and healing ministry in Galilee, his disciples, and the first signs of conflict with religious authorities and other outsiders (1:14–3:35; see especially 3:6).

As mentioned above, the parables discourse in chapter 4 serves as a turning point for Mark. It is at this point that the disciples begin to look like outsiders. Across the wider narrative section describing Jesus' continued Galilean ministry (4:1–8:26), that characterization of the disciples intensifies along with other conflicts increasing in Galilee. (Note that the section ends with the progressive healing of a person who is blind, after which the healed person is told to tell no one; 8:22–26.)

In 8:27–10:52, the focus shifts from Galilee to heading to Jerusalem (which the narrator repeatedly indicates by describing Jesus as being "on the way," although English translations sometimes obscure this repetition). Anchoring this section are three times when Jesus predicts his passion in parallel fashion. After each prediction the disciples act inappropriately: Peter, who just professed Jesus to be the Messiah, rebukes him (8:27–9:1); the disciples argue about who is the greatest, that is, who will succeed Jesus after he dies (9:30–37); and James and John request to sit at Jesus' right hand and left hand in his glory, a likely foreshadowing of the thieves crucified on Jesus' right and left (10:32–45). As with the previous section, this one ends with another healing of someone who is blind (10:46–52), only this time when Jesus tells him to go (without silencing him), the healed person follows Jesus "on the way."

Chapters 11–15 serve as Mark's Jerusalem narrative, in which Jesus takes on the religious authorities on their home court, prepares the disciples for his death, is arrested, and is executed by the Roman authorities at the behest of the religious authorities. As noted, it is in this section that the disciples become complete outsiders and abandon Jesus.

The final section of Mark is, of course, the odd story of the empty tomb (16:1–8). Even through the parable presents the scene without any disciples present and with the women leaving in fear and silence, this ending offers redemption to the disciples (and the readers!). By returning to Galilee—the parabolic representation of those places where people need good news, where healing and feedings take place, and where liberation from demons occurs—the disciples/readers can meet Jesus anew and become insiders in God's reign.

Luke

O. WESLEY ALLEN, JR.

The Gospel of Luke was written around 80–95 CE as the first half of a two-volume narrative often referred to as Luke-Acts. The full narrative tells the story of Jesus Christ in the first volume (Luke) and the beginning of the post-resurrection church in the second volume (Acts of the Apostles), which focuses especially on Peter and the Twelve in the first half and on Paul in the second half.

Although tradition asserts that the narrative was written by Luke the physician, a companion of Paul (see Col. 4:14), there is little evidence to support this claim. The identity of the author of Luke-Acts is simply unknown, but the traditional name ascribed to the author continues to be used for ease of reference.

While the author does not identity himself, he does specifically name his addressee in the prologue: Theophilus (1:1–4; see also Acts 1:1). Since, however, this name literally means "God-lover," it is unclear whether Theophilus is a real person (the patron of the publication) or simply a way to refer to any Christian reader. Regardless, the name shows that Luke is not writing to convert people who are hearing the story of Jesus for the first time, but instead is writing to (re)interpret elements of the faith to those already within the faith, a task many preachers face today.

In the prologue Luke claims to have researched other narratives, as well as reports from eyewitnesses (first-generation Christians) and servants of the word (second-generation preachers) that informed those narratives (v. 2), in shaping his reinterpretation. Scholarship generally holds that Luke used as his two main sources Mark and "Q" (a hypothetical sayings source used independently by Matthew and Luke) as well as other written and oral sources used only by Luke. While Luke valued these sources enough to build much of his first volume using them, he also critiqued them theologically as evidenced by the way he changed them. Preachers can compare and contrast Luke with Mark and Matthew to highlight its unique theology.

SALVATION HISTORY AND WIDER HISTORY

The cornerstone of Luke's theology is salvation history: the understanding that God's salvific work is found in the way God has acted and continues to act in history. Luke's salvation history extends beyond the events he narrates to a wider history in two significant ways. First, he presents his narrative as a continuation of the history of Israel, especially the prophets, as found in Scripture. Second, he locates his story in the context of world history (see Acts 26:26), in the Gentile world. In the opening chapters, for instance, he repeatedly references rulers and events outside the narrative proper (Luke 1:5; 2:1–3; 3:1–2) and traces Jesus' lineage back through Israel's history (cf. Matt. 1:1–17, which stops with Abraham) to the beginning of the human race (Luke 3:23–38).

At stake in connecting Luke's narrative to these two wider views of Israel's and Gentile history seems to be the question: How is the Gentile-inclusive church of Luke's day a fulfillment of God's promises to Israel, especially as revealed through the prophets (see 1:54)? While it is Acts that deals explicitly with the existence of the Gentile church, already in the Gospel Luke presents Jesus' mission as extending to the Gentiles (Luke 2:31–32; 4:23–27; 7:1–10; 8:26–39; 9:52–56; 10:33–37; 17:11–19; 24:46–47).

THE PROPHETIC PATTERN
OF SALVATION HISTORY

Although Luke presents God as doing something new in Jesus and the church that leads to the Gentile church, he presents many of his characters as typologically shaped in the likenesses of Abraham, Moses, and

Elijah. These characters are portrayed as Spirit-filled prophets standing in line with the prophets of old (in Luke, see 1:15–17, 26, 35, 41–42, 46–55, 67–79; 2:25–38; 3:3–4; 4:14–15, 17, 18, 24, 27; 6:23; 7:16, 26, 39; 9:7–8; 11:47–51; 12:11–12; 13:33–34; 20:6; 24:19).

This prophetic characterization leads to a recurring plot structure in Luke-Acts that follows the same orderly pattern Luke finds in Israel's story: The prophet who brings God's word is rejected and persecuted. God responds by redeeming the prophet, but in the process the prophet steps aside from being the central character in the story. God then deals with the persecutors, and the next prophet steps up to continue the work of God's reign. At the center of this progression in Luke-Acts is Jesus (Luke 1–24; Acts 1), followed by Peter and the Twelve (Acts 2–12), followed by Paul (Acts 13–28). Preachers should recognize that while the Gentile church is something new, it is also the providential fulfillment of God's ancient promise to Israel; thus preachers will avoid some of the anti-Jewish claims often made from the pulpit.

THE GOSPEL'S SALVATION NARRATIVE

While Luke presents Jesus as one prophet among many, he does not view him as a prophet among equals. In his first volume, Luke offers Jesus as the *paradigm* of the repeating prophetic pattern for the church. He is the center of salvation history (in terms of God's salvation effected in the past) and the model for how and the hope for why the church lives out its salvation, its eschatological life in the Spirit, in ongoing history. His story unfolds in the following manner:

Prologue (1:1–4). As discussed above, Luke opens with a declaration of his intent to offer his readers certainty concerning the faith they have been taught by providing them with an orderly account of the Christ/church event.

Beginnings (1:5–3:38). Luke's opening chapters tell of Jesus' conception, birth, growth, and baptism. The closing genealogy divides this section from the next. Unlike Mark, in which Jesus becomes Messiah at his baptism, Luke (similar to Matthew) has a Christology in which Jesus is born as the Messiah. While many in Luke's narrative are filled with the Holy Spirit (especially as prophets), Jesus alone is *conceived* by the Spirit (1:35) and receives the Spirit *in bodily form* at his baptism (3:22).

Jesus' ministry in Galilee (4:1–9:50). Whereas Mark and Matthew present Jesus' temptation as flowing forth from his baptism, Luke separates the two scenes with his genealogy (3:23–38). Thus the temptation story initiates Jesus' ministry of confronting evil in the world instead of concluding his preparation for ministry and is coupled with Jesus' inaugural sermon in Nazareth. As in the temptation, Jesus rejects the worldly approach to gaining power, so in the scene in the Nazareth synagogue, Jesus declares that his ministry is oriented toward those without power. Throughout this narrative section, that orientation is affirmed in healings and exorcisms, in conflicts with religious authorities, in table fellowship with sinners and crowds, and in calling and commissioning the apostles to preach the good news and to heal. Near the end of the section, it becomes clear that this type of ministry will result in Jesus' crucifixion (9:22, 44).

Jesus' ministry on the way to Jerusalem (9:51–19:28). The Lukan narrator indicates a major narrative transition by opening this section of the story with the words "When the days drew near for him to be taken up, he set his face to go to Jerusalem" (9:51). In the travel narrative that follows, a theological geography is established in which Jerusalem is the center of Luke's narrative world. In the Gospel, God's providence leads to Jerusalem (2:38, 41–50; 4:9; 9:31, 51, 53; 13:32–35; 17:11; 18:31; 19:11; 23:5); in Luke-Acts, God's providence flows forth from Jerusalem (Luke 24:46–47; Acts 1:8).

The journey to Jerusalem is itself a theological metaphor for Luke. As Jesus travels on the way/road to Jerusalem in accordance with God's plan (9:57; 19:36), so he sends his disciples out to minister on the way (9:3; 10:4; 14:23), and indeed the Christian movement itself is called "the Way" (Acts 9:2; 18:25, 26; 19:9, 23; 22:4; 24:14, 22). Luke offers the bulk of Jesus' teaching along the way to Jerusalem so that readers travel into discipleship, learning what it means to follow Jesus and to participate in the reign of God.

Jesus' ministry in Jerusalem (19:29–21:38). In this section Luke presents Jesus as entering Jerusalem triumphantly, cleansing the temple, and teaching the crowds there daily during his last days. Here Luke follows Mark fairly closely in terms of structure and basic content, but some small changes in language indicate significant theological differences. For instance, Luke must deal with the paradox of having Jerusalem as the geographical center of his narrative world while in the world of Luke's audience, the city and the temple had been destroyed by the Roman army 10–25 years earlier (70 CE). He does this by having Jesus explicitly predict the destruction as judgment for rejecting his coming (see 19:41–44; cf. 13:34–35).

Jesus' passion (22:1–23:56). Across the previous sections, conflict has increased between the religious authorities and Jesus until the leaders' chance to get their hands on Jesus finally arises when Satan enters Judas (22:3; see 4:13, where Satan leaves Jesus after the temptation until "an opportune time"). This narrative signals that his death is at hand and opens the door for Jesus' concluding preparation of the disciples for their leadership role in the church after he is gone. In contrast to Mark's portrayal of them as abandoning Jesus (Mark 14:50), Luke presents the disciples as faltering (exemplified in Peter's denial) but ultimately remaining faithful and near to Jesus (Luke 22:28; 23:49).

Once Jesus is in the religiopolitical authorities' hands, Luke repeatedly asserts his innocence (22:66–23:25). This is part of Luke's deemphasizing the cross as the point at which Jesus' messiahship is defined. In other words, for Luke the crucifixion is not the locus of salvation (note Luke's omission of Mark 10:45). Sermons in Acts repeatedly contrast that humans killed Jesus but God raised him (Acts 2:23; 3:15; 4:10; 5:30; 7:52; 10:39–40; 13:28–30). In Luke, therefore, Jesus' death is not so much that of a salvific sacrifice as that of an innocent, prophetic martyr that was a *necessary* part of God's providential plan, as revealed in Scripture.

Jesus' resurrection (24:1–53). For Luke, the resurrection instead of the cross is the axis of God's salvific action in history, the event from which the Spirit-filled life of the church flows (thus having the risen Jesus appear to followers in Jerusalem instead of Galilee, as in Mark and Matthew). Instead of the women fleeing from the tomb and telling no one what they had seen and heard and thus leaving the story to end on a note of fear (Mark 16:8), Luke presents the women as faithfully witnessing to what had occurred (Luke 24:8–9), leading to a chain of events so that the story ends on a note of joy (24:52–53).

LUKE'S SALVATION OF REVERSAL

Having examined ways that Luke "plots" out salvation in his orderly narrative, it is important to see as well how he unpacks the concept of salvation thematically in the gospel. Preachers will do well to contextualize Lukan passages both in terms of the Gospel's overarching structure and dominant themes.

Paradigmatic for Luke's thematic approach to salvation is the scene of Jesus' sermon in Nazareth (4:16–30). Luke takes this story from Mark 6:1–6 but moves it from the middle of the Galilean ministry to its beginning and edits it thoroughly. Jesus begins by reading from Isaiah 61:1 and 58:6: "The Spirit of the Lord is upon me, because he has anointed me to bring good news to the poor. He has sent me to proclaim release to the captives and recovery of sight to the blind, to let the oppressed go free, to proclaim the year of the Lord's favor" (Luke 4:18–19). He then declares to those gathered at the synagogue that he is the fulfillment of "this scripture" so that the whole of Luke's narrative can be seen as unpacking this claim.

The use of the Isaiah quote shows that, for Luke, salvation is reversal of the status quo. The use of the eschatological prophecy from Isaiah points to an overturning of the situations of the suffering and oppressed (cf. the Magnificat, 1:46–55; the Beatitudes and Woes, 6:20–26; and the parable of Lazarus and the rich man, 16:19–31). Thus for Luke salvation is social, not simply spiritual. It is less something that happens to an individual and more the overturning of social structures that keep some downtrodden while others lead a life of privilege and advantage. Indeed, in Luke there is a recognition that the oppressed cannot be lifted up as long as the oppressors remain in power, and the poor cannot be lifted up without the rich being brought down.

When looking at almost any passage in Luke, preachers will do well to see if some form of reversal is at play. Some prominent examples follow:

— In many of Luke's parables, the situation of the poor (and the wealthy) is reversed (8:14; 10:29–37; 12:13–34; 14:15–24; 15:11–32; 16:1–13, 19–31; 18:9–14; 19:11–27).

— While perhaps not as much as we would like, Luke lifts women above the status they would have been given in the first-century, patriarchal, Mediterranean world (1:26–53; 8:1–3; 10:38–42; 23:49; 24:1–11).

— Recovered health and liberation from demon possession are representative of God's providential will for the salvation of all whose situations need to be reversed (see 7:50; 8:36, 48, 50; 17:19; 18:42; in the Greek of these texts, Jesus refers to individual healings as being "saved").

— Forgiveness of sins, for Luke, is a reversal of the nature of the lost being found (chap. 15; see also 5:17–26, 27–32; 7:36–50; 19:10; 24:45–49).

— Although Luke does not emphasize eschatology in the same way Mark or Matthew do (see, e.g., 17:20–21), proclamation of God's reign (4:43; 8:1; 9:1–2, 11, 59–60; 10:8–11; 16:16) is the ultimate symbol of reversal, liberating the age from being under the reign of Caesar.

PARTICIPATION IN GOD'S SALVATION

In the Gospel of Luke, participating in God's providential purposes and responding to God's gift of salvation is manifested in a number of ways. Some of these have already been implied above (giving of possessions to the poor, an ethic of orientation toward the marginalized, and being brought into the fullness of community). There are others, however, that merit further discussion.

Repentance is a major theme for Luke (1:16–17; 3:3, 8; 5:31–32; 11:27–32; 13:1–9; 15:7, 10; 16:27–31; 17:3–4; 24:45–48). One must be careful not to view this repentance simply as an attitudinal turning (though it does include this, as in 18:9–14). For Luke, repentance is evidenced in one's turning toward an ethical life of discipleship that is in accordance with God's salvation of reversal (6:43–49).

Discipleship at times seems synonymous with repentance in Luke (5:4–11, 27–28; 9:57–62). The fact that it involves more, though, is seen in the use of *following* as a primary metaphor for discipleship (5:11, 27–28; 9:23, 49, 57–62; 14:27; 18:22, 28, 42–43; 23:49, 55). Following entails leaving all behind to be with Jesus continually, being *sent out* by Jesus, and risking persecution to the point of death (9:1–6; 10:1–20; 22:35–38; 24:44–49).

Prayer, for Luke, is an important element of discipleship. Jesus repeatedly models a commitment to prayer (3:21; 5:16; 6:12; 9:18, 28–29; 11:1; 22:32, 41, 44–45) and teaches his disciples to pray (6:28; 11:1–4; 18:1–8, 9–14; 20:47; 21:36; 22:40, 46).

CONCLUSION

Luke, especially when read in conjunction with Acts (which together make up a quarter of the New Testament!), is a gift to preachers concerned with connecting individual piety and discipleship with communal faith and the mission of the church in the world. Leading a congregation through extended conversation with Luke (for instance, throughout Year C of the Revised Common Lectionary, which Luke anchors) will expand hearers' thoughts about the scope of history under God's care, challenge clichéd understandings of salvation, and invite passion for social justice concerns.

John

RONALD J. ALLEN

While the name John is associated with authorship of the Fourth Gospel, three letters, and Revelation, almost all scholars today think the authors are three different people. Moreover, the name John does not appear in the text of the Gospel or Letters of John, but the church has used this name since the middle of the second century (and for convenience we will call the author "John" throughout this essay). This simple observation about authorship has an important implication for preachers. To honor the integrity of each figure named John, the preacher should not use one John to interpret another.

The preacher preparing sermons on the Fourth Gospel should honor a similar principle when it comes to the relationship of the Gospel of John to the other Gospels. Each Gospel has its own special character. Consequently, scholarship today advises preachers not to use one Gospel to explain another, but to interpret a text within the Gospel in which it is found. This is especially true of the Gospel of John. For John is quite different from Mark, Matthew, and Luke in literary style, in the chronology of the story, in its picture of Jesus, and in its overall theological outlook. When developing a sermon on a text from the Gospel of John, a responsible preacher will approach the passage from its Johannine point of view.

Many scholars think that John wrote the Gospel about 95 CE, but are divided on the location where John wrote and the location of the community to whom John wrote, proposing such places as Ephesus,

Syria, Antioch, and Alexandria. Since John's theology has a family similarity to a type of Jewish theology (represented by a writer named Philo) centered in Alexandria (and markedly different from that of the Synoptic Gospels: Matthew, Mark, and Luke), the writer and address-ees might have been in that area. However, Alexandrian thinking was found in many Jewish communities in the Mediterranean basin. For-tunately, we do not need firm conclusions about these matters to inter-pret the main lines of the Gospel of John.

THE DISTINCTIVE WORLDVIEW OF JOHN

The first three Gospels are all oriented to end-time (apocalyptic) think-ing. That is, they presuppose the idea that the current era of history is a broken, evil age, which God will destroy and replace with a new one—the realm (kingdom) of God. In the first three Gospels, Jesus seeks to alert people to the changing of the ages, invites repentance from collusion with the old age, and offers the opportunity to follow him and to be part of the new age.

In contrast, the Gospel of John draws on a perspective that was com-monplace in Greek philosophy and more oriented to the relationship of two spheres of ongoing existence: heaven and the world. John uses the word "world" (*kosmos*) in a specific sense, which is different from "the earth" as commonly understood. When working with John, the preacher should use John's designation "world." A preacher might be tempted to import the early twenty-first-century rediscovery of nature, with its emphasis on ecology, to fill out the notion of "world" in John. But the preacher must leave behind rapturous notions of creation. When John thinks of "the world," the Gospel writer has in mind the specific, narrow, and intensively negative sense described below. For convenience, we speak of heaven and the world in spatial terms, as a two-story universe with heaven above and the world below, although John understands these two spheres of existence to intermingle. John is not very concerned with the end of one age and the beginning of another, but with how people in the world (below) can have access to the things of heaven (from above).

For John, heaven is the sphere where God dwells. It is a sphere of love, life, light, fullness, grace, sight, truth, freedom, spirit, commu-nity, and abundance. (Jesus existed in heaven before descending to the world.) By contrast, the world is a sphere of hate, emptiness, darkness, legalism, blindness, falsehood (lying), slavery, flesh, division, and scarcity. The devil plays a dominant role in the world. "The Jews" belong to the world. (On John's use of the phrase "the Jews," see below.) Prior to Jesus, according to John, people in the world did not have real knowledge of heaven and its possibilities for existence in the present or in the future. By contrast, as we note below, those who believe in Jesus are already on the way to eternal life.

Although the analogy is inexact, the preacher might portray the world as a windowless basement of existence. People, along with other elements of creation, are locked in the dark, dank, stale basement, which is hermetically sealed. People grope in the dark, unable to see redemptive possibilities for life. Many people today do not experience the world in the comprehensively negative way that John portrays. Yet, qualities that John associates with "the world" do intrude on existence at every level: individual, household, congregation, and larger communities. The preacher in looking over the congregation, or paying attention to the news, will likely notice many people who long for lives with more qualities of the Johannine heaven.

JOHN'S PICTURE OF JESUS

John is the primary source of one of the church's beloved ways of speaking about Jesus: Jesus is the Word (the *logos*) who became flesh (1:1, 14), who descended from heaven and, after the resurrection, ascended to heaven (3:13). Although John uses additional designations for Jesus (e.g., Lamb of God, Son of Man, Christ, Lord), John always has the Word in the background. Different scholars put forward several different interpretations of what John means by "the Word" ranging from the conviction that God and Jesus are one (in the sense of the doctrine of the Trinity) to the idea that Jesus is God's closest agent.

Regardless of differences in interpreting the relationship of God and Jesus as the Word, virtually all scholars agree on what Jesus does. According to John, God loves the world (3:16). Love for John is less an emotion and more a decision that leads to action. To love is to act in behalf of the good of the other and the community. God's act of love was to send the Word as Jesus into the world *to reveal the possibility of heaven for those who are in the world.* Indeed, if the preacher is searching for one word that best summarizes the work of Jesus as presented by John, it is "reveal."

Jesus descended into the dark existence of the world and turned on the light, so to speak. In the language of 14:6, Jesus showed the Way to God. Two qualifications are important here. One is that a person follows the Way by believing in Jesus. Indeed, for John, believing in Jesus is the only way to God. Second, when a person believes in Jesus, that person begins to experience qualities of eternal life (heaven) in the present, in the very midst of the world: love, life, light, fullness, grace, sight, truth, freedom, spirit, community, and abundance. To use another imprecise analogy, a person who believes in Jesus already lives in a bubble of heaven. Of course, the believer continues to struggle with the world (14:18–24), but amid the struggle, the believer also experiences many qualities of heaven.

THREE SIGNIFICANT THEOLOGICAL
PROBLEMS WHEN PREACHING ON JOHN

The Gospel of John presents the preacher with three significant problems. The first is John's condemnation of "the Jews," a phrase that occurs more than sixty times in the Gospel and refers not to the Jewish people as a whole but to the Jewish religious authorities of John's day. John's attitude is summarized in an incident when "the Jews" have misunderstood Jesus. Jesus responds to them, "You are from your father the devil, and you choose to do your father's desires. He was a murderer from the beginning and does not stand in the truth, because there is no truth in him" (8:44). The Johannine Jesus claims that the Jewish leaders are not only unfaithful to their own heritage (they are no longer children of Abraham and Sarah, and of God), but also that they collude with the devil.

Many scholars today agree that this picture is an unfair caricature that comes not from Jesus but from John's frustration with Jewish leaders in John's time. This negative attitude in the Gospel of John is by no means singularly responsible for the church's long history of anti-Judaism and its more virulent outgrowth, anti-Semitism, but the negativity toward "the Jews" in the Fourth Gospel is especially pernicious. The preacher needs to help the congregation repudiate John's caricature and relate to Jewish communities in ways that demonstrate God's love (per 3:16).

A second problem is John's sectarian spirit. Ironically, Christians sometimes view the Gospel of John as "the universal gospel" in the sense that John wrote not just for Jews or gentiles but for everyone. However, a close reading of the Gospel of John reveals that John directs this book to the disciples of Jesus (who represent John's own community) to help them survive both internal tension among themselves and external conflict with "the Jews" and with the world.

Indeed, while John asserts God's love for "the world," John directs most of Jesus' teachings, including those about love, toward the community itself. For example, Jesus says to the disciples, "I give you a new commandment, that you love *one another*. Just as I have loved you, you also should love *one another*. By this everyone will know that you are my disciples, if you have love for *one another*" (John 13:34–35, emphasis added).

The Gospel of John is not entirely ingrown, but it does contain much less emphasis on outreach and mission beyond the congregation than do the other Gospels. The preacher needs to help the congregation recognize the limits of John's sectarianism and to seek to move beyond it. Indeed, it logically extends the notion of loving other disciples (as in 13:34–35) to the notion of joining God in loving the world.

A third problematic issue is John's exclusive idea of those who will be saved. To be sure, John was not dealing with a question that vexes many contemporary Christians regarding whether everyone will be gathered into heaven (universal salvation) or whether only a few will follow Jesus there (limited or exclusive salvation). Remember that John's understanding of salvation is related to access to heaven in the world now. Still, 14:6 famously puts John in the body of resources in support of the exclusive camp. After Jesus tells the disciples that he goes to prepare a place for them, one of the disciples wants to know the way that Jesus is going. Jesus asserts flatly, "I am the way, and the truth, and the life. No one comes to the Father except through me," that is, by believing in Jesus.

Some ministers are content to adopt John's viewpoint and to preach that those who believe in Jesus receive God's love into eternity, but others, like "the Jews" discussed above, are simply condemned. Some ministers who do not want to accept the notion of limited salvation seek to find exegetical grounds for claiming that universal salvation is the "real" teaching of John. I have not found any of these exegetical attempts to be plausible. For preachers whose larger theology presumes that God unconditionally and actively loves all, a better route is to acknowledge John's limited perspective while criticizing that perspective as inappropriate to the preacher's deepest convictions. Indeed, at a level unintended by the Gospel writer, John 3:16 itself moves in that direction.

THREE, FOUR, OR FIVE STEPS FOR
ENGAGING THE GOSPEL OF JOHN

The preacher can use a simple three-, four-, or five-stage approach to every passage in the Gospel of John. Different stages will play different roles in accord with particular passages in John and the preacher's particular contemporary context.

1. The preacher can note how "the world" is present in the passage, explicitly or implicitly, in the circumstances Jesus encounters: evidences of such things as hate, emptiness, darkness, legalism, blindness, falsehood (lying), slavery, flesh, division, scarcity, and death.

2. The preacher can identify how Jesus, in the passage, reveals the way to the possibilities of life, beginning now and coming to fulfillment in heaven: love, life, light, fullness, grace, sight, truth, freedom, spirit, community, and abundance.

3. The preacher can explore the possibility of points of contact between the situation of "world" in the passage and the experience of "world" on the part of the congregation today, for example, hate, emptiness, darkness, legalism, blindness, falsehood (lying), slavery, flesh, division, scarcity, and death.

4. The preacher can articulate the good news of the sermon by showing how Jesus continues to reveal possibilities for qualities of heaven (e.g., love, life, light, fullness, grace, sight, truth, freedom, spirit, community, and abundance).

5. The preacher may need to help the congregation name and deal with significant theological problems raised by the text, such as the issues discussed in the previous section.

Acts of the Apostles

STEPHEN FARRIS

The brief preface to the Acts of the Apostles (1:1–2) identifies this book as the continuation of the Third Gospel, traditionally attributed to Luke. Given the similarities in style, literary artistry, and theological emphases of the two volumes, the claim has been widely accepted by contemporary scholars. The preface addresses one Theophilus, as does the preface to the Gospel of Luke (1:1–4). The name means "friend of God," and it is sometimes argued that this is an indirect way of naming any reader of the work. Any honest inquirer into the story of Jesus and the life of the church is a "friend of God." While this represents a homiletically useful attitude toward any contemporary listener, such a reading may miss the mark with respect to the circumstances of composition of Luke and Acts. In Luke 1:3, Theophilus is accorded the title "most excellent," not a likely term of address for most early Christians who, as Paul reminds us in 1 Corinthians 1:18–31, were for the most part not of high social status. The most widely accepted reading is that Theophilus is a Christian of high status, likely the patron who paid the costs of producing the two volumes. With respect to contemporary preaching, the most significant consequence of this identification is to remind us that the right use of money is an important theme in both books.

The early church identified the author of the two volumes as Luke, a companion of Paul on his missionary journeys (see Phlm. 24; Col. 4:14; 2 Tim. 4:11). Acts tells us to pay attention to the early church, and it would be an ironic failure of reading simply to dismiss its opinion about the authorship of the book. The attribution of the author of the two-volume work as "Luke," however, is not explicitly indicated anywhere in the book itself. As with the other Gospels, we have no signed manuscripts with an author's name. It may be, then, that the identification of the author as Luke is a deduction from the names of the companions who were present with Paul in the "we passages," those passages in Acts in which the author seems to indicate that he was present on the described journeys (16:10–17; 20:5–15; 21:1–18; 27:1–37; 28:1–16). The use of the first-person plural here may be a literary device drawn from travel narratives in the ancient world or may indicate that the author has access to early accounts of Paul's journeys. Either way, there is no evidence that Luke the companion of Paul wrote Luke or Acts, but "Luke" remains a convenient name for the author of the work. "Luke" makes no claim to be an apostle. Rather, he is part of the early church, the subject matter of the book as a whole.

Contemporary scholars often call the two volumes "Luke-Acts," as if it were one work that should be read together. Why then are the two volumes not treated as a single work and printed consecutively in our Bibles? While a comparison of Luke's two volumes is often instructive, the early church separated the two. This position in the canon suggests that Luke is to be read primarily among the other accounts of the ministry of Jesus. Acts, by contrast, represents the transition to the life of the early church and introduces the collection of letters to young churches and early Christians, which make up most of the rest of the New Testament. It may be useful to consider Acts primarily *a book of transitions*, between Gospels and Epistles, between the ministry of Jesus and the ministry of Jesus through the Holy Spirit in the church, between Peter and Paul, and between mission to Israel and mission to the Gentile world.

Luke and Acts together provide the scriptural raw material for most of the church year, with Ascension and Pentecost coming from the latter work. The yearly rhythm of the church's life is chiefly drawn from Luke-Acts, and readings from Acts are assigned in all three years of the Revised Common Lectionary during the season of Easter. This accords well with the content of Acts. It is indeed history, but it is salvation history, the history by which the post-resurrection church lives. In his style Luke does echo both the historians of the ancient world and the historical books of the First Testament. He also links his history with the wider world: "This was not done in a corner," says Paul to Agrippa (Acts 26:26). Where he does so, he often seems to be accurate.

"Wider world" may be a misleading phrase, however. Salvation history is not for Luke a smaller and less significant thing that fits into the history of the "wider world," where the doings of kings and governors are of final importance. Rather, salvation history is the story of the way God touches the life of the world through Jesus and the work of the Holy Spirit in the church. This is not to suggest that Luke aimed at the factual accuracy that is theoretically the goal of historians of our day. It is not easy, for example, fully to harmonize the accounts of Paul's conversion in Acts (chaps. 9, 22, 26) with the autobiographical material in Galatians 1:11–16. Moreover, it is likely that Luke followed the pattern of ancient historians by composing the major speeches of his characters himself, which are so striking a feature of Acts. He may have had a sense of what happened on such occasions and even some source accounts of the events, but the wording as a whole comes from the author and not from the original speech itself. This was the acknowledged practice of the classical historians who served as models for Acts. More important for preaching, this means that the speeches can be understood as closely integrated into the narrative and theological purposes of Acts and not only records of the words of other individuals.

The author of Acts, then, is a historian but also a storyteller and a theologian. Acts displays the storytelling skills already evidenced in the Gospel. Stories of midnight escapes, imprisonments, and shipwrecks are inherently dramatic, but they are also recounted with great literary skill. Accounts such as the story of the conversion of Paul or the imprisonment of Paul and Silas in Philippi match in intensity anything in the Gospel of Luke. One could imagine a successful graphic novel based on this kind of story. Preachers might emulate this attention to the drama of a good story.

Acts is structured in line with the words of the risen Christ, "But you will receive power when the Holy Spirit has come upon you; and you will be my witnesses in Jerusalem, in all Judea and Samaria, and to the ends of the earth" (1:8). The story begins with the coming of the Holy Spirit at Pentecost, and the Holy Spirit continues to be the chief character in the story. Indeed, it is sometimes said that the Acts of the Apostles ought to be retitled as the Acts of the Holy Spirit. In Acts the Holy Spirit is the one who breathes life into the church and enables its mission. The Spirit is also the one whose presence validates the acceptability of hitherto unacceptable persons, first Samaritans and, after the conversion of Cornelius, the Gentiles.

Acts is divided into two sections of different length. The first section (chaps. 1–12) describes the creation of the church and its witness "in Jerusalem, in all Judea and Samaria," and Peter is the central character in the mission to Israel. The longer second section of the work (chaps. 13–28) shifts its focus to the mission to Gentiles and to the person of Paul. It is sometimes suggested that the turn to the Gentiles is the result of a failure of the mission to Israel. This interpretation is a result of too simplistic a reading of passages such as 28:28, which appears at the climax of Acts, "Let it be known to you then that this salvation of God has been sent to the Gentiles; they will listen." (See the very similar sayings in 13:46; 18:6.) By contrast, the first section of Acts consistently represents a mission that meets with considerable acceptance, beginning with the day of Pentecost, when "those who welcomed his message were baptized, and that day about three thousand persons were added" (2:41). In the end James and the elders in Jerusalem can say to Paul, "You see, brother, how many thousands of believers there are among the Jews, and they are all zealous for the law" (21:20). "Success" would be too strong a word to apply to this mission. There is, after all, also a crowd of Jews in the temple in the following chapter, doubtless similarly zealous for the law, who call for Paul's blood. Rather, according to Acts, the Jews are divided by the proclamation of the gospel. Division over the gospel is, in fact, the immediate context of the saying in 28:28. Nevertheless, the young church stands in essential continuity with Israel, and the renewed Israel within the church forms the foundation on which the Gentile mission is built.

The transition to the second section of Acts is anticipated in a series of stories about including in the church's life persons and groups who at first sight seem alien. The series begins with the account of the "first church fight" (6:1–6). Here the apostles make innovations in the formal structures of the church, naming the first deacons and more fully including Greek-speaking Jewish Christians in the life of the church. After a persecution arising from the preaching of Stephen, one of those deacons, a persecution arises, and the church is scattered. This leads to the conversion of the despised Samaritans, with whom the reader is already familiar from the Gospel of Luke. Next is the conversion of a sorcerer, Simon, and of the Ethiopian eunuch (Acts 8). Sorcerers trafficked with evil, and eunuchs were forbidden full membership in the people of God. But through the work of the Holy Spirit, even people who belong to these despised categories could become part of the church. It may be that the contemporary church is going through similar struggles and changes. The preacher who attends to these stories may be able to address these changes fruitfully and faithfully.

The series culminates in two key conversion stories, the account of the conversion of Saul/Paul (chaps. 9, 22, 26) and of Cornelius (chaps. 10–11). Both are unlikely converts, one because he is a persecutor of the faith and the other because, as a Roman centurion, he is a quintessential Gentile. Neither is welcomed easily into the fellowship of the church. As a consequence of these conversions, however, the strict Jew becomes the apostle to the Gentiles, whose mission becomes the focus of the second part of Acts. These stories are of such paramount importance that they are recounted more than once, the conversion of Paul three times! If readers fail to grasp the significance of these stories the first time, perhaps they will do so when they are repeated. Some Christian traditions will find stories of individual conversion congenial, while they may seem more foreign in other traditions. That stories of conversion play so central a role in Acts invites the preacher of any tradition to consider the nature of conversion in the contemporary church.

These are not, however, simply stories of the conversions of individuals or even of groups. They are stories about the conversion of the church. The conversion of an institution is always more difficult than the conversion of individuals, as can be seen in even the most cursory study of the history of the church, of which Acts is but the first volume. But Acts describes a process of conversion, under the influence of the Holy Spirit, that leads the church to accept those who were formerly unacceptable. This kind of conversion may also be addressed by preachers who attend to these stories.

The second section of Acts—following the dissolution of the ministry of the Twelve in Jerusalem, due to Herod's persecution in chapter 12—then focuses on Paul and his mission journeys. The value of the picture of Paul in Acts is sometimes underestimated by those who compare it unfavorably with Paul's own self-portrait in his letters. But a representation of what the wider church thinks about a person may be no less valuable than what a person thinks about himself. The representation of Paul in Acts has an inherent value regardless of any contrasts with the Epistles. In any case, this second section dramatically describes the transition to a largely Gentile church. This part of the story is structured around a series of journeys. Luke uses the same narrative technique in the Gospel, shaping the middle part of his story of Jesus into a journey from Galilee to Jerusalem. He then frames his story of the growth of the early church as a series of journeys from Jerusalem to the ends of the earth (1:8). Acts ends with the witness to the good news, if not at the geographical ends of the earth, at the other end of the earth politically and socially, the environs of imperial Rome itself (28:14–31).

The major human character in Acts may be neither Peter nor Paul, however, but rather the church itself. In our contemporary society, in which some within the church have a dangerously individualistic faith and many outside the church claim an equally individualistic and "spiritual but not religious" lack of faith, the claim of Acts that God works to establish a church and continues to work through that *community* of faith may be hard to hear. The claim may be rendered even harder to hear by the reality that the contemporary church is obviously flawed in so many ways. But then Acts paints a picture of a greatly flawed early church as well. Many of those flaws are startlingly familiar to any close observer of the church in our days. If the flaws are parallel, perhaps, in the mercy of God, the work of God may also be parallel. In any case, if something is hard to hear, that does not make it any less necessary to proclaim.

Romans

WILLIAM F. BROSEND II

The Letter to the Romans has long been set apart from the rest of the writings of the apostle Paul, treated as the final distillation and summation of his theology, surrounded by adjectives lauding the monumental, magisterial, and definitive quality of the epistle. The letter's impact on Christian theology is indeed unmatched, and it has more than once played an important role in seismic shifts in Christian history. Recent scholarship, however, has concluded that Romans is just as much an "occasional letter" of Paul as any other. On this reading the key to interpreting the letter is understanding what occasion prompted Paul to write to the church in Rome. The problem with Romans is that some of the questions are well below the surface.

This essay argues that preachers do best to read Romans as summative *and* occasional, because the issues addressed in the letter are ones the apostle has been wrestling with since his "revelation of Jesus Christ" (Gal. 1:12). The primary issue is the division within the community: whether social, economic, and religious; or between rich and poor, Jew and non-Jew. In Year A the Revised Common Lectionary offers the preacher fourteen consecutive Sundays in which to explore those divisions and Paul's response to them in Romans.

The basics of Romans are easy. It was dictated by the apostle Paul to

Tertius and most likely delivered by Phoebe, who supported its writing in Corinth, before Paul's final journey to Jerusalem. This dates the letter to 57 CE.

Drawing on a recognition of Paul's use of classic rhetorical approaches to argumentation, the letter is best outlined as follows:

1:1–17	Introduction
1:18–4:25	First proof, on God's surpassing righteousness
5:1–8:39	Second proof, on faith in Christ
9:1–11:36	Third proof, on the enduring salvation of the Jews
12:1–15:13	Fourth proof, on the shape of life in Christ
15:14–16:27	Conclusion

An approach to understanding and proclaiming each of the sections follows.

INTRODUCTION (1:1–17)

There is nothing exceptional about the first part of the introduction: a standard epistolary exordium identifying author and audience (vv. 1–6), followed by a blessing (v. 7) and thanksgiving (vv. 8–12). It is the *narratio*, Paul's statement of his long-frustrated desire to come to Rome (vv. 13–15), and especially the *propositio*, the thesis of the letter (vv. 16–17), that calls for special attention:

> For I am not ashamed of the gospel; it is the power of God for salvation to everyone who has faith, to the Jew first and also to the Greek. For in it the righteousness of God is revealed through faith for faith; as it is written, "The one who is righteous will live by faith."

This letter, Paul tells us, is about faith and righteousness, period. The righteousness of God and faith in, and the faith of, Jesus. The thesis is borrowed from Habakkuk 2:4, a verse with decidedly eschatological overtones as the prophet speaks from his watchtower of "a vision for the appointed time; it speaks of the end, and does not lie" (Hab. 2:2–3). It is a thesis that preachers should keep in mind as they work through any of the various sections of the letter.

FIRST PROOF, ON GOD'S SURPASSING
RIGHTEOUSNESS (1:18–4:25)

More so than the other sections of the proposed outline, 1:18–4:25 is a rhetorical unit that must be studied, taught, and proclaimed as a whole, even when preaching on a smaller pericope within the section. That said, we notice that the Revised Common Lectionary assigns only two short passages from this section and nothing from the pivotal and controversial 1:18–3:20.

Paul makes a sophisticated argument about human sin and divine righteousness that climaxes in his own paraphrase of Ecclesiastes 7:20, which reads, "Surely there is no one on earth so righteous as to do good without ever sinning." With his typical flair Paul writes, "None is righteous, no, not one" (3:10 RSV).

While neglected by the lectionary, this argument is central to the letter. It begins with Paul's reading of human nature and behavior (1:18–2:11), turns to the impact knowledge of the law has for awareness of sinfulness (2:12–3:8), and introduces questions about circumcision (2:25–29) and the "advantage [of] the Jew" (3:1–4). The latter portion of chapter 3 reaffirms that the righteousness of God proclaimed in the *propositio* (1:16–17) is righteousness to save, not just condemn.

Preachers need to be aware of a number of interpretive issues here, as it is important to make a right beginning when reading Romans. First, our chapter and verse divisions obliterate the point Paul made in arguing that those who condemn the behavior of 1:24–32 are themselves equally guilty: "You have no excuse, whoever you are, when you judge others; for in passing judgment on another you condemn yourself" (2:1). The rhetorical unit is clearly 1:18–2:11.

Second, this section introduces a rhetorical device favored by Paul, the unnamed "interlocutor" in whose mouth Paul places the opinions he wishes to refute, a practice that has at times confused interpreters into thinking such opinions were those of the apostle himself (e.g., 3:3–8).

Finally, we learn some important things about Paul's use of Scripture in chapter 4. Simply put, Paul idealizes, revises, and combines Hebrew Bible texts and traditions for the sake of his argument. Abraham falls on his face and laughs at the idea of Sarah giving birth in Genesis 17:17; for Paul, Abraham "did not weaken in faith when he considered his own body, which was already as good as dead" (4:19). It is not a matter of not letting the facts get in the way of a good argument. Rather, it suggests that Paul's encounter with the Septuagint (like that of other Jewish interpreters of his day) was lively, largely oral, and therefore fluid.

SECOND PROOF, ON FAITH IN CHRIST (5:1–8:39)

The first proof argues that the whole of humanity, Jew and Greek, is in need of salvation. The second proof argues that God has offered this salvation in Jesus Christ and that through participation "in Christ" one is saved (i.e., justified, made righteous). One of the limits of English, often pointed out by New Testament scholars, is the lack of a word to accurately translate the cluster of Greek words from the root *dikaios*. The word means "righteous," but English lacks a verbal form, "to righteous," so we translate the related Greek verb *dikaioō* as "to justify." The problem is the differing semantic fields conjured by the English words: "righteous" signifies something religious and moral; "justify" signifies something juridical. As one reads Romans 5–6, it is important to keep in mind that the Greek text means we are "made righteous by faith," not "justified by faith." To be "righteoused" is to be made acceptable to and unified with God, not be declared innocent of wrongdoing and freed from punishment by a judge. Its force is positive, not the avoidance of a negative: it is saved *for* rather than saved *from*.

The section begins with the claim that "we" are "righteoused" by faith, have peace with God, and thus by grace have the hope of a share in God's glory. Because of this "we" boast in our suffering and go on to climb Paul's rhetorical ladder to endurance, character, and a hope that does not disappoint (5:3–5). Paul is making a powerful statement of the benefits of being "righteoused" by faith in response to the need for salvation expressed in the first proof. In the rest of this chapter and the next, he will explain how this "righteousing" takes place. Before exploring that explanation, we have an obvious question to answer: who is the "we" of which Paul speaks?

Paul invites himself, if you will, into the communities of his audience through use of the first-person plural. In doing so, he hopes to bridge the Jewish, non-Jewish divide in that audience because one of the most important questions occasioning the letter is the relationship in the church that consists of Jewish and non-Jewish believers in Jesus, and relations between believers and nonbelievers.

Chapter 5 explains the mechanics of "righteousing" in a syllogism about the first man, Adam, and the new man, Jesus. As Adam's sin brought death to all, now Jesus' death and life brings life to all who believe. Chapter 6 explains how "we" participate in this "righteousing" through our baptism, in which we experience our own death and res-urrection. And because we are now dead to sin and alive to God, we must no longer act as slaves to sin, but "present your members as slaves to righteousness for sanctification" (6:19).

In chapter 7 Paul more fully addresses the concern that will absorb his attention through chapter 11: how will Jews share in this salvation? It is a complex and frustrating argument, with the conclusion clearer than the reasoning. First, preachers should remember that recent schol-arship has concluded that Paul was a Torah-observant Jew throughout his life, including his life after the revelation in Damascus. Paul argues, however, that non-Jews need not become Jews in order to be saved, and he maintains that the law is not binding on non-Jews. In fact, the law can be detrimental for non-Jews. Nevertheless, the law is holy and good (7:12). Salvation is, for Jew and non-Jew, to be found in and through Jesus, the Messiah. The famous struggle in 7:14–25 is summarized in 7:19, "For I do not do the good I want, but the evil I do not want is what I do." Here Paul's argument is abstract, not autobiographical. He is speaking not about himself, but about the whole of humanity, both Jew and non-Jew. Thus "I" should be understood in the third person as "one." "One does not do the good one wants, but the evil that one hates is what one does."

The turn here is strong, and it is in chapter 8 that the language becomes intimate, if not autobiographical. Paul concludes his second proof with analogies of participation, specifically the kind of participa-tion found only in families: the believer becoming much more than a member of the household, but, like Jesus, a child and heir. All of this is mediated by the work of the Spirit, who helps in times of weakness and intercedes for the saints, all according to God's eternal plan. The proof concludes with Paul likely appropriating an early confessional hymn, climaxing in the claim that nothing "will be able to separate us from the love of God in Christ Jesus our Lord" (8:39).

THIRD PROOF, ON THE ENDURING
SALVATION OF THE JEWS (9:1–11:36)

Paul returns to Abraham to explain what he as a Jew knows must be true, that salvation is "to the Jew first and also to the Greek" (Rom. 1:16). The third proof is filled with quotations from the Septuagint, more so than any other passage in Paul's Epistles. Paul, however, is not addressing only Jewish believers in this section of the letter. In 11:13 he specifically names that he is "speaking to you Gentiles" (*tois ethnesin*). He is explaining to all how the heirs of the covenant of Israel are also heirs of the promise made in Christ. It is a passionate, often eloquent explanation of a surface impossibility, and Paul wisely (shrewdly?) uses a vast array of verses from the Septuagint to make the case.

The outline of the argument in the third proof is clear. Paul shifts his language from Jew to Israelite to better ground his reasoning in the history of Israel, demonstrating that the righteousness of God is shared with the world through the people of the covenant. "My heart's desire and prayer to God for them is that they may be saved" (10:1).

A second shift in language is in the use of third-person plural pronouns, that *they* might be saved, but note that this apparent distancing is not Paul contrasting himself with Jews, but with those who do not share his belief in Jesus. And we must acknowledge a truth of Paul's style of argumentation that preachers still use today: when all else fails, break into song. "O the depth of the riches and wisdom and knowledge of God!" (11:33).

FOURTH PROOF, ON THE SHAPE
OF LIFE IN CHRIST (12:1–15:13)

Paul generally ends his letters with instruction. Like any good preacher, Paul knows that his audience needs guidance in applying the wisdom of the letter to daily practice. Paul writes of how believers should live in community, in an empire of great power and a deep distrust of religious communities. Some of the instruction is an extension of Torah, much of it sounds as if it came from Jesus, and most of it would not be out of place in a Greek philosophical document. It is conventional wisdom, not alternative, and definitely not subversive wisdom.

With ageless resonance, 14:1–15:13 deals with a topic specific to the emerging communities of believers in Rome and other large urban areas, instructions for a particular time and place. In a city of more than a million people, filled with Roman shrines, temples, and statues and ruled by those suspicious of the new, it was a challenge to live faithfully as a follower of Jesus. There was as yet no guide to discipleship, though examples were soon to appear in the form of the Didache and deutero-pauline letters. One problem stood out for Paul, in Rome as elsewhere: what can one eat, with whom, and when? Eating may also have been a metaphor for other issues or practices, and if so, Paul's instructions would remain valued: "Let us then pursue what makes for peace and for mutual upbuilding. Do not, for the sake of food, destroy the work of God" (14:19–20).

CONCLUSION (15:14–16:27)

The first verses of the conclusion remind the Romans that Paul is raising money, for the saints in Jerusalem and for his hoped-for journey to Spain. He also asks for prayers and concludes chapter 15 with what reads like a benediction, "May the God of peace be with all of you. Amen."

Manuscript traditions differ here, and many scholars argue that chapter 16 is a later addition to the text, whether by Paul or one of his disciples, in part because we have nothing remotely like this in the other undisputed letters. Paul asks for greetings to be shared with twenty-six people and the "church [ekklēsia] in their house" (16:5). Did he know them all? Unlikely. Rather he hoped to get to know them, making the greetings aspirational.

The preacher must guard against so compartmentalizing the letter that Romans becomes only the fodder for current debates, while missing the great argument the letter itself makes: the good news of Messiah Jesus is "the power of God for salvation to everyone who has faith, to the Jew first and also to the Greek." Lectionary preachers are confronted with the "summer of Romans" every three years. At least once in one's preaching career, preach it, all sixteen Sundays. You might launch a reformation.

1 Corinthians

MICHAEL P. KNOWLES

Against a tendency today to idealize the church of the first century and to conceive of congregational ministry in terms of returning the church to its pristine form, Paul's letters to the believers in ancient Corinth offer a sobering corrective, painting a picture of social, doctrinal, and ethical turmoil that the apostle must correct against the standard of Christ. The situation that Paul describes has an important impact on the manner in which we may preach from these letters. One approach is to distill from them timeless principles of doctrine or ethics so as to explain or insist on their relevance for the present day. Another is to preach the collective "life story" of the congregants to whom Paul writes, inviting our own hearers to enter into a similar theological narrative that redefines their existence. Yet a third approach—one that encompasses elements of doctrine, ethics, and identity alike—is to join the apostle in bearing witness to Christ and the ongoing vitality of his ministry in the life of the church. On this view, to preach from 1 and 2 Corinthians is less a matter of abstracting their contents or entering imaginatively into their world (neither of which is inherently transformative), and more a question of receiving their testimony to the ways of God in Christ, from whom transformation proceeds.

Refounded and completely rebuilt as a Roman colony under Julius Caesar, Corinth occupied a strategic military and economic position as a port city and gateway to the Isthmian peninsula. According to Luke, Paul established the church there in the course of an eighteen-month stay (Acts 18:1–11), likely around the years 50–51 CE. Following his departure, Paul learns that the congregation has fallen into disarray, split by allegiances to different preachers (1 Cor. 1:10–17) and by a wide range of moral, social, and theological disagreements. In an attempt to remedy the situation, Paul writes the Corinthians as many as four times (for Paul's references to multiple letters, see 1 Cor. 4:17; 5:9; 2 Cor. 2:3–4; 7:8). The first letter is lost to us, and 2 Corinthians is likely Paul's fourth letter, but it contains fragments of other letters. First Corinthians is the second of Paul's letters to the church in Corinth, likely written from Ephesus (1 Cor. 16:8). Its structure is relatively straightforward: the apostle deals first with three issues (factionalism, sexual immorality, and a lawsuit between members) reported to him by those who have brought correspondence back from Corinth, and thereafter with questions contained in the letter itself.

Ancient letters typically began with a thanksgiving section, and this one is no exception (1:4–9), but Paul is likely impelled as much by theology as by literary convention: before he moves to exhortation or discipline, he must first recall the foundation on which his pastoral relationship with the congregation is based. Because their conduct falls short, he emphasizes that divine fidelity and the call of Christ, not their response to that call, is what sustains them. Preaching from this letter can do no better than to begin where Paul begins, by seeking to discern the work of Christ in the congregation as the anchor for whatever instruction, discipline, or encouragement may need to follow.

FOOLISHNESS AND WISDOM, WEAKNESS AND POWER (1:18–2:16)

Reflection on his own ministry at Corinth leads Paul to reiterate the nature of his calling, which is "to proclaim the gospel" (*euangelizesthai*, 1:17), despite the apparent foolishness and futility of the cross (1:18–25). This Greek term describes the proclamation of divine victory, indicating the hand of God in human affairs. As such, it allows for the careful parsing of human and divine responsibilities, drawing a sharp contrast between homiletical eloquence and human wisdom, on the one hand, and the power of the cross, on the other. Whether in Corinth or today, speakers are susceptible to the lure of technique, relishing affirmation in the form of public prestige; for their part, audiences both ancient and modern prove vulnerable to promises of spiritual or material prosperity. By contrast, Paul's description of the message of the cross is paradoxically distasteful, to all appearances nothing more than a humiliating social, physical, and intellectual failure both for its original victim and for those who are shaped by its terms. To preach and live by such a message, then, runs counter to our natural desire for self-reliance, recognition, and reward, forcing us to turn instead to God (1:26–31). Just so, Paul describes his original preaching in Corinth as characterized by "weakness, . . . fear and . . . much trembling," in marked contrast to the "power of God" that made such preaching paradoxically effective and led to the founding of the congregation (2:3–5). As he declares in a famously compact summary of the matter: "We impart this in words not taught by human wisdom but taught by the Spirit, interpreting spiritual truths to those who possess the Spirit" (2:13 RSV).

DISARRAY IN THE CHURCH (CHAPS. 3–6)

Next Paul responds to the problem of congregational factionalism. He repeats his earlier contrast between human effort and divine agency so as to relativize the contribution of any one pastor or preacher: "So neither the one who plants nor the one who waters is anything, but only God who gives the growth" (3:7). More pointedly, he refers all human judgments to the judgment day of God, thereby encouraging us to view all ministry in light of an ultimate, eschatological horizon and the accountability that this implies (3:13–15; 4:4–5). Still, Paul is conscious that the spiritual immaturity of his congregants requires delicate handling: he reminds them of his founding role, yet he does not want to be overbearing in response to the enthusiasm that has led them to prefer other leaders and leadership models. And since news has now reached him of serious ethical breaches within the congregation, he must respond with pastoral sensitivity as well as theological firmness.

One such issue is a matter of inappropriate sexual conduct, whereby a member of the congregation is cohabiting with his mother-in-law (5:1). Here Paul is concerned with the reputation of the fledgling community in the eyes of society (cf. 10:32): even in Corinth, with its well-deserved reputation for sexual liberty, such conduct would have seemed abhorrent. He is equally concerned that no one else in the church has thought to intervene: on the contrary, the congregants seem to consider themselves above correction. For Paul, the obligation of holiness as an essential feature of Christian identity requires expulsion of the offending member (5:2, 5, 13). While marital and sexual mores may differ between cultures, and Western models of congregational leadership are unlikely to accommodate the radical disfellowshipping that Paul commends, his response challenges preachers to consider the profound implications of being "in Christ." Not least, his invocation of Passover imagery (5:7–8) implies a break with non-Christian forms of identity and conduct (so 6:9–11) in ways that may prove newly relevant for preaching in today's post-Christian era. On this model, Christian preaching calls its hearers into conformity with Christ himself.

A similar critique applies to the question of congregants taking one another to court (6:1–8) and patronizing local prostitutes (6:15–18). On both fronts, Paul responds by insisting that however highly they may think of themselves (4:8; 5:2!), they have failed to grasp the greatness of Christ in them. Here, too, an eschatological logic applies: they have no need for lawcourts since on the last day they themselves will have a role in judging creation (6:2–3). As to sexual immorality, such is their union with Christ that it excludes union with any in whom the Spirit of God is not also alive (6:19). Not least, Paul insists on the practical implications of calling Christ "Lord": "Do you not know that . . . you are not your own? For you were bought with a price; therefore glorify God in your body" (6:19–20). To preach in such a manner is not simply to insist on obedience, maintaining one's reputation or purity, or even pursuing principles of justice and equity. Rather, this is christological reasoning, as preachers call their congregants to live out the reality of Christ's transforming presence at work within them.

"CONCERNING THE MATTERS ABOUT WHICH YOU WROTE" (CHAPS. 7–14)

Recognizing the distance of their own social contexts from that of ancient Corinth, preachers may initially struggle to make homiletical sense of the next several chapters, in which Paul responds to specific questions concerning marriage, family life, slavery, circumcision, and idolatry. Yet the apostle is guided by two basic principles to which preachers should attend. The first is pastoral pragmatism: "It is to peace that God has called you," he insists (7:15). "Let each of you remain in the condition in which you were called" (7:20). "I want you to be free from anxieties" (7:32). The second principle, by contrast, again concerns theological vision. Whatever the circumstances of one's life, Christians are ruled by the gifts (7:7) and call (7:17) of God. Whereas the difficulty of applying his directives today in anything more than a general sense might encourage a reductionist sort of pragmatism (Paul does, after all, advocate the promotion of "good order"), his primary responsibility, he says, is to secure their "unhindered devotion to the Lord" (7:35).

Similarly the lengthy and difficult discussion concerning consumption of food consecrated to idols poses questions of cosmology and praxis with which contemporary preachers may be unfamiliar (chap. 8). Here Paul's concern is again both pastoral and theological: he warns the community that whatever their actions, they must avoid causing injury to the faith or fidelity of other members (8:11–13). This is notwithstanding the sovereignty of God the Father and of the "one Lord, Jesus Christ," whom they acknowledge as the sole true source of their existence (8:6). Thus Paul would have us preach with theological clarity, but not at the expense of charity, and with practical wisdom that is nonetheless constrained by absolute fidelity to Christ.

Next Paul turns briefly to consider the nature of congregational leadership, evidently defending himself against those who have questioned his right to remuneration (chap. 9). He speaks of preaching the gospel (using the same term as before, *euangelizesthai*) not as a career choice or path to social prominence, but as an obligation, divine commission, and constraint (9:16–17). Implicit in his self-description is a servant Christology and a form of ministry that seeks to model its conduct on that of Christ himself. Hence he writes, "I have made myself a slave to all. . . . I have become all things to all people, that I might by all means save some" (9:19, 22). Such ministry requires careful focus and discipline: while he may benefit from the gospel that he preaches, sharing in its "blessings" (9:23), he is not above its demands. Paul is no less responsible for obedience than those to whom he ministers (9:27). Here he instructs us less in *what* to preach than in *how* to preach, namely, as those who are constrained to live by the words that we speak.

Returning to his earlier subject (food offered to idols), Paul summarizes his instructions in a twofold principle that transcends the circumstances of the moment: "Whether you eat or drink, or whatever you do, do everything for the glory of God. Give no offense to Jews or to Greeks or to the church of God" (10:31–32). Focusing on this twofold mandate of doxology and beneficence will help preachers to interpret the otherwise difficult passages that follow, on the veiling of women (11:2–16) and appropriate conduct at the Lord's Supper (11:17–34).

With respect to spiritual gifts (chaps. 12–14), preachers will likely be guided by the constraints of their confessional context. Yet here, Paul employs a principle similar to those named above: "To each is given the manifestation of the Spirit for the common good" (12:7). This is not to reduce the historical and theological specificity of Paul's response to a universal truism (as happens frequently with his discussion of love in chap. 13). On the contrary, the constraint of a canonical text requires us to acknowledge its testimony to the ongoing work of God in reconciling, unifying, and empowering the community of faith as the expression of divine intent for all humanity. Where spiritual gifts can be a source of pride and division (then as now), Paul is concerned to emphasize mutuality and the edification of believers (12:12–14, 25–26; 13:4–7; 14:4, 12, 26, etc.), even as they direct us to their giver and source, whom believers will one day see "face to face" (13:12). Preaching on spiritual gifts, then, must be unabashedly theocentric, just as Paul is concerned to remind his congregants that these are, precisely, gifts *of God*. Such recognition, Paul predicts, will come from visitors who witness their manifestation among members of the congregation: they will "bow down before God and worship him, declaring, 'God is really among you'" (14:25). Again, to expound these chapters today invites preachers to discern and explain the operations of the Spirit of God at work within their own congregations.

RESURRECTION (CHAP. 15)

Returning to the content of his own preaching, Paul now reiterates the importance of the resurrection and its implications for the life of the church (15:1–58). In addition to responding to specific misunderstandings (e.g., 15:34), he notes that God's action in raising Jesus from death provides the fundamental basis for Christian identity, assuring us that God bends the trajectory of our common existence toward life and grace. Accordingly, Jesus' resurrection is axiomatic for Christian proclamation: "If Christ has not been raised, then our proclamation has been in vain [Gk., *kenon*, "useless"] and your faith has been in vain" (15:14). Not just the veracity of the apostle's own preaching (or Christian preaching in general) is at stake (15:15), but the more foundational conviction that God gives life to a moribund creation, which is why Paul characterizes resurrection, that of Christ and of Christians alike, as God's definitive victory over death as the "last enemy" (15:26, 54–57). In the context of Hellenistic body-spirit dualism, Christian death is not therefore a release from material existence but, on the precedent of Jesus' physical resurrection, its affirmation. Resurrection preaching will therefore affirm the goodness of material creation as that which God both ordains and makes new.

CONCLUSION (CHAP. 16)

The letter concludes by addressing situational concerns: a financial collection for the poor of Jerusalem (16:1–2), Paul's own travel plans (16:3–9), those of other Christian workers (16:10–12, 17–18), and personal greetings (16:13–16, 19–24).

To summarize, 1 Corinthians models theologically articulate testimony to Christ amid pastoral turmoil and conflict, in the vivid assurance of God's sustaining work even when the preacher is, like Paul, under siege.

2 Corinthians

MICHAEL P. KNOWLES

Unlike most Pauline letters, 2 Corinthians focuses less on Christian doctrine or lifestyle than on the qualifications required of a preacher or congregational leader. The reason for this is that the relationship between Paul and the church that he founded (cf. Acts 18:1–11) appears to be at the breaking point.

Refounded and completely rebuilt as a Roman colony under Julius Caesar, Corinth occupied a strategic military and economic position as a port city and gateway to the Isthmian peninsula. According to Luke, Paul established the church there in the course of an eighteen-month stay (Acts 18:1–11), likely around the years 50–51 CE. Following his departure, Paul learns that the congregation has fallen into disarray, split by allegiances to different preachers (1 Cor. 1:10–17) and by a wide range of moral, social, and theological disagreements. In an attempt to remedy the situation, Paul writes the Corinthians as many as four times (for Paul's references to multiple letters, see 1 Cor. 4:17; 5:9; 2 Cor. 2:3–4; 7:8). The first letter is lost to us, and 1 Corinthians is likely Paul's second letter.

In what may be his fourth letter to the congregation, Paul responds (likely around 54–55 CE) to complaints about his leadership, some of them occasioned by a recent visit that has not gone well. He finds himself accused of being "carnal" or "worldly" (10:2–3), of being an unpolished speaker and of unimpressive appearance (10:10), of causing needless pain and upset (1:23–2:9), of acting dishonorably (11:7–11), perhaps even of having misled them with regard to his travel plans (1:17; 12:16). There has evidently been a call for new leaders and a different style of leadership (11:12–13; 12:11).

Complicating matters further is the fact that in its present form, 2 Corinthians seems to contain fragments of earlier letters (e.g., 6:14–7:1, as well as chaps. 10–13 that could represent some or all of the "severe" letter that he mentions in 2:3, 9; 7:8). As a result, establishing the literary structure of our "2 Corinthians" and reconstructing the sequence of events to which the present document refers both prove extraordinarily difficult. Nonetheless, certain themes appear consistently throughout, in particular that of discipleship and leadership, shaped by the cross of Christ. Where congregants seek divine affirmation and blessing, together with leaders who can champion their cause in the public arena, Paul proclaims a Savior who was shamefully rejected and "crucified in weakness" (13:4). In a society for which religious affiliation serves as a means of social advancement, Paul insists on humility, self-abasement, and a form of spiritual transformation that remains largely invisible to outsiders (4:16–18). In short, he presents a vision of discipleship and ministry that is diametrically opposed to the self-promotion and prosperity theology of ancient Corinth.

SUFFERING AND SUFFICIENCY

Second Corinthians opens with a frank discussion of suffering and consolation, as Paul describes his identification with the sufferings of Christ: "For just as the sufferings of Christ are abundant for us, so also our consolation is abundant through Christ" (1:5). In this regard, Paul's theology is of a piece with his life experience. He has been forced into absolute reliance on God as the basis not only for discipleship or ministry to the church, but also for survival itself: "We were so utterly, unbearably crushed that we despaired of life itself. Indeed, we felt that we had received the sentence of death so that we would rely not on ourselves but on God who raises the dead" (1:8–9). This contrast between profound human inadequacy and the assurance of divine favor is the leitmotif that runs through every part of the canonical letter, whatever the complexities of its compositional history. It also governs Paul's focus as he deals with conflict, for as he explains his change of travel plans (1:15–16, 23) and assures church members of his love for them even when they cause each other pain (2:1–11), the apostle directs attention away from himself and toward Christ, through whom God establishes the church (1:21–22).

COMPETENCE FOR MINISTRY

In similar terms, Paul addresses the question of ministerial qualifications. Contrary to custom both ancient and modern, which codifies authority in the form of written documents, Paul is willing to be judged simply by the results of his preaching, above all the fact that his detractors were themselves converted under his ministry (3:1–3). Even so, he admits that none of the normal qualifications—whether his Jewish heritage and learning, his extensive record of suffering and sacrifice (11:22–28), or even his service to the church—make him equal to the task of proclaiming a counterintuitive gospel. On the contrary, he writes, "Our competence is from God, who has made us competent to be ministers of a new covenant, not of letter but of spirit; for the letter kills, but the Spirit gives life" (3:5–6).

To preach Christ, says the apostle, entails both the stench of death and the fragrant aroma of new life (2:15–16). Such is the human impossibility of this task that it obviates normal means of persuasion: by way of technique, all that remains is the "open statement of the truth" (4:2), not accommodating the gospel to the expectations of one's audience, but speaking "in Christ . . . as persons of sincerity, as persons sent from God and standing in his presence" (2:17). Although this sense of divine authorization allows for confidence (3:4), even boldness (3:12), Paul continues to assert his own weakness and inadequacy (cf. 12:5, 9). "For," he insists, "what we preach is *not ourselves*, but Jesus Christ as Lord, with ourselves as your servants [slaves] for Jesus' sake" (4:5 RSV note). In this way, Paul highlights the importance of spiritual identity and authenticity for preaching, and of relying on the "mercy" of God for ministerial or homiletical efficacy (4:1).

Notwithstanding his own unimpressive bearing, on the one hand, and the congregation's spiritual immaturity, on the other, the apostle nonetheless insists that Christian ministry results in the transformation of believers via the agency of God's Spirit, "from one degree of glory to another" (3:18). And despite the low esteem in which the congregants hold him, he says, preachers in particular are "ambassadors for Christ, since God is making his appeal through us" (5:20).

TREASURE IN CLAY JARS

At the core of Paul's vision of reliance on God instead of self (for both discipleship generally and ministry in particular) lies a contradiction that is central to Christian identity. "We have this treasure," he explains, "in clay jars, so that it may be made clear that this extraordinary power belongs to God and does not come from us" (4:7). Just as with Christ, for whom the humiliation of death was reversed by exaltation to new life, so Christ's followers are "always being given up to death for Jesus' sake, so that the life of Jesus may be made visible in our mortal flesh" (4:11).

Identification with Christ also accounts for the affliction lists that are a prominent feature of this letter (see 4:8–9; 6:4–10; 11:23–28; cf. 1 Cor. 4:10–13). What this suggests is that Christians (and their pastors) should not expect to be spared the afflictions characteristic of a broken creation. The difference, as Paul sees it, is that rather than implying condemnation or abandonment by God, suffering represents an opportunity for divine consolation and identification with Christ (see 12:10). This is Paul's own experience, as he speaks repeatedly of experiencing personal "comfort" and "consolation" (1:3–7; 7:4–13), of not "losing heart" (4:1, 16), and being "of good courage" (5:6–8 RSV), even in the face of affliction. To offer this perspective to a congregation will require preachers to avoid the extremes either of fatalism or triumphalism, encouraging hearers to discern God graciously at work even amid human suffering. For God dwells tangibly even amid imperfect saints, he says, making them "the temple of the living God" (6:16).

FAITH AND GENEROSITY

Assurance of God's help in the face of frailty is not, however, at the expense of appropriate human obligation. Paul encourages the Corinthian believers to share the benefits they have received by contributing to the relief of others who now find themselves in need (8:1–9:5). His rhetoric, however fitting for its day, may strike us as overly forceful, yet its theological foundation remains the same as throughout the rest of the letter, since he insists that generosity toward others is only made possible by God's prior generosity toward those who now have opportunity to share (9:6–15). The Macedonians themselves, he says, "gave themselves *first to the Lord* and, by the will of God, to us" (8:5), leading them to contribute over and above their means. In this way, Paul consistently situates responsibility for the needs of others within the context of faith and devotion. This is ethical preaching at its best, which empowers the response that it seeks by highlighting God's work of grace.

It is essential that we read Paul's extended discussion of Christian generosity (8:1–9:15) in light of the preceding chapters, with their emphasis on a cruciform vision of discipleship. Doing so will keep us from interpreting his metaphor of "sowing" and "reaping" (e.g., 9:6, 10) out of context, as if to imply a principle of automatic return on one's charitable donations. In contrast to such a "prosperity gospel" approach, Paul's clear emphasis on "the generous act [grace] of our Lord Jesus Christ" (8:9 note) does not suggest giving so as to generate a larger recompense, but hinges rather on unrepayable divine beneficence, which inspires generosity in return.

APOSTOLIC AUTHORITY

The final four chapters show Paul once more on the defensive, as he again responds to his detractors. Even if we ourselves cannot, like Paul, claim to be apostles, the manner in which he asserts his authority is nonetheless instructive. If he has been granted authority, he says, it is "for building you up and not for tearing you down" (10:8; cf. 12:19); his intention is to facilitate "the knowledge of God" (10:5) and "a sincere and pure devotion to Christ" (11:3). This narrow theological and devotional focus provides a helpful corrective to the many forms of institutional authority that preachers typically wield and sometimes misuse. That being said, and despite his claim that "it is not those who commend themselves that are approved, but those whom the Lord commends" (10:18), Paul nonetheless "boasts" (11:17–18) of his religious heritage and his suffering for Christ (11:22–28), of personal revelations (12:1–5), even of "signs and wonders and mighty works" (12:12). Yet he is equally willing to concede that what defines him as a servant of Christ is not strength but weakness, for he says, "Whenever I am weak, then I am strong" (12:10). His example indicates the proper place of autobiography in preaching, since it serves primarily to illustrate his need of Christ.

CONCLUSION

The foregoing summary suggests that preaching from 2 Corinthians will focus on identification with Christ as the proper avenue for addressing more particular questions of suffering, conflict, or social obligation, as well as of congregational leadership. With Paul, contemporary preachers will seek to explain what it means to be part of God's "new creation" in Christ (5:17) and, more particularly, "ambassadors for Christ" (5:20) whose shortcomings and liabilities are preconditions rather than disqualifications for discipleship. Especially for churches alarmed by the tempo of their own decline, split by internal dissension or moral failure, or grieving their loss of prominence and social privilege, Paul reorders our theological priorities and redefines the task of preaching itself.

Galatians

DAVID SCHNASA JACOBSEN

Trying to interpret Galatians is a bit like trying to understand an angry phone call while overhearing only one side. You can tell that the caller on your end is alternately frustrated and passionate with the person(s) on the other end of the line, but you are not always sure why. What is clear is that such an animated conversation is conflicted and revelatory . . . of something. While other Pauline letters are written to communities we know something about (such as the Corinthians), we know precious little about the Galatians and the context of Paul's angry communication with them. We only know that from Paul's side the conversation touches on exceedingly vital and revealing issues: the nature of the gospel itself, Paul's apostleship, struggles over works of the law and faith, and practices around circumcision in a Gentile Christian context, in what we today call central Turkey.

ADDRESSEES

Preachers who interpret Galatians need to start by being honest about what we do not know. Scholars have long debated who the actual intended audience was. The two main proposals are that the addressees, "the churches of Galatia," are an ethnic group in a small geographic area or they are Christians throughout a much wider geographic province. For preachers the issue might prove important insofar as the former would be more of an ethnic identity; the latter a broader, foreign imperial designation.

STRUCTURE

The letter's broad structure includes a salutation (1:1–5), a more doctrinal section (1:6–4:31), an exhortation section (5:1–6:10), and a conclusion (6:11–18). This simple structure, however, barely contains the conflict underneath. The doctrinal section is sometimes rough on the Galatians and includes Paul's own difficult experiences and troubling biblical texts about Abraham, Hagar, and Sarah. The exhortation and conclusion soar, but sometimes are sore and personal as local struggles come into view. The problem with determining how ideas in the letter develop is, again, that we only have one side of the conversation.

GALATIANS IN RELATION TO PAUL'S
OTHER LETTERS

Fortunately, there are places where preachers can stand on firmer scholarly ground. In Galatians we may have only half of a "revealing angry phone call" to people we do not know, but we *do have access to some of Paul's other communications.* If we limit our comparison to those six other Pauline letters that contemporary scholarship largely agrees are authentic to Paul (Romans, 1 and 2 Corinthians, Philippians, Philemon, and 1 Thessalonians), we can discern some important unique features of Paul's correspondence with the Galatians in particular. Two such features of Galatians stand out.

First, the opening of the Letter to the Galatians lacks the typical thanksgiving of the other authentic Pauline letters. Even Paul's more routinized forms of communications carry a bit of an "ouch" with them in Galatians. This formal ouch continues deep into a letter where Paul is frustrated about opponents who seem to advocate an observance of Jewish works of the law (more about this below), especially circumcision for male, Gentile Christians. Paul even says he hopes these opponents will "castrate themselves" (Gal. 5:12).

Second, Paul draws special attention to himself, as he often does in his letters, specifically his apostleship and his personal experience as an apostle. Along the way, Paul discloses more about himself in this letter than in most of the others. The letter even ends with Paul "writing in [his] own hand" (Gal. 6:11). This communication in Paul's Letter to the Galatians is thus even at the level of form both angry and revealing.

It would be less than adequate to the subject matter of Galatians, however, to treat it as just another letter from one human being to other human beings. Galatians is, of course, just that and like Paul himself bears all the marks of a very human document. At the same time, however, the letter's mysterious language pushes its readers (and perhaps those who read over their shoulders centuries later) beyond what we already know to something even more controversial and even more revealing: Galatians points ultimately to an apocalyptic gospel of Jesus Christ, revealed to Paul when he was initially called to be an apostle.

PAUL'S APOSTLESHIP AND APOCALYPTIC GOSPEL OF JESUS CHRIST

Right after the letter's salutation (1:1–3) and Paul's confession of astonishment that there could even *be* a gospel different from the one he preached among the Galatians, a confession accompanied by curses (1:6–10), Paul decisively aligns the revealed gospel he preached with his apostleship narrative (1:11–2:10). Paul claims that, like the other apostles, he received his commission from Jesus Christ. This commission involved no other human sources or teaching. Therefore in Galatians Paul describes the gospel he preaches as through an "*apokalypsis* of Jesus Christ," that is, an apocalypse or revelation (1:12).

This theological claim is important for the whole letter. The narratives about Paul's life leading up to and including his apostolic call buttress the same revealing theological claim (1:16): Paul does not confer with other people nor does he go to Jerusalem (1:13–17). The narrative continues three years later, when Paul does go to Jerusalem and sees Peter and James, but does not meet with other apostles (1:18–24); the churches of Judea know about Paul by his prior reputation and glorify God as a result of his conversion, but they are not the ones who authorize. Paul's narrative jumps ahead fourteen years later to Jerusalem (2:1–10). Again, a revelation/apocalypse guides Paul there (2:2). He speaks with the leaders in Jerusalem but does not submit his revelatory, apocalyptic gospel of Christ to them for their approval, nor does he submit his Gentile partner Titus to circumcision. The upshot of the narrated conference is a confirmation that Paul has indeed "been entrusted with the gospel for the uncircumcised," while the Jerusalem leaders are "entrusted with the gospel for the circumcised" (2:7).

This issue of the revelation of the gospel and Paul's apostleship represents the core of the conflict that plays out in Paul's communication with the Galatians: the rough words of the beginning greeting (1:1–10), the cutting words about his opponents at the end (6:12–13), and all the sarcasm and name-calling in between (3:1; 5:12). Yes, Paul's Letter to the Galatians is like an angry, revealing phone call; but preachers should attend to the fact that even more so it is theologically revealing as Paul's direct claim to apostleship and direct apocalyptic revelation of the gospel, Jesus Christ.

KEY THEMES IN PAUL'S CONFLICTED COMMUNICATION

Over the centuries, Paul's animated response to the Galatians has sometimes made dualistic, either/or ways of thinking attractive to his interpreters. The either/or language that seems to animate Paul's discussion about law/works, circumcision/uncircumcision, and flesh/spirit in Galatians 2:11–16 has not had a neutral history of effects. At its extreme, anti-Jewish Christians and some contemporary anti-Semites have misused Paul's conflicted language for attitudes and actions that contemporary preachers have an ethical duty to oppose. Faithful contemporary interpreters in particular need to recall that Paul's letter was written to address a specific situation and not intended to be a universal treatise; he is doing pastoral theology more than systematic theology. The flame that burns in these pages is actually a local fire, not one that is necessarily fueled by universal binaries about essentialized "Jews" and reified "Christians." In fact, at the time of Paul's Letter to the Galatians, Christianity was still a movement within Judaism. The leaders in Jerusalem were Jews, but so was Paul, and quite possibly, his opponents in the Galatian church as well.

For this reason, scholars and preachers puzzle over just how to interpret Paul's strong words in Galatians in a way that honors his identity as a Jew as well as his local context, enmeshed as it is in Jewish/Gentile relations within a community only now differentiating within Jewish traditions. Without this critical contextual and pastoral check on the reading, Paul's dualistic claims about Spirit and flesh, promise and law, works of the law and faith, are turned into eternal either/or ways of thinking about persons. So what is a preacher to do as a local theologian in our contemporary world? Let us consider three exemplary either/or ways of thinking in light of three different ways of interpreting Galatians contextually.

Spirit and flesh. Scholars attuned to the revelatory apocalyptic language in Paul like to point out that Paul's communication about flesh/ Spirit presupposes an eschatological turning of the ages, not either/or identities. The age of the flesh is an apocalyptic age even now passing away; the age of the Spirit is part and parcel of God's new creation in Christ. Here the mistake would be to read Galatians as if it embraces Greek philosophical dualisms about body and soul. Paul's conflicted communication here is not about the essence of human beings. It is about the new creation even now dawning amid the old. For Paul, this "new creation" (6:15) means more than any either/or in the end.

Faith and works. From yet another new perspective, some scholars are keenly aware of Paul's conflicted language about works of the law and faith in Christ but are concerned that such words are misread if faith and works are treated as an undifferentiated dualism. They argue that some interpretations of Paul run the risk of portraying all Jews as legalistic and Christians as justified by faith. Such an essentializing move about identities has led scholars to look more deeply into the local causes of the conflict in Galatia. The argument some make is that "works of the law" refer not to a general, universal principle but to the specific local issue concerning circumcision. Elsewhere in Galatians, Paul is happy to remind the Galatians about what works they need to do (5:1–6 in particular). Thus, when Paul refers to "works," he is using a technical term that refers to a specific "work" that gives one entry to a Jewish covenant identity: the rite of circumcision for men. This specific practical context has the advantage of revealing the nature of the local conflagration that is Galatia. A community of Gentile Christians, perhaps confronted by Jewish or Judaizing Christians, needs to decide whether faith in Christ is sufficient for entry, or whether the Jewish work of entry needs to be observed.

Promise and law. A final either/or way of thinking concerns promise and law. In contrast to interpreters mentioned in the previous section, some scholars argue that a broad distinction between works of the law and faith still matters, but that the all-encompassing promise to Abraham *relativizes both law and Jewish (or even Gentile) identities.* For them, the distinction between promise and law is not so much an eternal dualism as it is a way of renarrating Israel's story: the narration of Abraham's promise interprets and thus relativizes law for Jewish and Gentile Christians alike. This is also crucial for the local situation of the Galatians, namely the texture of their communal life.

CONCLUSION

Paul's Letter to the Galatians requires discernment on the part of preachers who interpret it, to keep it local both then and now. Paul's vocabulary and conflicted way of thinking in context is difficult to grasp. Yet the difficulty of understanding the Gentile Christian and Jewish Christian context Paul has in mind requires interpreters to join in the struggle of reading and discernment for our own very different pluralistic times.

The good news is that for Paul the call is to struggle in our own conflicted, revealing ways with the gospel itself: its nature, its audience, and its newly creative purpose in relation to a concrete community in Galatia and in the end to us, too.

Ephesians

LISA MARIE BOWENS

Although some scholars maintain Pauline authorship of Ephesians, many believe that because of its style, language, and eschatological perspective it is pseudonymous, written by a disciple of Paul to Gentile believers. Also, since "in Ephesus" (1:1) does not appear in some early manuscripts, some interpreters argue that the letter functioned as a circular epistle that was to be read to different congregations, with the different church names appended. Moreover, Ephesians contains similar language and ideas found in Colossians, which indicates a close relationship between the two letters. More than likely, Colossians precedes Ephesians. Preachers today need not focus on the authorship issue, for many ways exist in which to analyze Ephesians for the preaching moment, and one of the best ways is to think about a particular passage's relationship to one of the overarching themes and purposes of the letter, the nature of the church.

ALL THINGS GATHERED INTO CHRIST

In Ephesians, Paul provides his audience with a number of metaphors to describe the beauty of the church: "household of God" (2:19–22), "holy temple" (2:21), Christ's "fullness" (1:23), Christ's "body" (1:23; 4:12, 15–16), and bride of Christ (5:23–33). Paul writes that the believing Gentiles, who were once aliens and without God in the world, are now the people of God through the blood of Jesus (2:11–13). Christ has broken down the dividing wall and made Jews and Gentiles one, providing all people access to the Father through the Spirit (2:18). Paul declares to his Gentile audience that they are citizens with the saints, members of the household of God, and growing into a holy temple, a dwelling place for God's presence (2:22). In fact, Christ creates in himself "one new humanity" (2:15), which the church made up of both Jews and Gentiles embodies and displays to the world.

Paul further underscores this unity brought about through the Christ event with the image of the church as a body intricately connected to Christ's body, which God raised from the dead. In 1:20, the apostle speaks of God's great power, which the Divine displayed in Jesus' resurrection. This emphasis on God's power to raise a dead body and to seat this resurrected body at God's right hand above all authority and every name—this power has implications for the church. By echoing Psalm 8:6 when he states that all things lie under Jesus' feet, Paul illustrates the power of Christ's resurrected body (1:22) and rounds off this part of the discussion by juxtaposing Jesus' feet and head. Whereas all things are under Christ's feet, he is at the same time the head of the church, who is the fullness of his body, implying that the church participates in God's triumphant victory in Christ. In fact, Paul says that when God raised Christ and seated him in heavenly places, God seated believers in the heavenly places with him (2:6). Believers, in some sense, have already experienced resurrection. They have a heavenly vantage point from which to view their life and calling in relation to God's cosmic purpose for the world, which is to gather all things in heaven and earth in Christ (1:9–10).

This divine purpose, however, was a mystery (*mystērion*) until now. The apostle uses the term *mystērion* several times in the letter (1:9; 3:3, 4, 9; 5:32; 6:19), and he elaborates upon what this mystery entails: "a plan for the fullness of time, to gather up all things in him, things in heaven and things on earth" (1:10). Gathering all into Christ includes the Gentiles, who were once alienated and without God (2:11–22).

THE APOCALYPTIC NOW

This *mystērion* hidden to previous generations is what God now reveals by the Spirit to the apostles and prophets (3:5). The presence of the "now" in 3:5 highlights Paul's dichotomy of periods: *before* God's mystery was unknown, but *now* the Spirit reveals the *mystērion*. The Ephesians live in the *apocalyptic now* in which what was previously hidden has been unveiled. Apocalyptic in this context means an unveiling or uncovering made possible by the Spirit's revelation.

Before their conversion, the Gentiles were aliens, strangers, and without hope, but now they have been "brought near by the blood of Christ" (2:13). This *apocalyptic now* reveals what life was like before God's radical intervention in Christ and what life entails now through salvation and revelation. Before Christ, the Gentiles practiced lifestyles of greed, impurity, and corruption (4:17–24), but now the apostle encourages them to live "worthy of the gospel" (4:1), clothing themselves with the new self, which is righteous and holy, thereby signifying the inbreaking of God's mystery. The apostle describes the mystery of the now with three *syn* (with) adjectives (3:6): *sygklēronomos* (fellow heir), *syssōmos* (member of the same body), and *symmetocha* (sharer or participant). By using these adjectives, the apostle underscores the unity of the community of faith in which a new body is formed, one in which divisions and the wall of hostility (2:14) disappear.

Paul's view of the apocalyptic now, however, is not naive talk of utopia. He sees the church's new way of existence as displaying God's power to rulers and authorities in heavenly places that continue to be hostile to God's rule (3:10). The concept of hostile powers located in the heavenly realms occurs in apocalyptic writings, in which angels and spirits war against God and God's people (cf. Job 1:6; Dan. 10:13, 21; 2 Macc. 5:2). Paul depicts these powers elsewhere in the letter as evil entities that need subjection and against which believers fight (2:2; 6:12–17). The existence of the church does not eliminate these cosmic powers but reveals to them that God's power, despite their repeated opposition, prevails. The reappearance of "now" in 3:10 heightens the apocalyptic sentiment of this epistle. *Now* God's plan has been revealed to the powers, and the task of disclosing this revelation is not limited to the apostles and to the prophets but is that of the church as a whole.

Paul's acknowledgment of continued conflict (6:12–17) tempers the apostle's earlier statement about believers already sitting in heavenly places. Although believers are raised with Christ and experience the powerful presence of the Spirit (1:13; 4:30), they contend with cosmic powers of darkness and spiritual evil. Accordingly, Paul admonishes the Ephesians to put on the whole armor of God and to equip themselves for the struggle. The vantage point from which believers fight these powers, however, is from a seat of victory.

HOUSEHOLD CODES

The final salient image of the church is the bride, an image which appears in 5:22–33, the first section of the household codes (5:21–6:9), the name given to this section of the letter because of its focus on household members' duties. Paul depicts the church as Christ's bride, which Christ purified by giving his life. The apostle portrays Christ as a tender, loving husband who nourishes and cherishes the church with such deep love that he is willing to give himself up for her needs and well-being. Paul once again weaves the imagery of the body with the imagery of the bride. As the husband and wife are one body, so too the church is Christ's body, underscoring the divine care with which Christ deals with the church. In 5:21 Paul sums up the way he views the marriage relationship and the church: "Be subject to one another out of reverence for Christ." Husbands are to love their wives in such a way that, as Christ submitted himself to the needs of the church, they too submit their needs to that of their wives. Thus the mutual submission outlined in 5:21 instructs how one reads 5:22–33. This idea of mutual service and submission coheres with the apostle's repeated statements that God through Christ brings all things into unity and oneness. Mutual submission on the part of the husband and wife bears witness to God's work of unity and oneness in bringing all creation into God's saving work.

The last part of the household codes in which Paul instructs slaves and masters is problematic to modern ears but fits within the framework of mutual submission in 5:21. While he reminds slaves to obey their masters, he reminds masters that they too are slaves because their master in heaven surveils them (6:9). Thus, their position as masters mean nothing to God; Roman law defines for God neither the slave's nor the master's identity. To God both are equal. The cosmic unification of all things in Christ includes masters and slaves, which means that even this societal division disintegrates. With his words Paul attempts to undercut the hierarchy present within the congregation. Understandably, to many people today his attempt falls short and does not go far enough to abolish the institution of slavery. Yet his language, *in its time and place*, does allow a means to subvert the practice.

Preaching from Ephesians needs to involve an understanding of how these household codes have been used throughout church history to justify the unjustifiable, such as women staying in abusive marriages, children obeying their parents in ways that are harmful, and African

Americans suffering in slavery. The Roman society of Paul's day that legitimized patriarchy and slavery no longer holds today. Thus, the Spirit's work from Paul's time until now is bringing to pass what the apostle saw in relation to the Jews and Gentiles, the abolishment of the dividing wall between these groups, and what he could only have imagined in relation to male-female and master-slave relationships. God creates a new humanity in Christ where no divisions remain.

In this letter ministers find a range of grand images of the church and the wonderful entity God calls it to be. Yet the reality of life for pastors and congregations is often antithetical to the portrayals the apostle gives. Communities of faith are often fractured, broken, hurting, sitting at ground level, and not in heavenly places. On the surface, it seems that Paul does not live in the "real world" and writes to a perfect church. Upon closer inspection, however, we see that Paul writes to a church who, like us, experiences the effects of sin, such as brokenness, anger, and division (4:22–6:9). Thus, Paul the pastor employs the right images for such a church: the broken need to know they are restored, the divided have been united, the lost have been found, the dead have been raised, the lonely have become part of a body in which every part is necessary, those deemed inferior by society stand equal before God, and the fractured have been made whole. Likewise, those locked in ground position, so to speak, believing that there is no way for them to rise higher, hear that they sit with Christ in heavenly places. As Paul in Ephesians reminds his audience of their identity and calling, so too pastors today in preaching from these texts remind congregations to transform their vision, to follow the Spirit's lead, and to redescribe reality, proclaiming that the apocalyptic now, the fulfillment of God's revelatory activity, continues.

Philippians

LISA MARIE BOWENS

Many scholars argue that Paul wrote Philippians from a Roman prison in the early 60s CE, whereas others insist on a prison in Ephesus (mid-50s) or Caesarea (late 50s). Although his whereabouts when writing this epistle are uncertain, we know that Paul writes from confinement (1:7, 13–14, 17), and he expects some type of resolution to his predicament soon (1:19–26), whether life or death. He prefers life for the sake of his beloved Philippians (1:23–26), whom he believes need him for their own growth and maturity in the faith. Scholarly convention divides the letter more or less in the following manner:

Introduction (1:1–11)
Body (1:12–4:1)
Conclusion (4:2–23)

Paul's purpose in writing the letter is to encourage his audience, in light of his possible impending death, to thank them for their assistance, and to urge them to be citizens of the gospel who strive for unity amid earthly and spiritual struggle. When contextualizing a passage for a sermon, then, preachers should notice how the passage relates to the recurring themes of joy, sharing, struggle, unity, and citizenship, all of which appear in the very first chapter, foreshadowing Paul's weaving them together throughout the rest of this short but powerful exposition of the gospel.

JOYFULNESS

Despite its prison origin, joy and rejoicing are prominent motifs in the letter, appearing sixteen times (1:4, 18, 25; 2:2, 17–18, 28, 29; 3:1; 4:1, 4, 10) and indicating that Paul views joy as central to the believer's life. Indeed, Paul starts out by stating that he thanks God for the Philippians and prays constantly for them with joy (1:3–4). His frequent references to his deep affection for this congregation cause some to label this epistle a love letter (1:7–8; 2:17; 4:1, 14). He also rejoices that even though others preach Christ from a variety of motivations, some to harm him and others for selfish gain, Christ is still proclaimed (1:18). For him, the fact that the gospel spreads is sufficient for elation.

The Philippians were naturally concerned for Paul during his imprisonment, but the fact that he continues to rejoice serves to console and reassure them. If he, a prisoner in chains, can be joyful in his present circumstances, they can in their own trials and tribulations be joyful (1:29–30; 3:17; 4:9). Paul presents himself as a model of what he tells them in 4:11 and 4:13. He has learned how to be content with whatever he has and knows that he can do all things through Christ, who strengthens him. Paul's call to imitate him in 3:17 includes his ability to rejoice and be thankful in difficult situations. Preachers will do well to focus not only on Paul's joy in adversity but also on why he feels this way: the gospel proclamation continues, Christ remains present with him in his suffering, and he has the support and prayers of the Philippians.

SHARING IN THE MIDST OF STRUGGLES

In the opening of the letter, Paul thanks God for the Philippians because of their "sharing" (*koinōnia*) with him "in the gospel" from the very beginning (1:5). This concept of sharing occurs repeatedly in the letter. The Philippians share the same faith in Jesus Christ as Paul, and when no other church partnered with him, they assisted him in all that he needed so that the gospel would continue (4:15–16). Along with sharing in the gospel, the Philippians also share in his imprisonment by meeting his needs through the gifts they have sent through Epaphroditus (2:25–30; 4:14–18).

Moreover, the Philippians are fellow sufferers with Paul since they have the same struggle (Gk., *agōn*, a word with athletic and military connotations) which he is currently experiencing. This language indicates that they are undergoing some sort of persecution for the sake of the gospel (1:30). He views the believer's life as one of conflict; for when one proclaims the gospel, adversaries invariably arise.

In light of their shared struggle, Paul admonishes the Philippians in 1:27 to remain "standing firm" (*stēkō*), another athletic and military term, which denotes an athlete's steadfastness in position despite any difficulty and the soldier's resolution to remain in place no matter how difficult the fight. Paul's notion of sharing speaks volumes for the preaching moment. In a society that emphasizes individualism, believers embody a counternarrative: their lives are inextricably linked with others through faith, resources, and suffering.

UNITY

One stands firm (*stēkō*) in the midst of opposition (*agōn*) by remaining unified. Extending this metaphorical cluster, Paul uses another athletic or military term, *synathleō*, which means "striving *together* with someone" or "fighting *alongside* someone." For Paul, this term highlights the significance of unity among believers. He urges one spirit (1:27); the same mind that was in Christ Jesus (2:5); and despite disagreements (2:1–4, 14–15; 4:2–3), gentleness with one another so that their behavior witnesses to the world (4:5). Paul discourages any hindrance to unity from within or outside of the congregation. The Philippians are to avoid those who distort the gospel for selfish gain and those who add to the gospel anything other than the cross (3:2, 18–19). By repeating his call to unity, Paul reveals that believers' lives are communal and that they remain steadfast if they fight, not against each other, but together assisting one another in the struggle.

The themes of unity and sharing converge in Paul's and the Philippians' prayers for each other. Paul fervently prays that their love would overflow, that their knowledge and insight may grow, so that they may be able to discern *ta diapheronta*, a phrase that means "what matters, what is most important, most valuable" (1:9–11). For the apostle, love ought to increase in knowledge and insight, all of which are worth petitioning God. Paul, then, does not see knowledge or the ability to think critically as antithetical to the gospel but integral to the believer's perception of what really counts.

As Paul prays for the Philippians, they too pray for him; and he believes that their prayers, along with the Spirit of Jesus Christ, will aid in his deliverance from prison (1:19). Here the apostle underscores a divine/human partnership where his future freedom from incarceration comes about through human intercession and divine activity. He espouses an important spiritual principle: God mysteriously links the divine will on earth to the prayers of the righteous.

Just as unity and sharing converge in the letter, they also converge in believers' lives. Thus pastors today, like Paul, need to challenge their congregations: to pray because prayer participates in the divine will, to unify because such action witnesses to God's identity, and to think critically so that they may discern what is most important.

CITIZENSHIP

Finally, along with joy, sharing, struggle, and unity, Paul emphasizes the theme of "living as citizens, citizenship" (*politeuomai, politeuma*) throughout Philippians. In the opening of the letter, he urges the Philippians to live as citizens worthy of the gospel of Christ (1:27). In the rest of the letter, then, he fleshes out what it means to fulfill this mandate. Since Philippi was a Roman colony and since many of its inhabitants, including those in the Philippian congregation, were likely Roman citizens, Paul's semantic decision of choosing *politeuomai* would have resonated with his audience. Yet Paul subverts the understanding of citizenship that many in his congregation would have held. Having Roman citizenship meant status since one belonged to what was believed to be the greatest empire in the world at that time. Nevertheless, Paul counsels his audience to live as citizens *"worthy of the gospel of Christ"* (1:27), not Rome: the two are not identical. Indeed, his imprisonment proves that to defend the gospel is often antithetical to the laws of ruling authorities. To live worthy of the gospel may mean persecution and death at the hands of the empire. For Paul, one's citizenship is defined by a life lived according to God's grace and the gospel, not by national identity. He offers important paradigms to the Philippians of what it means for love to increase in knowledge. As Paul discerned that what was most important was not his imprisonment but the gospel and its proliferation, so too, he learned to distinguish that what mattered most was the gospel, not Roman citizenship.

Again, in 3:20 Paul reminds the Philippians of their heavenly citizenship, and though it relativizes earthly citizenship, it has earthly implications. As citizens worthy of the gospel, the Philippians live in humility, looking out for others more than for themselves. Likewise, they do not seek to promote themselves but live as compassionate people who have the mind of Christ (2:1–5). Verses 2:6–11, known as the Christ hymn, serve as an example to the Philippians of Christ's humility and self-emptying, demonstrating to them God's call upon their own lives. Yet this hymn serves as more than an example: it is a proclamation of empowerment as well. The same Christ—who became human, suffered, obeyed even unto death, and was subsequently raised and exalted—is present with the Philippians, empowering them and enabling them to live in unity and love and to be all that God destined for them. Paul calls upon the Philippians to imitate him in discounting the past and pressing forward to know Christ (3:4–17), to share in Christ's sufferings as well as in the power of his resurrection (3:10). How the Philippians treat one another and how they live demonstrate to the world to which commonwealth they belong.

Preachers should note that Paul subverts the notion of citizenship; he knows that the name of Jesus is above every name (2:9–10), including the name of Rome, and that allegiance to country is not the same as allegiance to God. Christians today share with Philippian believers the tendencies toward pride and division, but as the apostle reminds his audience of Christ's humility, so too will current preachers do well to do the same, not only through words from the pulpit, but also in how they themselves live their lives inside and outside of the church.

THEMATIC CONVERGENCE

Paul ends the letter with several calls to action. First, he urges Euodia and Syntyche to be unified, and he implores the Philippians to help these two women who have "fought beside him in spreading the gospel" (4:3, my trans.). Paul returns to athletic and military imagery by using the same word (*synathleō*) that he uses in 1:27. By using this term, Paul undoubtedly characterizes a unified preaching team in which he, these women, Clement, and others fight together to proclaim the gospel.

Second, along with the call to assist these women preachers, Paul reminds the Philippians to rejoice and to continue to pray. When they make their requests known to God with thanksgiving, Paul assures them that the peace of God will guard (*phroureō*) their hearts and minds in Christ Jesus (4:7). Paul resumes military imagery in this promise, for *phroureō* means to guard in a martial sense. Paul depicts God's peace, like a warrior, protecting and standing guard over the Philippians' minds and hearts. As citizens of heaven (3:20), the Philippians do not look to Roman soldiers for protection, but to God and God's peace.

CONCLUSION

The fact that Philippi was a Roman military colony may have played a role in Paul's decision to insert martial language throughout the epistle. This language enables Paul to connect the themes that permeate the letter—joy, sharing, struggle, unity, and gospel citizenship—themes that enrich sermons because they describe the believer's life so well.

Colossians

LISA MARIE BOWENS

The Letter to the Colossians contains some of New Testament's richest expositions about the cosmic nature of Christ's role, believers' participation in Christ, the defeat of cosmic powers, and God's reconciling action in the Christ event. Disputes remain over two primary issues in the letter: its relationship to Ephesians, since the two letters treat similar topics with corresponding wording and imagery, and whether Paul or one of his disciples wrote the letter. Many interpreters believe Colossians precedes Ephesians in time and that Paul (or the author) reiterated some of the Colossian material in the Ephesian correspondence. Preachers today need not focus on the author debate, but rather on the letter's content and themes, and in doing so will find that this approach is a fruitful way of engaging the rich material this letter provides for the transformation of both preacher and congregation.

The epistle addresses a congregation in which a deceptive teaching threatens to lead them away from the gospel (2:8). As he refutes this teaching, Paul espouses a robust Christology that grounds the letter's soteriology and ecclesiology while emphasizing both a realized and future eschatology, all of which serve to encourage the Gentile audience in Colossae, who need continued guidance and instruction in the faith.

CHRISTOLOGICAL HYMN

The christological hymn (1:15–20) sets the tone for the rest of the letter by emphasizing Christ's role in creation, salvation, and reconciliation. Christ is the image of the invisible God and the firstborn (*prōtotokos*) of all creation (1:15). The term reappears in 1:18, where Christ is the firstborn from the dead. Such terminology denotes Christ's status as first temporally, sovereign over all things, and the assurance of the future resurrection of the righteous.

Paul goes on to assert that all things were created in, through, and for Christ (1:16). Christ is the goal or telos of creation, for everything created exists for and because of him, which includes all powers, both visible and invisible, heavenly and earthly. The acknowledgment of cosmic powers aligns with Jewish traditions regarding angelic beings who affect human existence (Dan. 7–12; 2 Macc. 3:24; 1 Enoch 61.10; 2 Enoch 20–22). Here Paul declares that even these entities are subject to Christ.

This cosmic preeminence of Christ corresponds with Christ as the head of the church, which is his body (1:18). Here Paul makes a wordplay with *kephalē*, a noun that can mean physical head and can denote a leader or ruler. In addition, the term also has connotations of origin or beginning. The reason Paul emphasizes Christ's preeminence comes to the forefront in 1:19: in Christ "all the fullness of God was pleased to dwell." In other words, all that God is, Christ is. Paul returns to this topic in 2:9, writing that in Christ "the whole fullness of the deity dwells bodily." Christ's preeminence and God's supremacy cohere in such a way that God reconciles all things, heavenly and earthly, through Christ. Here Paul does not explain how or why all things need reconciliation. Instead, he simply emphasizes God as the agent who initiates and completes the reconciliatory act. Preachers can emphasize the apostle's focus on Christ's preeminence, God's supremacy, and the reconciliation that takes place through the blood of the cross, which brings peace to a chaotic cosmos taken over by hostile cosmic powers. The blood of the cross defeats these powers and restores peace to God's creation, in effect signifying to these powers their incontrovertible defeat.

NEW LIFE AND THE DEFEAT OF COSMIC POWERS

Paul returns to the topic of the defeat of these powers in 2:15, indicating that he views them as working behind the scenes of the deceitful philosophy that has crept into the Colossian congregation. In 2:13–15 the apostle explains further the soteriological ramifications of the cross for his audience. Before the cross, these Gentiles were dead in trespasses and uncircumcised (2:13), but God has erased their record, forgiven their sins (2:14), and made them alive together with Christ (2:13). Paul declares, then, that this record, which contained all these deeds, was erased and nailed to the cross, so that no believer's deeds count anymore against them. Any power that would try to condemn a person before God has no ground upon which to stand.

The powers have not only been stripped of their ability to accuse believers, but they have been stripped or disarmed of all their power (2:15). Therefore, the Colossians should not trust in a teaching that follows after the elemental spirits of the universe (2:8), observe certain days of the calendar, eat or abstain from particular foods or drink (2:16), or worship angels (2:18). Christ's cross has dealt decisively with the powers of the cosmos, and the Colossians need no further addendum to their salvation. Indeed, Paul writes that God has made a "public example of them, triumphing [*thriambeuō*] over them in it" (2:15). The word *thriambeuō* denotes a military triumphal parade in which the Romans would march after a victory over an enemy. In these parades, the victor displays the conquered foe in the procession. Paul depicts God as defeating these powers in the cross and then leading these vanquished powers in a spectacle for all to see.

Thus Paul tries to paint such a clear picture to the Colossians of God's complete work in Christ and Christ's preeminence that they would begin to understand the sufficiency of all that God accomplished in Christ's death and resurrection. When Christ died, the Colossians died to the elemental spirits of the universe and so no longer need to live as if they still belong to this world. Instead, the apostle declares their rising with Christ (2:12; 3:1) and that this metaphorical resurrection orients them to a new way of seeing and existing (3:1–4), that is, seeking things above, where Christ sits at God's right hand.

In 3:5–11 he advises the Colossians in relation to this new life by instructing them to avoid vices, such as fornication and greed. Conversely, in 3:12–17 he urges them, as God's chosen ones, to live by virtues, that is as people who have compassion, meekness, and patience. Although Paul depicts believers as already risen with Christ (3:1) and as rescued from the power of darkness and transferred into Christ's kingdom (1:13), he recognizes that these same believers are people who still need to "put to death, therefore, whatever in you is earthly" (3:5).

In other words, Paul is not naive: even though the believer is already victorious in Christ, conflict continues, and the believer has to put to death certain practices. There is an "already" and "not yet" quality to the apostle's exposition. The inbreaking of the new age means that the future breaks into the present. Nevertheless, the old age still exists, and its complete destruction awaits the eschaton. Whereas Paul depicts vices as part of the old age under the rule of the defeated powers, he portrays virtues as gifts given by God, who enables and empowers believers to live this new existence.

The language of clothing in chapter 3 provides a tangible way of viewing the old and the new. In ancient baptismal practices, the one being baptized stripped naked before entering the water and was clothed anew after coming out of the water. Paul states that the vices are part of the old self that the Colossians have stripped off. They in turn have clothed themselves with the new self, which is renewed in knowledge according to the image of Christ. Paul reminds the Colossians that their baptism continues to have ongoing, everyday effects. Going down in baptismal waters means death with Christ and death of their old self, while coming up out of the water means resurrection, new life, and putting on the new self.

This new self has implications for individuals and the believing community as a whole, for Paul goes on to write in 3:11 that "there is no longer Greek and Jew, circumcised and uncircumcised, barbarian, Scythian, slave and free; but Christ is all and in all!" Societal divisions and identities no longer hold sway in the new community that God creates through the Christ event. The presence of Christ abolishes the divisions and makes them irrelevant.

Christ's preeminence and power permeate the epistle and offer preachers a way to communicate to believers the irrefutable victory that they have in Christ, who defeated all powers and because of whom God leads a victory parade, showing to the world evil's defeat. This theme of supremacy also provides an opportunity to preach about what it means to live victorious in the midst of a world still ravaged by the old-age order of things, where it looks like the powers still reign and principalities still prevail. In such a world, believers may be tempted, like the Colossians, to look for another philosophy, another gospel, one that can add to what Christ has already done. Yet preachers have the task of declaring like Paul that there is no other gospel whereby one can be saved because it is only through the blood of the cross in which the flesh of the image of the invisible God (1:15) brought peace and reconciled all things on earth and in heaven (1:20).

HOUSEHOLD CODES

Upon first glance, Paul's statement in 3:11 contradicts what is known as the household codes in 3:18–4:1, the name given to this section of the letter because of its focus on household members' duties: wives are told to submit to their husbands, children to obey their parents, and slaves to be obedient to their masters. In the context of the letter, Paul sees the preeminence of Christ as reigning over these household roles as well. The phrase "there is no partiality" at the end of 3:25 has implications for all of the household codes, especially in light of 3:11. For the sake of Greco-Roman society, differing roles may exist, but in God's economy such distinctions are irrelevant since Christ is all and in all.

The household codes are problematic to modern ears, and preaching from Colossians involves understanding how these household codes have been used to justify the unjustifiable, such as women staying in abusive marriages, children obeying their parents in ways that are harmful, and African Americans suffering in slavery. The Roman society of Paul's time that legitimized patriarchy and slavery no longer holds today. With his language that reminds his hearers to love (3:19), to consider that with God no partiality exists (3:25), and to remember that God as Master in heaven sees all (4:1), Paul attempts to undercut the hierarchy present within the congregation. Understandably, to many people today his attempt falls short and does not go far enough. Yet it does allow *in its time and place* a means to challenge these expected roles.

As Paul in Colossians reminds his audience of Christ's sovereignty, so too preachers can follow Paul's lead today in reminding congregations that Christ's lordship means something, and it means something for our everyday lives, in how we treat others, including those deemed "other," in how believers refuse to allow society's polarities and divisions to become our own, and ultimately in how we live out this new life in the midst of the old age.

1 Thessalonians

WILLIAM F. BROSEND II

Scholars and preachers may like to think otherwise, but there are only a handful of dates about which we may be certain in the study of the New Testament: when Pilate was prefect of Judea, when Gallio was proconsul of Achaia, and the date of the Jewish War. One thing on which all agree is that the First Letter of Paul to the Thessalonians was the first written document among the twenty-seven books of the New Testament. Most further agree that it was written in 50–51 CE, in Corinth. That, however, is the easy part, and knowing it was the first letter by Paul does not tell us to whom in Thessalonica it was written, why, or how it was received.

Thessalonica was an important Roman city, the capital of the Roman province of Macedonia, and blessed with two gifts, one natural and one constructed, that made it a significant center of commerce and trade. First, it was founded as a port city on the coast of the Aegean Sea, and the important east-west Roman road, the Via Egnatia, passed through it. As a major commercial center, it attracted a mixed population of Macedonians, Greeks, Romans, Jews, and others. It also featured an assortment of religious shrines, temples, and the deities to which they were dedicated. Second, the imperial cult was prominent in Thessalonica as throughout the empire, and Thessalonica was also known for the worship of Egyptian gods and the *Theos Hypsistos* (God Most High; see Acts 16:17). Perhaps most prominent was the cult of Cabrius, a figure whose legend includes dying and rising, thus inspiring conjecture about the relation of Cabrius to Christ from a history-of-religions perspective. So when Paul praises the addressees for "how you turned to God from idols, to serve a living and true God" (1 Thess. 1:9), he knew that they had made a choice with many alternatives.

AUDIENCE

Paul also told us something else important in that verse (1:9). Because Jews who came to believe that Jesus was the Messiah, like the Jewish Paul, did not need to turn from idols, the believers to whom Paul was writing in Thessalonica were non-Jewish believers in Jesus. (This claim is bolstered by the account of Paul's visit to Thessalonica in Acts 17:4, "Some of them were persuaded and joined Paul and Silas, as did a great many of the devout Greeks and not a few of the leading women," and the depiction in Acts 17:5–9 of "the Jews" becoming jealous and turning on Paul, Silas, and their host Jason.)

The final evidence that these believers were not Jewish comes in the instructions on sexual behavior in chapter 4, where Paul admonishes the readers to act, "not with lustful passion, like the Gentiles who do not know God" (4:5). Paul is here admonishing non-Jewish believers not to conduct themselves like their unbelieving neighbors, so that the distinction he is making is not between Jew and Gentile, but between believers and unbelievers.

We should also remember that these non-Jewish believers in Jesus were new to their faith, had experienced only two to three weeks of instruction (Acts 17:2), and were hearing from Paul only a few months after he left their city. That there was considerable room for misunderstanding seems inevitable, as 4:1–8, 13–18; 5:4–8, 12–22 show. Preachers will do well to realize that such misunderstanding is just as likely today.

PAUL'S RELATIONSHIP WITH THE AUDIENCE

As in all his letters, First Thessalonians was an opportunity for Paul to deepen his connection with the readers, here a group of believers for whom he felt great tenderness, and not a little pride. Paul wrote primarily to commiserate, but also to encourage, instruct, and exhort.

The *tenderness* is seen in a commonplace, "As you know, we dealt with each of you like a father with his children" (2:11–12) and in a surprising metaphor at 2:7b–8: "But we were gentle among you, like a nurse tenderly caring for her children. So deeply do we care for you that we are determined to share with you not only the gospel of God but also our own selves, because you have become very dear to us." The word translated as "gentle" in the NRSV literally means "infant" or "child" (so Gal. 4:1), and the word used for "nurse" can also mean "nursing mother." Paul was using the gentlest metaphors he could imagine, casting himself as father and mother to the Thessalonians.

The *pride* is expressed in two ways: Paul's pride in the addressees (1:9; 3:6–10) and in himself (2:1–6; 3:4, 7; in 1:2–6 and 2:9–12, 13 he combines the two).

Commiseration is seen in chapter 2 and the first half of chapter 3, and brings us to the topic of persecution in the letter, which includes challenging language about "the Jews" (2:14–16). Paul writes of his own experience of being persecuted (2:2; 3:4, 7) and alludes to the Thessalonians' persecution (2:14; 3:3). An examination of 2:14–16 is especially illuminating:

> For you, brothers and sisters, became imitators of the churches of God in Christ Jesus that are in Judea, for you suffered the same things from your own compatriots as they did from the Jews, who killed both the Lord Jesus and the prophets, and drove us out; they displease God and oppose everyone by hindering us from speaking to the Gentiles so that they may be saved. Thus they have constantly been filling up the measure of their sins; but God's wrath has overtaken them at last.

Paul indicates that the persecution experienced by the Thessalonians was at the hands of "your own compatriots," non-Jews, just as Jewish believers in Jesus in Judea were persecuted by Jews. This raises two issues: (1) What is the nature of the persecution Paul describes? And (2) if the Thessalonians were being persecuted by non-Jews, why is the short diatribe against "the Jews" in 2:15–16 included?

When we see the word "persecution" (Gk., *thlipsis*, 3:3) today, we imagine imprisonment, torture, and violent death, but this was hardly the norm for most believers most of the time. Instead, persecution covers a broad range of behavior, such as what happened in Thessalonica to Jason (Acts 17:5–9), any attempt to hinder the proclamation of the word about Jesus (see 1 Thess. 2:16a above), or a scorning of those who do accept that word. Persecution is here best understood as resistance and difficulty, not trial and execution.

Why, then, does Paul speak about "the Jews" so vehemently? Some scholars argue that 2:14–16 is a later interpolation from another hand, reflecting Paul's death and the destruction of Jerusalem: "God's wrath has overtaken them at last." Paul's later writing, especially Romans 9–11, reflects this view, but there is no textual basis to support the claim of an addition to the text. Here we need to remember that Paul does get mad, best shown in Galatians, and sometimes he gets mad at his fellow Jews. The language is intemperate, but like it or not, this is what Paul writes like when he is angry, an anger best explained by Acts 16–19. Preachers must realize that using Paul's anger to justify contemporary supersessionism or anti-Semitism is unwarranted and counter to Paul's larger project.

But he is not always angry. Paul can also *exhort* and *encourage*, as the *instructions* at 4:1–12 (e.g., v. 9, "You yourselves have been taught by God to love one another") and 5:12–22 ("Rejoice always, pray without ceasing, give thanks in all circumstances," vv. 16–18a) give eloquent evidence.

ESCHATOLOGY

Paul's eschatological outlook is present in every chapter of this letter (1:10; 2:19; 3:13; 4:13–18; 5:1–11) and especially prominent in chapters 4 and 5. Paul is responding to the community's concern over the fate of brothers and sisters who have died since his visit (4:14). His words in 4:13–18 and 5:1–11 are grounded in an eschatology more akin to Mark 13 than the book of Revelation, explaining how the Lord's return will happen (4:15–17), encouraging the Thessalonians to console one another (4:18; 5:11) and to live with expectant hope as children of the light, awake and sober (5:5–10). The timeless quality of his words is attested by their continued use in contemporary funeral liturgies.

Paul's ethic, founded on the expectation of an immediate return of the Lord, endures throughout Paul's writings, even as the expectation dims and eschatology ceases to be an important theme in later letters. The letter feels eminently Pauline, even while themes such as righteousness, the cross, circumcision, and food laws are not mentioned, and faith is named only rarely, without elaboration (e.g., "your faith in God," 1:8 and 3:5–6).

First Thessalonians is important not just for our understanding of Paul. The gentleness and encouragement, along with the instruction, is an example for the Thessalonians and for those who would preach from this letter today.

2 Thessalonians

WILLIAM F. BROSEND II

Did the apostle Paul write 2 Thessalonians? If he did, when did he, and how should we understand the difference in tone, eschatology, and ethics between it and 1 Thessalonians? If he did not, who did, when was it written, and why did the author go to such lengths to make it appear that Paul wrote a second letter to the same community? More importantly, how do questions of authorship, date, and provenance matter to the preacher? This is a question for 2 Thessalonians and for other writings traditionally ascribed to the apostle Paul that for a variety of reasons are now held by scholars to have been written in Paul's name but not by the apostle himself.

The traditional argument for Pauline authorship of both letters to the Thessalonians is straightforward: the author of the second letter said so, twice, and at the end of the letter emphatically: "I, Paul, write this greeting with my own hand" (3:17). Moreover, the order of the second letter is like the first, as is its focus on eschatology. But here the similarity also suggests the key difference: while both letters speak of the coming of the Lord, they do so in completely different ways. First Thessalonians includes in each chapter a reference to the coming of the Lord (1 Thess. 1:10; 2:19; 3:13; 4:13–18; 5:1–11, 23); 2 Thessalonians does so in only one focused passage (1:5–2:12), in a different tone, and with a different scenario. It is fair to say the two letters have radically divergent eschatologies. Preachers, therefore, should treat 2 Thessalonians as pseudonymous.

Pseudonymity affects preaching indirectly. No matter whom scholars determine is the likely author, and whether the preacher agrees or disagrees, the text is Scripture. We do not decide what is Scripture and what is not. In other words, determining that someone wrote 2 Thessalonians in Paul's name (instead of Paul writing it himself) in no way diminishes the authority of the letter as part of the canon.

The difference pseudonymity makes for preaching, then, is through our interpretation of Scripture. For example, based on vocabulary, style, tone, and eschatology that differs between 2 Thessalonians and the undisputed Pauline letters, preachers should envision this letter as addressing a later period than Paul's original writings, a time when the emerging communities of faith were facing different issues than during Paul's ministry. Pseudonymity was viewed differently in antiquity, not as fraud but as a way of the author claiming that if Paul had been around at this later date, this is what he would have thought and written. In other words, while 2 Thessalonians was written by someone else after Paul's death, it was written in his spirit, claiming Paul's authority for an extension of Pauline theology in a new day. Whatever the preacher decides about authorship, 2 Thessalonians has been chosen or assigned and must be interpreted and proclaimed as Scripture with as much faithfulness and rigor as the preacher brings to a passage from Romans or the Gospel of John.

Second Thessalonians begins in the traditional manner of a Greco-Roman letter, and much like 1 Thessalonians, with a salutation (1:1–2) and thanksgiving (1:3–4). Verse 5 continues in this way, acknowledging the suffering of Thessalonians (cf. 1 Thess. 1:6), and then the letter takes an abrupt turn toward the vengeful punishment of those who persecuted the community: "For it is indeed just of God to repay with affliction those who afflict you, . . . when the Lord Jesus is revealed from heaven with his mighty angels in flaming fire, inflicting vengeance on those who do not know God and on those who do not obey the gospel of our Lord Jesus" (2 Thess. 1:6–8).

This transition makes clear that we are in a very different eschatological world than in 1 Thessalonians. Whereas in 1 Thessalonians, Paul speaks with hope and encouragement concerning the coming of our Lord Jesus, the author of 2 Thessalonians 2 tells the faithful that the Lord will not come "unless the rebellion comes first and the lawless one is revealed, the one destined for destruction" (2:3). (There was no rebellion or lawless one mentioned in 1 Thessalonians.) The letter continues with a description of the lawless one, who "opposes and exalts himself above every so-called god or object of worship, . . . declaring himself to be God" (2:4). The author connects the lawless one with Satan and all his powers and "wicked deception for those who are perishing, because they refused to love the truth and so be saved" (2:9–10). "For this reason God sends them a powerful delusion, leading them to believe what is false" (2:11). In other words, the Lord has not returned because there has not yet been a Satan-led rebellion of those who persecute the believers and themselves refuse to believe, thereby triggering a powerful delusion *sent by God* so that they will never believe. It is understandable if the readers think they have stumbled into the Letter of Jude.

After this outburst the author calms down, offering a blessing (2:16–17) and praying that the word of the Lord will quickly spread. Then the pendulum swings between "wicked and evil people" without faith and the Lord who is faithful and will guard against the evil one (3:1–3). Who is this lawless one/Satan/evil one, and who are those deceived by him (and deluded by God)? We do not know, nor do we know who are the "idlers" brought up in 3:6. But we would not be wrong to think we have now wandered into the book of Revelation, to the Dragon (Rev. 12) and the Beast (Rev. 13) and their followers. The author is clear on one thing, however. "We gave you this command: Anyone unwilling to work should not eat" (3:10). Then the author backtracks in conclusion, saying to shun those who do not obey so they will be ashamed. "Do not regard them as enemies, but warn them as believers" (3:14–15).

Two things are at work here: dissension within the community and a heightened eschatology that introduces actions and characters that sound much more like the Apocalypse of John than 1 Thessalonians. Preaching this letter is a challenge. Lectionary preachers will find it assigned to the last three Sundays of Year C, where it is paired with Zacchaeus, the Sadducees' question about the dance card in heaven, and a snippet of Luke's eschatology, which does warn about being deceived and being persecuted, but not of the lawless one or a rebellion. The letter offers preachers an opportunity to preach a series on biblical eschatology, a series in which the listeners are best served by preaching through 2 Thessalonians, not around it. Second Thessalonians allows the preacher to talk about the different eschatological scenarios in the Bible.

Preachers shy away from focusing on apocalyptic eschatology because it is often seen as the topic of charlatans and fanatics in today's world. In lectionary traditions the preacher is rarely given a passage with sufficient range to demonstrate the essential message of *all* biblical eschatology: God is in control, Jesus is coming (soon), keep the faith. Second Thessalonians provides the rare opportunity to explore and explain a particular eschatology and also the place of eschatology in Christian faith and thought. Eschatologies are written to encourage and offer hope. For a variety of reasons, preachers often ignore or forget that purpose, leaving the conversation about eschatology to those who would use it to terrify. We can and should do better.

1 Timothy

DEBORAH KRAUSE

As a collection of writings, 1 and 2 Timothy and Titus are often called the Pastoral Epistles. This label is due to the fact that they appear to be letters written by Paul to two of his closest emissaries in ministry. The history of the collection is remarkable in that it always appears as a unit, and its ostensible component parts never appear in manuscripts separate from one another. When this element is considered alongside the fact that most scholars argue they were not written by the apostle Paul, but by an interpreter of Paul several generations following him (a practice known as pseudepigraphy), this collection can be seen as a rhetorical performance of Paul by a leader in the church teaching on matters of proper church leadership in the decades following his ministry.

In a context of the church where the interpretation of Paul's letters was fraught with conflict (e.g., 2 Pet. 3:16), a clear exposition of Paul's mind on any number of subjects would have been welcome. Moreover, the discovery of a trove of private instruction between Paul and his close friends would likely have been seen as divinely ordained by those who valued and benefited from their teaching. For those whom the instructions silenced, disparaged, or marginalized, we can only (in light of the Christian canonical evidence) wonder about their reactions. Reading these interpretations of Paul's teaching invites preachers to explore ideas related to scriptural and ministerial authority and to consider how challenges related to finances, gender, and power inform the church even to this day.

First Timothy is written in the form of an ancient Greco-Roman letter. Following this convention, the letter opens with the naming of the sender (Paul) and of the recipient (Timothy) (1:1–2).

Following the initial greeting, the letter veers from epistolary protocol and seems to displace what should be a thanksgiving section for instructions related to controversies and the law (1:3–11). The writer returns to convention in 1:12–20 and offers thanksgiving to Christ Jesus for strengthening him in service of the gospel. This stated object of thanks is unique in the Pauline tradition, where thanksgiving is typically offered to God (e.g., Rom. 1:8; 1 Cor. 1:4; Phil. 3:3; Col. 1:3; 1 Thess. 1:2). For Christians today who affirm the divinity of Christ, this may seem immaterial, but for the historical Paul as a Jewish person, it would have been highly significant. This shift from praising God to praising Christ (combined with evidence regarding concepts, vocabulary, and structures) provides a basis for noting that the writer of this letter is not Paul, but a church leader writing in his name in a later context of the church. Importantly, such an insight is not about discrediting the writing, but appreciating that in it we can see developments in the theology of the church into the latter first and early second century.

After the thanksgiving the letter writer commences to take up a series of instructions, including prayer for those in authority (2:1–7); the comportment of prayer among men and women in the assembly (2:8–15); requirements for the offices of bishop and deacon (3:1–13); the delineation of personnel and resources for the offices of widow and elder (5:3–22); and instructions for slaves (6:1–2). This focus on ecclesial offices, matters of church administration, and their relationship to the Christian household is what earned the letters the designation of "a rule, so to speak, for pastors" by Thomas Aquinas. The administrative content of the writing may appear mundane to contemporary preachers, but assessing these rules and instructions for what they presume about leadership offers a perspective on what some scholars consider "struggles of power" within the early church. Reading between the lines of the writer's instructions offers a dramatic perspective on these struggles, how authority was constructed within this part of the early church, and how that authority impacted the lives of those who lived within the structures of the church. One example of reading between the lines of the writer's instructional rhetoric can be seen in scrutinizing his seemingly balanced approach to offering directions to both men and women regarding their comportment in worship. On the one hand, men are summarily commanded to pray "in every place, . . . lifting up holy hands without anger or argument" (2:8). On the other hand, women are directed in detail on how to dress, wear their hair, not speak, and finally considered in terms of their origins as less trustworthy than men (in relation to Gen. 3:6, 13). As such, what is framed as instruction to men and women in worship is clearly developed with more scrutiny on the behavior of women and ultimately on a foundational argument regarding their lack of fitness to teach or have authority within the church. Read for the dimensions of power within the rhetoric, these instructions disclose far more than a list of expectations for men and women in the church. They reveal a context in which women's leadership (already well attested in the Pauline tradition, e.g., Rom. 16:1; 1 Cor. 11:5; Phil. 4:2–3) is being challenged and reassessed in the name of Paul. No doubt the author's preoccupation with reinforcing the unsuitability of women to lead the church is motivated by the fact that, even while he commands their silence (several times!), there are women speaking (teaching and preaching) authoritatively in the church. In this sense it is helpful to remember that his rhetoric is more prescriptive in his context than fully descriptive of it.

The reorganization of authority in the church around gender roles goes further than the mere allocation of speaking parts in leadership. In 5:3–22 the letter writer takes up the issue of women who occupy the role of "widow" in the church and seeks to delineate between those who are "real" widows (those whom the church will support financially) and those who are not. In the midst of this discourse on widows, the writer works to curtail the number of women on the "list" who garner material support from the church. The section opens and closes with admonition that private households with widows must provide for them (5:3, 8, 16) so that "the church not be burdened" (5:16). And yet, in the following section, the writer commands that elders who rule well in preaching and teaching (who have already been delineated as men) be afforded a raise in compensation ("double honor," 5:17). In this sense, thrift is not at issue so much as a redistribution of resources to certain offices, while others, such as widows, are reduced and marginalized.

In addition to curtailing the ministry of widows financially, the letter writer also works to circumscribe the social power of the office. One strategy he uses is to redefine the qualifications that make one a "real widow." At once the writer demands that real widows must have been the wife of only one man, must have raised children (though currently have no children to provide for them), and must be over sixty years old. The net result of these qualifications would mean that

very few women would qualify, and those who did would have little social power. Another strategy is to disparage the work of widows,
which included moving between members' homes and speaking with
members as "gadding about from house to house" and being "gossips"
(5:13). Overall the writer, drawing on the authority of Paul, at once
empowers the office of elder while sidelining the office and trivializing
the work of widows. Preaching on this portion of 1 Timothy can focus
on the dynamics of leadership at work between the lines and behind
the scenes of this text. In the early church and today, leadership and
ministry are more diverse (and at times more contentious) than official
statements and publications of the church make plain. Then and now
God's Spirit is often present with and among those who are pushed
to the margins, demeaned, and relegated to last place. Shining a light
on the widows' plight in 1 Timothy offers an excellent opportunity to
speak to how the church and society have subjugated women's social
and economic empowerment, a chance to illumine the ways in which
women have and continue to work for their liberation.

The series of instructions moves from speaking about widows and
elders to slaves (6:1–2). In a remarkable rhetorical twist from Philemon, where Paul calls upon Philemon to receive Onesimus back into
his household "no longer as a slave but more than a slave, a beloved
brother" (Phlm. 16), the writer of 1 Timothy portrays Paul appealing
to slaves not to be disrespectful to their masters on the ground that they
are brothers, "believers" (6:2). In the former context the fictive kinship
brought about by baptism provides the ethical case for not imposing
the expected punishment for a runaway slave. In the latter context, kinship through baptism provides the grounds to reinforce the institution
of slavery and call on slaves to serve their masters "all the better" as a
means toward strengthening the church. Understandably the Revised
Common Lectionary avoids this text in the cycle of epistolary readings.
Certainly its prescriptive authority should be challenged and avoided
in preaching; however, there are ways to teach with this text even in the
context of church leadership that confesses the legacies of this particular interpretation of the Pauline tradition, yet still lift up how others in
the early church (and beyond) have understood that the gospel of Jesus
Christ means liberation for all.

The writing draws to a close with the challenge to "urge these
duties" (6:2) and to avoid controversies (6:4). The writer names Timothy (6:20) in the closing greeting and offers a brief benediction, "Grace
be with you" (6:21).

2 Timothy

DEBORAH KRAUSE

As a collection of writings, 1 and 2 Timothy and Titus are often referred to as the Pastoral Epistles. This label is due to the fact that they appear to be letters written by Paul to two of his closest emissaries in ministry. The history of the collection is remarkable in that it always appears as a unit, and its ostensible component parts never appear in manuscripts separate from one another. When this element is considered alongside the fact that most scholars argue they were not written by the apostle Paul, but by an interpreter of Paul several generations following him (a practice known as pseudepigraphy), this collection can be seen as a rhetorical performance of Paul by a leader in the church teaching on matters of proper church leadership in the decades following his ministry.

Second Timothy builds on the authoritative space constructed between Paul and his coworker in 1 Timothy by evoking the additional nuance of Paul writing the second letter to Timothy, anticipating the end of his own life (4:6). In this sense, the author of 2 Timothy draws on the lifetime of Paul's witness, the authority of his whole ministry, and the premise that these are his last words written just before his death, to his most trusted friend.

Second Timothy reflects on the connection between Timothy and Paul, and offers the summons to suffer as Paul suffered (1:8; 3:12) and to continue in what he has learned from Paul. Timothy is characterized as one whose piety has been shaped by his grandmother and mother's faith (1:5) and as one who is grounded in the knowledge of

315

"the sacred writings" (3:15). Paul is drawn as an apostle reflecting on his call to proclaim the gospel among the Gentiles (4:17) and as one who has fought the good fight and will be awarded the crown of righteousness (4:7–8). Importantly, both these leaders would be dead in the experience of those who first read the letter. Their connection and the naming of their attributes would serve as examples of faithfulness and dedication for subsequent generations of leaders in the church. On the other hand, the opponents of the writer are characterized as those who threaten the faith with their "godless chatter" that "will lead people into more and more ungodliness" (2:16 RSV). These opponents were also church leaders who held differing interpretations of the faith. Polemical language, such as "godless chatter," is descriptive of the writer's perception of his opponents. It is not an accurate description of the opponents themselves, their motivations, or their beliefs. What is clear from the writer's rhetoric is that he understands holding fast against the opponents is essential to maintaining the faith. Their ideas and their speech are "like gangrene" (2:17) that infects the health of the whole church. His rhetoric (again presented in the authoritative voice of Paul) demands that his readers join this oppositional stance.

In the midst of this polemical rhetoric, the writer offers metaphors for faithful leadership formation and for the life of the church that express a desire for particular virtues of church leaders and church members. Drawing on idealized portraits of virtue among different professions, the writer holds up the good soldier, the victorious athlete, and the hard-working farmer (2:3–6). Through these portraits the writer of 2 Timothy outlines the expectations for leaders in the church: those who can follow the authoritative guidance of others and are focused on the mission; "faithful men" (2:2 KJV) sought by the church and not virtuous for their bravery or their power, but rather for their focus on the job (a soldier not entangled in civilian pursuits); their commitment to authority (an athlete who follows rules); and their dedication (a hard-working farmer who is entitled to the first share of the crops).

The odd detail of the farmer who not only works hard but also is entitled to the first share of the crops stands out in this teaching. To what extent does the writer signal that "faithful men" who serve as church leaders are entitled to financial gain in the church? Coupled with the call to "double pay" (GNT) for elders in 1 Timothy 5:17–18, on the basis of the saying that "the laborer deserves his wages" (NIV), the teaching about the hard-working farmer promises quid pro quo for those who rule and teach well under his authority. This detail may be precisely the "understanding" that the writer promises (perhaps with a wink) that the Lord will grant if the reader "thinks over" what he says in 2:7. The fact that Paul in his own ministry refused to take payment for his teaching and preaching of the gospel (e.g., 1 Cor. 9:12) underscores just what a successful reformulation the Pastoral Epistles' writer has made of the Pauline tradition.

In addition to portraits of leadership, the writer also draws a metaphor to articulate a way of understanding membership and belonging within his understanding of the church. In his authentic writings (1 Cor. 12 and Rom. 12), Paul draws a metaphor of "the body of Christ" that offers a way to describe the interdependent relationships between all members of the church, in which everyone in the church is an important and honored component of the whole.

The metaphor of the body, however, is not used in the Pastoral Epistles to describe the life of the church. In 2 Timothy 2:20–21 the writer instead draws on the imagery of a large house complete with its varied utensils, some of gold and silver and some of wood and clay, some for special and some for ordinary usage. Unlike Paul's body metaphor, where every member is an integral component of the healthy functioning of the whole, the large house metaphor reinforces the class division of "special" and "ordinary" utensils (members) and imagines that those who "cleanse" themselves in the church as the writer has taught will "become special utensils."

As part of this hierarchical view of the church, one component that carries over from the rhetoric of 1 Timothy to 2 Timothy is the disparaging of women as particularly susceptible to errant teachings and thereby as unfit for leadership in the church. In 2 Timothy 3:1–9 the writer describes the "last days" as times in which people will embody a whole host of general vices such as disobedience, pride, and arrogance (among many others). These people, according to the writer, are to be avoided, as among them "are those who make their ways into households and captivate silly women, . . . who are always being instructed and can never arrive at a knowledge of the truth" (3:6–7).

The imagery of opponents moving into households and of women who are particularly susceptible to their errant teaching offers another hint about the front on which the writer of the Pastoral Epistles and his opponents were struggling within the early church. Households and their maintenance, women and their relationship to male heads of households, teaching and its impact among different people in the community—these were all spaces in which the church struggled to discern the meaning of the gospel of Jesus Christ in relationship to existing social structures. What is clear in 2 Timothy is that the writer (in the name of Paul) worked diligently to maintain structures of households and social power within them against what appeared to him as a threatening and errant tide of women's ministry and teaching in the church. The legacy of his rhetoric, as it took on canonical form and scriptural authority in suppressing women's religious leadership, cannot be overstated even to this day. These elements of 2 Timothy pose challenges for contemporary preachers, but they also provide an excellent case for how church leaders must always be vigilant to issues of social ethics and power in the project of managing church crises and conflicts.

Titus

DEBORAH KRAUSE

As a collection of writings, 1 and 2 Timothy and Titus are often referred to as the Pastoral Epistles. This label is due to the fact that they appear to be letters written by Paul to two of his closest emissaries in ministry. The history of the collection is remarkable in that it always appears as a unit, and its ostensible component parts never appear in manuscripts separate from one another. When this element is considered alongside the fact that most scholars argue they were not written by the apostle Paul, but by an interpreter of Paul several generations following him (a practice known as pseudepigraphy), this collection can be seen as a rhetorical performance of Paul by a leader in the church teaching on matters of proper church leadership in the decades following his ministry.

The final component of the collection presents Paul as writing yet another personal letter, but in this case to his coworker Titus instead of Timothy. Paul describes Titus in Galatians 2:1–3 as his traveling companion to the Jerusalem Council, a Greek who is not compelled by the Jerusalem church leadership to be circumcised. Additionally, Paul names Titus as his trusted steward of the Jerusalem collection in Corinth (2 Cor. 8:6, 16–17, 23). With this additional recipient, the writer of the Pastoral Epistles collection evokes the reach of Paul's ministry across the Mediterranean—including Rome, Greece, Asia Minor, Syria, and Judea/Jerusalem—the beginning of an imagination of a global church.

The author poses that Paul is writing to Titus where he had left him

319

on the island of Crete to establish and build up the church "in every town" by appointing elders (1:5). This framing of the author's literary fiction of the writing anticipates that the Letter to Titus takes up the work of establishing and administering the leadership of churches. In this regard, like 1 Timothy, Titus addresses the guidelines for church leadership and the challenges facing building the church and holding to the faith.

The opening of Titus offers language that reflects a concise summary of early Christian theology as it developed in the second century, to address theologies of the replacement and displacement of Israel's scriptural tradition (amid, for example, Marcionism, which rejected the God of Israel's Scripture). Titus 1:1–3 offers a vision of a trustworthy and providential sovereign God who before all time promised eternal salvation, who has revealed God's word, and who now is making that word manifest in the teaching and preaching of Paul. Such a framework offers a means toward affirming the revelation of God's saving purposes in Israel's scriptural tradition, connecting that witness with the revelation of God's "word," and grounding that revelation in the teaching and authority of the apostle Paul. Importantly, however, Paul's writings also serve as a resource for those who would discredit this theological heritage. The interpretation of Paul's letters was essential to all sides in the struggle over how to construct the theological framework of the Christian gospel. Titus finds its place in this important theological argument of the church.

Mirroring the content of 1 Timothy 3:2–4, the writer of Titus moves quickly into outlining the expectations of elders and bishops in the church (1:6–9). While elders are expected to be "blameless" and "not rebellious," bishops are required to be "blameless" and to maintain self-control while being able to teach and preach sound doctrine in ways that stand up to the challenges of those who contradict the faith. In this sense, both elders and bishops must be above reproach, but where elders must know how to take commands, bishops are required to be able to inspire confidence for those within the church and to withstand controversies and conflict for those outside of the church. The delineation of these roles offers insight into the chain of command in the early church that developed after Paul's day.

In contrast to blameless church leaders, the writer outlines that there are many "rebellious people," especially those "of the circumcision," who upset whole families (literally, "disrupt households") and teach "what it is not right to teach" (Titus 1:10–12). The reference to conflict over the practice of circumcision may reflect the writer's intention to connect with a detail from the ministry of Paul (as seen in letters such as Galatians and Philippians). Whatever the generation of church leadership, one thing seems to be guaranteed: there are always plenty of rebellious opponents. Titus is organized around much the same polemical rhetoric of 1 and 2 Timothy.

As the writer continues, he summons Titus to teach "sound doctrine." This theological expectation, however, is followed by an overwhelming amount of information on household codes and social conventions where older and younger women (2:3–5), younger men (2:6–8), and slaves (2:9–10) are all called upon to show reverence, to manage their households well while being submissive to their husbands, to be self-controlled, and finally to be submissive and show perfect fidelity to their masters. When the rhetoric of domestic social order is contrasted with concerns about how "rebellious" teachers disrupt families (1:10–12), it is clear that households were the primary social space for struggles of power in the early church. Where this writer (in the name of Paul) yearns for order, peace, and quiet, others in the Pauline tradition (such as Thecla in the noncanonical Acts of Paul) yearn for freedom outside the structure of the patriarchal household to preach and teach the gospel.

The last major instruction of the letter summons Titus to remind the church to be subject to rulers and authorities. This teaching on obedience to worldly authorities (see also Rom. 13:1–7; 1 Tim. 2:1–2) extends the writer's desire for order in the household to order in civil life. Those who rule and are in authority in government parallel the office of the bishop in the church and the father in the patriarchal household. For this pseudepigraphal interpreter of Paul, order, peace, and quiet within the church and between the church and the government reflect the truth that the loving-kindness of God our Savior has appeared (in Jesus Christ; vv. 3–7). Arguments, quarrels, dissension, envy, and anger, on the other hand, show a church in rebellion against God. Reflecting back on the contentious rhetoric of Paul in his leadership (e.g., 2 Cor. 10–12; Gal. 5:12), it is hard to imagine that he could ever serve as a paragon of order, peace, and quiet in the administration of the church. This is the remarkable power of the rhetorical innovation of the Pastoral Epistles. They construct a space in which the contextual particularity (and grit) of Paul's leadership of the church are construed toward a general ecclesial rule, and in this way they provide a remarkable platform for the management of not only the Pauline tradition, but also the church that followed.

Preaching from Titus provides the opportunity to explore the dynamics of power at work in the leadership of the church and its ministry. Far from needing to affirm the writer's interpretation of Paul on the issue of women's leadership or slavery, for example, the preacher of Titus can engage the writer's rhetoric as illustrative of a yearning for peace, order, and calm in the midst of a church that was clearly facing many social challenges. We would all love for our opponents to agree with us and for our antagonists to toe the line. We also all know that life in the church is seldom that cut-and-dried. When we see Titus as a construction of a second-century church leader's desire for order in the church and peace between the church and society, we can entertain the array of visions of church, community, and ministry that are present between this interpretation of Paul and his own likely historical letters. In this sense, the writing invites the preacher to wonder with the congregation about the kind of community we are building in the church and toward what purpose.

Philemon

MICHAEL P. KNOWLES

Philemon is by far the shortest Pauline letter (with only twenty-five verses), inviting preachers to treat the whole letter in a single sermon (the Revised Common Lectionary incudes the whole letter except the closing during Ordinary Time, Year C). It is also one of the most difficult from which to preach, primarily on account of the approach Paul takes to slavery. In addition, his rhetoric and the social conventions to which he appeals are unrecognizable from the perspective of our day.

The situation behind the letter can plausibly be reconstructed as follows: Paul writes to Philemon, a slave owner, on behalf of a slave named Onesimus, who has either run away or otherwise incurred his master's wrath. Importantly, Onesimus has recently professed faith in Christ (v. 10). Paul sends Onesimus back to his owner, perhaps as the bearer both of this letter and of the Letter to the Colossians (since Col. 4:9 refers to Onesimus as "the faithful and beloved brother, who is one of you"). Whatever circumstances may have caused this rupture or led Onesimus to avail himself of Paul's assistance, the apostle urges Philemon to receive his slave as a Christian brother (i.e., not to punish him), and he promises to repay whatever costs or damages may be outstanding.

Resisting simple categorization (on the basis, for example, of modern examples), the Roman institution of slavery is a complex phenomenon. On the one hand, self-sale into limited-term slavery for the purpose of debt relief or social advancement was not uncommon, and even those

323

kidnapped, captured in war, or born into servitude could be manu-
mitted later in life. Still, the slave owner's power was absolute: slaves
were no more than chattel and in a strongly hierarchical society were
sometimes considered as less than fully human. In short, Onesimus has
every reason to fear his master.

In contrast to the bondage of slavery, Paul appeals to personal relationships and the moral obligations they imply, first recalling Philemon's love for God and the apostle, then Paul's own love for Philemon
and, in that context, their mutual obligation to treat Onesimus with
love. The apostle's deliberative rhetoric appeals to honorable conduct
and character, with Paul essentially declaring that Philemon owes him
obedience. Although wholly appropriate by the conventions of its own
day, such an approach sounds in modern ears too much like flattery and
manipulation, when we might prefer a more direct (and prophetic!)
denunciation of self-evident injustice.

In this way, and in contrast to the radical individualism that characterizes many contemporary Western cultures, Paul emphasizes the
organic connections that constitute Christian community. This letter
comes not just from his own hand, but from "Paul, a prisoner of Christ
Jesus, and Timothy our brother" (v. 1); five fellow believers also send
greetings (vv. 23–24). More importantly, this is not a private letter,
but one addressed "To Philemon, . . . to Apphia our sister, to Archip-
pus our fellow soldier, and to the church in your house" (vv. 1–2).
Philemon cannot presume to act in isolation: the situation concerning
Onesimus is public knowledge, and its resolution should reflect the
moral constraints of membership in a community that lives by forgiveness of "legal demands" (Col. 2:13–14). Paul's hope for an imminent
visit (v. 22) further underscores his personal connection to the congregation, again as the context for appropriate moral conduct. Such coun-
tercultural openness and accountability would be revolutionary for the
church today. Stated differently, prominent Christian leadership (since
Philemon generously hosts the church in his house, vv. 5–7) implies
responsibility for modeling Christian virtue. Preaching from this letter
will seek to fashion congregations into communities that understand
ethics as an expression of their Christian identity, for which all members hold one another mutually accountable.

No less unexpected is Paul's wholesale avoidance of larger moral
issues. Where today's preacher might prefer to call for social change,
confident in the ability of ordinary people to "make a difference" in
society, Paul has little more than prayer (v. 6) and personal persuasion

to rely on. As followers of Jesus whose distinctive piety and social allegiances set them apart, Paul and his readers represent an infinitesimal minority in the world of their day, most lacking in prestige or social influence. Preaching from this letter calls us to consider the dilemma of powerlessness, when Christians must submit to the norms and structures of an unjust society. In such a context, Christian counterculture and the testimony of a community that lives by shalom becomes all-important.

Paul takes this principle even further. Instead of focusing on his apostolic authority, he emphasizes the fact that he is in prison (vv. 1, 9, 10, 13, 23), a highly unusual circumstance for a Roman citizen. In other words, he writes from a position of powerlessness, shame, and legal jeopardy, the same situation in which Onesimus now finds himself. For us, preaching about powerlessness and indignity is difficult enough; choosing to preach from a position of powerlessness is more challenging still. Yet in so doing, Paul models compassion for the powerless and the powerful alike (in this case, Onesimus and Philemon), both of whom have been converted under his ministry (vv. 10, 19). By sending back an escaped slave (at great risk) and entreating the master to receive him (with no guarantee of success), he calls both to live by the same ethic of radical, risky Christian transformation that governs his own life.

If we are to follow the model proposed by this letter, how might we exhort the powerful or "preach for change"? First, we do so on the grounds that reconciliation to God through Christ necessitates reconciliation between perpetrators and victims of injustice. Second, therefore, social transformation should be a direct reflection of new identity in Christ. The theology on which Paul bases his argument implies that neither piety nor social action alone suffice; for followers of Jesus, each entails the other. This excludes any possibility of a privatized faith or for the compartmentalization of life between Sunday conduct and "business as usual" throughout the remainder of the week. Collectively, becoming a community of visible reconciliation, justice, and the reversal of social inequity will remain essential whether or not we have power to effect wider change. As with Onesimus, Paul, and Philemon, learning to base our own social relations on shared Christian confession (rather than prevailing social models or structures) will require vulnerability and risk for power holders and powerless alike. Perhaps unexpectedly, the same principle will apply to the pulpit also, as preachers cede their perceived right to compel compliance and instead risk less forceful appeals to mutual love (v. 9), goodwill (v. 14), and confidence in their (manifestly imperfect!) hearers (v. 21).

We should not imagine that Paul's Letter to Philemon addresses every social injustice or explores the full range of possible responses to the evil of slavery. Much more simply, this letter models redemptive, faith-filled weakness as one such response, but without any guarantee that it will prove effective or elicit the desired outcome. As a matter of historical fact, we do not know whether Philemon complied or Onesimus escaped retribution. Yet the letter itself has survived, which encourages us to continue preaching regardless, calling for relationships that subvert injustice and communities that confound social expectation, not because of what we ourselves can accomplish but on the basis of what Christ makes possible in us.

Hebrews

STEPHEN FARRIS

The Letter to the Hebrews may seem alien to many Christians. It operates on the premise that there is a heavenly realm, more truly real than our earthly reality, and moreover that the ultimate work of Christ does not take place in an earthly location, either spatial or temporal, but in heaven, where Jesus, the eternal high priest, offers the perfect and complete sacrifice on our behalf. This is not the way contemporary listeners normally think about reality. Nor will many listeners be familiar with the details of sacrificial worship of Judaism or aware of the example of obscure biblical characters such as Melchizedek. That Jesus is a priest after the order of Melchizedek, for example, is not obvious comfort to listeners, who worry about their jobs and what the kids are up to. "Relevance" is not the first word that comes to mind when reading Hebrews.

Nevertheless, this work has richly funded the work of many of the great preachers of the church. Texts drawn from it appear frequently in the lectionary, on, for example, some of the major feasts of the Christian year, such as the Annunciation, Christmas, and Good Friday. For two separate stretches the Revised Common Lectionary directs us to Hebrews. These are Year B, the season after Pentecost, Proper 22 through 28, and Year C, the season after Pentecost, Proper 14 through 17. Lectionary preachers will be able to expose their listeners to a representative range of texts from Hebrews on those occasions.

WHEN, WHERE, TO WHOM, BY WHOM?

We know little about the origins of Hebrews. We do not know where, when, to whom, or by whom it was written. Theories both ancient and contemporary about these matters abound but are more obviously inspired guesswork than with other books of the New Testament.

Unlike the letters of Paul, the text itself does not tell us the identity of the intended recipients of the work. It is normally titled "The Letter to the Hebrews" or the "Epistle to the Hebrews." Given the lack of internal evidence, "Hebrews" is likely a very early deduction from the general content of the work. Perhaps it was assumed that only a largely Jewish Christian community would be interested in and familiar with the abundant Hebrew Bible references in the work and with the detailed comparison of the priestly work of Jesus to worship in the temple. Of course, an ancient supposition is not necessarily incorrect.

There is one geographical reference at the end of the epistle: "Those from Italy send you greetings" (13:24). This may mean either that the author wrote from Italy to an unspecified group of Christians elsewhere in the early church or, equally, that the letter is written to a group in Italy, probably Rome, and the author therefore also brings the greetings from Christians who are originally from Italy.

A little more can be said about when the book was written. The author consistently speaks about the sacrificial practices of traditional Judaism in the present tense, as a continuing reality, which might indicate that the work was composed before the destruction of the temple and the end of sacrificial practices, in 70 CE. We know, however, from parallels in Judaism that materials on temple worship and sacrificial practices continued to be written long after that disaster. Temple worship can continue to be described in the present tense in these materials, as in the work of the Jewish historian Josephus. Still, it may be significant that a reference to the end of sacrificial worship could easily have been worked into the author's thesis that the sacrifice of the heavenly high priest, Jesus, was superior to the earthly sacrifices at the temple. The author does not do this. Does this mean that the temple is still standing and its sacrificial worship continues? Such "arguments from silence" are notoriously problematic.

Hebrews is sometimes dated to a later period because of its "high" and complex Christology, which, it is argued, require a period of time to develop. Yet this kind of dating depends on developmental theories of early Christian theology that are themselves questionable. More significant for preaching purposes is that the first flush of enthusiasm for the faith has had time to subside. The Hebrews, as we shall continue to call the recipients, have had enough time to grow weary in the faith. This suggests at least some passage of time since the early days of the church. We shall return to this point shortly for this matter leads us into the purpose of the letter.

We also cannot say by whom the book was written. In older editions of the King James Bible, Paul is named as the author, but this identification has long been rejected by most scholars. Attribution of Hebrews to Paul is an ancient opinion (and may have helped Hebrews earn a place in the canon), but rejection of the attribution is also very ancient. The early third-century scholar Origen argued that the Greek style of Hebrews simply does not sound like Paul, a conclusion accepted by most contemporary scholars. Questions of style are always debatable. It is very difficult to imagine, however, that the Paul who so vehemently insisted that he owed his revelation directly to the Lord and not from any other source could write, "It [the revelation of God] was declared at first through the Lord, and it was attested to us by those who heard him" (2:3).

Over the centuries the work has been attributed to a gallery of early Christian figures, such as Barnabas, Silas, Epaphras, Luke, Apollos, or Priscilla, perhaps writing in conjunction with her husband, Aquila. In the end, most scholars agree with another conclusion of the venerable Origen, "But who wrote the epistle, in truth, God knows."

Questions such as all these are determined, for the most part, by similarity. To what other writings or traditions in the ancient church is the Letter to the Hebrews similar? The answers to this kind of question lead to no reliable consensus and, in any case, may be of little use to contemporary preachers. This uncertainty is not necessarily a disadvantage for the preacher, however. It makes us turn away from questions behind the text to the material within the text itself. The uncertainty with respect to ancient similarities also invites us to ask what similarities there may be between Hebrews and the situation of churches in which contemporary preachers do their work, a more homiletically useful question.

WHAT?

We may be able to answer the question of *what* the writing is. It has been frequently observed that the Letter to the Hebrews displays a high degree of rhetorical skill and, in many ways, reads more like a sermon than a letter, with some epistolary material added at the conclusion. It may be a sermon in its entirety, or it may be composed from a combination of elements from different sermons, but the rhetorical nature of the material seems clear. Thus, while we do not know *who* the author was, we can reasonably guess *what* the author was: a preacher. We can take one important step further: the author is a preacher addressing problems similar to those addressed by preachers in the present day. The church to whom the preacher is writing has grown weary in the faith. It is a church that is just hanging on. That, manifestly, is true of many of our churches and congregations today, and that also is why Hebrews, despite its often-alien language, needs to be preached.

WHY?

If we think of the author as a preacher and the "epistle" as a sermon, we may be able more clearly to answer a question more important than any addressed to this point: *why* was Hebrews written? To do so, we ought to consider the challenge the preacher lays before the congregation.

The first exhortation in the sermon is, "Therefore we must pay greater attention to what we have heard, so that we do not drift away from it" (2:1). The Hebrews must not "neglect" the message (2:3). The theme recurs at various point in the work: "Let us hold fast to our confession" (4:14). There is a real danger that the Hebrews may "fail to reach" the promised rest (4:1 alt.). The exhortations to endure and hold fast to the faith are particularly vigorous in chapter 10 (vv. 23, 35–36, 39). And finally, near the climax of the sermon, we hear, "Therefore lift your drooping hands and strengthen your weak knees" (12:12).

Preachers should not consider these exhortations to be mere homiletical noise, the kind of thing preachers say in any circumstances. One particular detail shows us how central they are to the sermon's purposes: "And let us consider how to provoke one another to love and good deeds, *not neglecting to meet together, as is the habit of some*, but encouraging one another" (10:24–25, emphasis added). To put it in contemporary terms, the preacher knows that some people have quit going to church. His message is "Don't do what they have done." It looks as if their hands are drooping, their knees are weak, and they are in danger of abandoning that confidence of theirs. Even the popular litany of the saints of faith in chapter 11 functions as an indirect exhortation to a church that needs renewed commitment. The preacher speaks with great passion about the danger of falling away from the good that God offers in Jesus Christ. The similarity to the situation that faces many contemporary preachers in today's church is striking. The hands of many in contemporary churches are drooping, and our weak knees need strength. And "God knows" that many in our day have quit going to church. This similarity to a common situation in our churches is the starting point for effective preaching on Hebrews.

While a consideration of the preacher's exhortations in Hebrews is a good starting point for reflection on the ancient sermon, it would be a mistake to think that the main thing in the book is a homiletical harangue to shape up and get going in the faith. Hebrews displays a series of movements that many of us use in our own sermons. The pattern is to lay out an exposition of a section of the Scripture (our Old Testament) such as a text or series of texts or an episode within it. The preacher then moves to the work of Christ for the listeners, which is anticipated by the scriptural material. The movement then concludes with exhortations to faithfulness, on the basis of that work. This pattern is repeated throughout the sermon.

The pattern is thoroughly christological in its orientation. The author thinks that the best answer to the problem of a tired church is not really exhortation to take one more step. It is to say that Jesus has traveled the journey before us, and therefore we can take that next step with confidence. The sermon to the Hebrews is first and foremost about what Jesus has done. The book begins with an exposition of Jesus as the one through whom God has spoken finally and authoritatively. It ends with a benediction in the name of Jesus, "our Lord Jesus, the great shepherd of the sheep, by the blood of the eternal covenant" (13:20). The call of Hebrews, therefore, is not simply to a renewed or greater dedication to the faith. It is, rather, the assurance that such a rededication will be fruitful and worthwhile because of what Jesus has done. To give but one example, the message is not simply "Hold fast to your confession" but "Since, then, we have a great high priest who has passed through the heavens, Jesus, the Son of God, let us hold fast to our confession" (4:14; cf. 10:23). Any exhortation in Hebrews is based on the work of Jesus, which forms the motivation for hearing and accepting the preacher's call to action.

The main emphasis of Hebrews, therefore, is a complex and spiritually profound exposition of the work of Jesus, the great high priest. The author makes an audacious wager that Christians will go *further* if they go *deeper* into the mystery of Christ. Preaching on Hebrews does not lead primarily to sermons with titles such as "Six Steps to a Deeper Spiritual Life." It points, rather, to Jesus, who has passed through the heavens ahead of us and offered a spiritual sacrifice that is superior to anything merely earthly.

The challenge of preaching Hebrews is that to many of us a Christology based on what might be called a two-realm worldview may not only be hard to grasp but seem to demean the importance and value of this earthly realm and our life within it. It may also cause listeners to forget that Jesus "suffered under Pontius Pilate," that is to say, lived, died, and was raised to defeat the powers that claim to still rule that earthly realm. The thoughtful preacher on Hebrews will have to ask whether we need to convert listeners to Hebrews' worldview before we can ask them to convert to Jesus.

An introduction to Hebrews cannot answer that question for the preacher. Hebrews does, however, invite the contemporary preacher to testify to the work of Jesus with a carefully thought-through Christology. The Christology of Hebrews does not limit Jesus to a particular, long past, historical time. The great high priest of Hebrews is present to help believers of all times and places, including ours. Moreover, the work of Jesus in Hebrews is not merely a matter of a moral example to those who follow him. Hebrews asserts with confidence that the sacrifice of Jesus has changed reality itself, for our eternal good. Preaching on Hebrews may not demand a Christology identical to that of the book, but it does demand a Christology that is equally serious and profound. That Christology becomes, in turn, the basis for any call to renewed commitment.

So what? Is all this worth preaching? It may be helpful to remember that the falling away from the faith, which is traditionally called apostasy and which is so marked a feature of life in the church in contemporary Western culture, is nothing new. The church both faces apostasy and survives it, says the Letter to the Hebrews. In the challenging circumstances of the contemporary church, both preacher and congregation may need that assurance.

James

RONALD J. ALLEN

The document we call the Letter of James has hit several potholes in
its journey through the history of the church. Some early church leaders wanted to exclude James from the canon because they doubted its
author was a first-generation follower of Jesus. Martin Luther, who
started the Reformation, described James as "right strawy" because he
did not think James places enough emphasis on grace and places the
wrong emphasis on justification by works.

While we speak of the book of James as a "letter," it lacks several
key characteristics of ancient letters. Moreover, James does not write in
the coherent style of most of the other Gospels and letters but appears
to put together a random collection of thoughts. But the preacher who
follows a reliable exegetical GPS discovers that James is a theological
roadway leading to important destinations.

In the opening (1:1) the writer identifies himself as "James," but we
know nothing else about who this James is. He names the addressees
as "the twelve tribes in the Dispersion," referring to communities of
Jesus' followers, largely Jewish, who lived around the Mediterranean
basin. The English word "assembly" in the NRSV of 2:2 translates the
Greek for "synagogue." In positive manner, James quotes and alludes
to many passages from the Torah, Prophets, and Writings. Preaching
from James, thus, gives the preacher an ideal opportunity to show continuity between the Testaments.

We can understand the purpose and style of James by considering the broader background of the writing. At the time of James, many people believed that desire for lesser things distracted self and community from achieving the highest purposes. Hence, many people believed that mastering desire, sometimes called self-mastery, was a goal of life.

James shares the view that inappropriate desires undermine community (e.g., 1:14–15; 4:1–2). Scholars note that James speaks explicitly of only one misbehavior in the community, the wealthy defrauding the poor (2:4, 6–7; 5:4), but themes throughout the book imply that members of the community are likely struggling with many other issues that detract from community life as well. When the community follows such desires, it condemns itself (2:13; cf. 2:12; 4:12; 5:9, 12).

The primary focus of James is to offer wisdom to members of the community of faith so they can master things that distract them from fulfilling God's purposes. The author uses a range of expressions to name this purpose: reaching maturity (1:4), wearing "the crown of life" (1:12), bearing the first fruits of the creatures of God's renewal of the world (1:18; 2:5), being "blessed" (1:25), living on the basis of "the law of liberty" (1:25) and "the royal law" (2:8), and receiving "treasure for the last days" (5:3).

From the perspective of the literary style of antiquity, the book of James is an exhortation to a community to continue a way of life to which it is already committed. The technical name for this approach is "paraenesis." Such hortatory discourses assume that the congregation has a basic grasp of its core values but needs a reminder to put those values into practice.

James offers the reminder in a manner reminiscent of biblical wisdom (e.g., Proverbs) and other Jewish and Greek writings of the time. Such documents bring up, in rapid-fire sequence, a series of subjects that do not appear to be directly related or have a clear flow of thought. Such writers often admonish listeners to self-mastery by the use of relatively short, pithy imperatives. Indeed, in its slim 108 verses, the book of James contains more than 50 imperatives! The warnings in James are pastoral alerts prompting the community to take corrective actions that lead to the goals above.

While the ancient writer intended for the audience to take individual injunctions seriously, the larger purpose of the document was to call to mind a way of life (a life of self-mastery) whose qualities are represented by the specific precepts. By covering many different subjects, the imperatives reveal the threads in the fabric and quality of life God intends. As we note more fully below, preaching on individual passages from James should contribute to the wider goal of helping the congregation see how the individual admonitions contribute to the larger life of self-mastery.

James previews the major themes of the book in the first chapter. By examining these themes together, we can gain an overview of the book's approach to self-mastery. The following table correlates themes in James 1 with other passages in James.

James 1; correlate passages	Issue(s) that James addresses	James's pastoral admonition to the ancient congregation
1:2–4, 12–18; 5:7–11	Facing trials and temptation	The community is tempted to yield to desire. In the face of desire, the people should endure (persist in living faithfully). God does not tempt: temptation comes from our desires. By enduring, believers master temptation.
1:5–8; 5:13–18	Prayer	In the face of temptation (including illness), the community should pray for wisdom (including healing) in the confidence they will receive it. Prayer is a means to endurance and self-mastery.
1:9–16; 2:1–6; 4:13–5:6	Inappropriate relationships between the wealthy and the impoverished in community	The wealthy disrespect and even defraud the poor. Those with material resources should relate appropriately to the community and use their material resources for the good of all. Sharing is a means for the wealthy to master their greed and to sustain the poor.
1:17–18; 3:13–4:10	God's gift of truth (wisdom from above) in contrast to cravings (friendship with the world)	Although God gives wisdom from above that would create supportive community, people often choose to follow their cravings, which leads to personal isolation and social chaos (e.g., envy, selfish ambition, wickedness, conflicts, murder, and coveting). As a means to self-mastery, believers should seek the wisdom from above, which builds community.

James 1; correlate passages	Issue(s) that James addresses	James's pastoral admonition to the ancient congregation
1:19–20; 3:1–12	What we say (the tongue) in relationship to behavior	Because what people say (symbolized by the tongue) significantly shapes themselves and community, people should master the tongue and commend things that create mutually supportive community.
1:22–27; 2:14–16	Hearing about God's purposes in relationship to living them	True religion consists of both hearing and welcoming God's message as well as acting out that message: hearing *and* doing.

With knowledge of these core themes in hand, preachers developing a sermon from a passage in James might make four moves. (1) Recall the issue that James addresses. (2) Explain the pastoral admonition that James offers to the ancient congregation, relating it to the wider issue of self-mastery. (3) Identify perspectives and behaviors in today's congregation and larger world that are similar to those in the community to which James wrote. Is something wrong that the assembly needs to correct? Is something going rightly on which the community needs to build? (4) Help today's congregation imagine how its attitudes and actions can more fully express the qualities of life in community that James commends.

Preachers can often move easily from the themes in James's ancient context to today. Many Christians today are tempted to yield to the desire for individual pleasure and to forgo the values and practices of the community-based life that God desires. Many congregations need a deeper life of prayer that opens them to the wisdom that empowers them toward a life of self-mastery. Discrepancy between the wealthy and the poor encourages the idolatry of wealth on the part of the rich and leaves many people in painfully impoverished circumstances. Many individuals and groups, who settle for friendship with the world, that is, friendship with such things as envy, selfish ambition, and reliance upon violence (murder), would benefit from friendship with God and exposure to wisdom from God. In the early twenty-first century, the tongue is increasingly uncivil and disrespectful in public life: self-mastery in speech is a first step toward mutually supportive community. Today, as then, many Christians hear and welcome God's promises but do not live in the requisite ways. James is on target: Christians still need to be doers of God's way of life, and not hearers only.

1 Peter

RONALD J. ALLEN

Interpreters sometimes puzzle over the authorship of this letter. Scholars are divided as to whether "Peter" was the apostle with that name, or someone following the custom, commonplace in the ancient world, of writing anonymously but using the name of a respected leader. While I incline toward the latter, I join other interpreters in using the name "Peter" to refer to the author of this letter. However, today's preacher does not need to be distracted by this issue, for regardless of the author, the letter of 1 Peter can prompt preacher and congregation toward an important if sometimes difficult conversation about the relationship of the church to the larger culture and the mission of the church.

Peter describes the congregation to which he writes as "exiles of the Dispersion" (1:1, 17; 2:11). A traditional interpretation held that Peter meant simply that Christians are in exile on earth while they are awaiting their true home with God after the second coming. Peter's meaning, however, is more complex, as we can see when looking at the context of the letter and its purposes.

THE SITUATION

The congregation was made up of Gentiles who have turned away from idols and embraced the God of Israel through Jesus Christ. Yet Peter indicates that the community is suffering (e.g., 1:6; 3:17; 4:16; 5:9).

A question arises: what does Peter mean by "suffering"? While many Bible students once thought that the Roman government was officially, systematically, and violently opposing the church, there is no historical record of such activity at the time Peter wrote (early 90s CE).

The key to understanding the suffering referenced in the letter is to recognize that social expectation and community membership were much more powerful in the ancient world than in today's highly individualistic culture. Roman society expected people to participate in Roman civil religion (including idol worship) and to support the values and practices of Roman society. Members of the church, however, were not to partake of attitudes and behaviors contrary to those of God (e.g., 4:3–4). Scholars today think that when people became part of the church, many of their neighbors, friends, and family regarded them not only with suspicion, but sometimes broke long-standing ties, thus leaving the church, figuratively speaking, in exile from their former communities and from the larger culture. Unconverted Gentiles verbally abused and ostracized members of the church (2:12; 3:9, 15).

Against this background, we can easily see the central purposes of 1 Peter: not only to encourage the congregation to remain faithful during the present season of exile so God will find them faithful at the second coming (e.g., 1:7, 13; 2:12; 4:5–6, 7, 17–19; 5:5), but also to believe that the circumstances of exile create distinct opportunities for witness. Peter counsels the congregation to make its witness in a way that will not unnecessarily offend those outside the congregation. Indeed, most of the time, outsiders should be able to regard the holy living of the community as exemplary conduct from the perspective of the larger culture (e.g., 2:12, 15; 3:16; 4:15–16).

Given this paradoxical emphasis on being a distinct, holy community while also offering an appealing witness to the wider culture, we need to consider the hermeneutical spectrum along which the preacher must place today's congregation and the purpose of the sermon. At one end of the spectrum, the contemporary community may be in a situation similar to that of the community to which Peter wrote. Because of its witness, the contemporary congregation may be in exile, in the position of aliens: criticized, harassed, or otherwise persecuted. In this case, the preacher could use texts in 1 Peter to assure the congregation of God's continuing presence and support. At the other end of the spectrum, today's congregation may be acculturated to the point that its values and practices are so closely aligned with those of the dominant capitalist culture of North America that it is difficult to distinguish the qualities of life in the congregation from the idolatrous, unjust, and exploitative assumptions and actions in the larger culture. This preacher may want to use the text as a challenge to the community to manifest attitudes and actions that point to the living hope that God makes possible through Jesus Christ. Preacher and people today will often struggle with Peter's dual imperatives: to live as a holy people but in such a way as to fit into the larger community. Where should the contemporary congregation be on the hermeneutical spectrum to maintain holy witness without inappropriate compromise with the larger world?

STRUCTURE

We can divide 1 Peter into the following units of thought, each one about the right length for a preaching text. These divisions could form the structure of a sermon series on this letter. (A semicontinuous series of readings from 1 Peter are assigned by the Revised Common Lectionary during the season of Easter in Year A.) Of course, thoughts and images overlap from division to division.

First Peter 1:3–12. Peter assures the listeners that they have made the right choice by believing in God through Jesus. Although they suffer now, they can endure in the confidence that they have the future that is summarized in 1:5–6.

First Peter 1:13–22. Peter calls the congregation to continue to turn away from their former Gentile behavior (1:14, 18) and instead to be holy in the way that God is holy (1:16, citing Lev. 19:2). The work of Christ has made the congregation holy (1:18–19).

First Peter 2:1–10. Peter further specifies the vocation of the community. They are "a chosen race, a royal priesthood, a holy nation, God's own people." These designations (from Exod. 19:6 and Isa. 43:21) indicate that God has chosen the church, like Israel, to point to God's ways of blessing for the Gentiles.

First Peter 2:11–3:7. On the one hand, this passage is part of the strategy of winning the approval of the larger culture through exemplary conduct (2:12). Peter simply commends the hierarchical social pyramid assumed by most people in antiquity, which saw rulers having authority over the community (2:13–17), masters having authority over slaves (2:18–24), and husbands having authority over wives (3:1–7). On the other hand, many preachers find 2:13–3:7 so theologically problematic they must reject its arbitrary hierarchical perspective. Such preachers argue theologically that this pyramid violates God's intent for people to live together in egalitarian mutual support through love, peace, justice, and abundance for all.

First Peter 3:8–22. Peter exhorts the community to do what is good (what is holy) even if outsiders respond by causing the community to suffer. In doing so, Christians follow the model of Christ, their example (3:18; cf. 2:21–25).

First Peter 4:1–19. Peter prompts the congregation to remember that the final day of judgment is ahead (4:7) and that they must renounce human desires (4:3–4; cf. 2:1) and, instead, they are to live as stewards of "the manifold grace of God," exemplified in 4:8–10 (cf. 3:8–9). Indeed, while God will call the Gentiles to a final accounting for their destructive living, God will first judge the household of God (4:17).

First Peter 5:1–11. Peter instructs the elders, leaders of the congregation, to lead the congregation in the manner of a shepherd responsible for a flock. While shepherds lead the sheep to nourishment and provide tender care, they also defend the flocks from wolves and thieves and discipline the sheep as needed. Indeed, Peter manifests all of these qualities in this letter: theological nourishment, empathetic care, warning against threat (e.g., 5:8–9), and calling the community to maintain the discipline necessary to endure. Those who do so will join God and Christ in eternal glory (5:10).

2 Peter

RONALD J. ALLEN

As with 1 Peter, interpreters of 2 Peter often dwell on the question of who wrote this letter. Relatively few scholars today think that Peter, the apostle of Jesus, wrote 2 Peter. Most scholars agree that an anonymous person wrote in the name of Peter to add to the authority of the writing (but they continue using the name "Peter" to refer to the author for the sake of convenience). While modern people today may regard this behavior as fraud, it was a common custom in antiquity. Regardless of authorship, the letter is part of the New Testament canon and can spark provocative conversations.

While 2 Peter has the formal characteristics of an ancient letter at the beginning and ending of the document (1:1–2; 3:17–18), the main part of the document is a farewell discourse, the ancient analogy to a "last will and testament." In such addresses, speakers or writers summed up the main lines of their thought for the next generation. Congregations in antiquity were familiar with such statements from such respected biblical figures as Jacob, Moses, Jesus, and Paul (e.g., Gen. 48–49; Deut. 32–33; Mark 13//Matt. 24–25//Luke 21; John 17; Acts 20), as well as from final discourses in wider Jewish and Greek circles.

The form of 2 Peter, as a farewell discourse, suggests that the preacher might shape the sermon as one's farewell discourse. If you had just one sermon left to preach, what are *the* most important things you would say? The preacher could use the same approach with the congregation as a community. If the congregation were coming to the completion of its life, what would be its last will and testament? The preacher might invite members of the congregation to consider: what are *the* most important things they want to leave behind?

Whereas 1 Peter was sparked by hostility of people (Gentiles) outside the congregation, 2 Peter seeks to help the congregation think theologically about issues on which the congregation was internally conflicted. Specifically, Peter deals with a question that continues to vex today's congregation: what to think about the fact that Jesus has not returned (3:1–16). Peter takes up this issue because teachers have come into the community with a way of thinking that Peter considers false (2:1–22). Peter urges the congregation to trust the prophets and the apostolic tradition (1:12–21). In the back of the specific issue (what to believe about the second coming) are larger issues that also vex today's church: the question of how to make judgments among different and even competing authorities in the church (and world) and which ones to trust.

Second Peter 1:1–12 lays out the foundation for the letter's authority: it is an apostolic witness, coming from the tradition of Jesus. In a shrewd rhetorical move, the author explains that the addressees already share the perspectives of the letter and only need a reminder of things they already know (1:12–15).

In 1:16–18, Peter invokes the tradition of the transfiguration of Jesus, emphasizing the heavenly voice giving direction to the disciples (cf. Mark 9:2–8//Matt. 17:1–8//Luke 9:28–36). Peter uses the motif of the heavenly voice to confirm the validity of true prophecy (1:19–21). Apocalyptic writers, including 2 Peter, thought of prophecy as identifying and criticizing unfaithfulness that God will condemn, as well as inviting repentance and urging faithfulness in the face of opposition on the way to the apocalypse. According to Peter, true prophets hear the voice of God and transmit it to the community. Prophecy is not "a matter of one's own interpretation" (1:20).

In 2:1–22, the letter exposes the instruction of the false teachers as "destructive opinions" (2:1). The false instructors denied that Jesus will return for judgment (3:4; cf. 1:16). They contend that life will continue just it has since creation without the possibility of divine intervention (3:4), and therefore people are free to do what they want without fear of consequences (2:18–19).

The false teachers scoffed at sacred tradition and misinterpreted the Scriptures (3:3, 16). Peter indulges in rhetorical caricature typical of the time in illustrating the life that the false prophets teach. This life is characterized by such things as licentiousness, greed, deception, slander, reveling, dissipation, adultery, unsteady souls, going astray, transgression, desires of the flesh, and indulging in lusts (2:2–3, 12–14; 3:3). The false teachers and those who follow them end up as "slaves of corruption," for people "are slaves to whatever masters them" (2:19). These attitudes and behaviors do nothing more than provide momentary sensual pleasure to the individual and do not contribute in lasting ways to the well-being of community. Consequently, God has already condemned the false prophets and will punish them at the last judgment (2:3b–5a, 6, 12–13, 17, 20, 22; 3:7, 10).

Peter explains why the congregation needs to order its life in the way of the holy prophets and Jesus in light of the coming apocalypse. God has the power to effect cosmic transformation as evidenced by the fact that God destroyed and punished with the great flood (3:5–7). Human perception of time is different from God's point of view. For God, "a thousand years are like one day" (3:8). The congregation does not know when Jesus might return (3:10). The community should consider the delay in Jesus' return as an expression of divine patience (3:9, 15). God wants people to repent (3:9). While the community waits for the new heaven and new earth, the waiting is not passive but active, striving to live in holiness and godliness, at peace and without spot or blemish (3:11, 14; cf. 1:5–8), in the manner of Noah and Lot (2:5, 7–9) and in the way of the prophets and Jesus (1:19; 3:1–2).

In addition to using 2 Peter to preach about conflicting teachings in the church, preachers dealing with 2 Peter can also help the church think critically about what to believe concerning the second coming. The preacher who accepts Peter's logic will help the congregation consider why they should continue to anticipate the apocalypse and how to live in response to this anticipation. God has delayed the apocalypse to allow time for repentance. Because we do not look at history from God's point of view (a day with God "is like a thousand years," 3:8) we cannot know the time, but we need to be ready. Moreover, the godless receive what they deserve when God condemns them as the world dissolves with fire.

For other Christians, however, the apocalypse belongs to a mythological three-story first-century worldview (God in heaven above, the world in the middle, an underworld below) they no longer share. Members of this group typically adhere to a scientific worldview. They do not anticipate God interrupting history, destroying the world with fire, and replacing it with a new heaven and a new earth. They interpret Peter's language about the new heaven and the new earth as a figurative way of saying that God is dissatisfied with the present quality of life in the world and seeks to renew that life. Many in this camp believe that God is constantly present, offering the human community the possibility of participating with God in helping the world move toward the values and practices associated with the new heaven and new earth. Ironically, this latter view has some elements in common with the perspective of the false teachers, who did not expect Jesus to return in a singular moment of judgment and redemption, and whom this letter condemns. It differs, however, in believing that the world is not prisoner of the way things are and that God is ever seeking the renewal of the quality of life in the world. It also differs in believing that people are accountable for living faithfully in response to God's purposes. While God may judge in a singular, dramatic moment, these Christians believe that unfaithfulness leads to collapse in personal and corporate lives that is similar in effect to the consequences of divine judgment as pictured by Peter.

1 John

KAROLINE M. LEWIS

The Johannine Letters, as 1, 2, and 3 John have come to be known, gar-
nered their title from a preliminary connection to the Fourth Gospel.
Early on, the three were yoked with the Gospel of John and Revelation,
largely due to similarities in both vocabulary and theological themes.
More recent trends in scholarship advocate for authorship separate
from the Fourth Gospel, an important development when it comes to
preaching these letters. The letters deserve to be read and preached on
their own terms, without the lens of the Fourth Gospel or the Apocalypse filtering their unique perspective on Christian belief and practice
at the end of the first century. The author, therefore, is unknown, but
with the noted resemblances between the three: "the elder" referred to
in 2 John 1 and 3 John 1 is the commonly identified author of 1 John.

The letters were likely written somewhere between 90 and 110 CE.
While the determination of a precise date does not have much bearing
on the preaching of these letters, knowing the general time of writing
helps to tease out the letters' themes and issues. Representing "later
Christianity," the letters offer a glimpse into the period of time when
the Christian faith is making claims and decisions for the long haul.

As one of the "General Letters" (so called because they do not name
specific addressees), 1 John is a little out of place. It reads more like a
sermon or an essay than a letter and lacks conventional epistolary elements, such as a salutation. Its sermonic feel provides an initial key to
preaching the first of the Johannine letters. Acknowledging the genre as

possibly different from its counterparts should have some implications for its interpretation. As such, while there are certainly polemical qualities to 1 John and warnings against adversaries who try to thwart the truth, the dominant tone is one of encouragement.

Addressing a congregation experiencing division, "the elder" reassures those who are holding fast to the essential tenets of the faith. The identity of the persons advocating for unfaithful reiterations of the Christian faith is not known, but the issues that the letter addresses provides clues to the group's points of dissension. It seems that the group being called out for false teachings has questioned that Jesus actually came in the flesh, the nature of God's love, the kind of love that should be expressed in the community, morality, the definition of sin, and the end of times.

Moving through the letter for the sake of preaching, 1 John's concerns about Christian identity and Christian community should have a familiar ring in the ears of contemporary listeners. Before Christianity became the dominant religion, it first had to find its way through the myriad of assertions made by both other religions and those vying for a say about this new faith's orthodoxy. The letter gives testimony to this inherent aspect of the Christian faith: the perpetual need for articulation and definition of core beliefs. First John is an example of what a confessing faith looks like, especially as it seeks to justify its principal creeds over and against voices trying to stake a claim of authority.

The sectarian sense of 1 John is felt most palpably in the writing's dualism, but it also brings out the main themes of the letter. Light reigns over darkness, truth over false teaching, eternal life instead of certain death, and love will have sovereignty over hate. These are not simply antithetical existences but also point to the nature of God and the identity of Jesus. Thus, central to 1 John is what it reveals about God and what this then means for the believer. The exhortation to the true Christian calling is 1 John's timeless message.

First John opens with a sweeping history of Christian proclamation, setting out the themes to which the author will return repeatedly (chap. 1). "What was from the beginning" establishes immediately the origin and authority of the author's testimony. What will come next is not an argument based on extant proofs, but a witness to the experience of God. The first characteristic connected to God is life: this life comes through the presence of Jesus, which also makes a difference for how the Christian life is led. Critical to the interpretation of 1 John is to recognize that the kinds of beliefs one holds have an impact on what discipleship looks like. God is also light, in whom there is no darkness. Those who insist that they live in light but then do deeds of darkness are liars. First John 1:8–10 will be familiar to many as words of confession of sin in various liturgical traditions. At the same time, it calls attention to a primary dimension of Christian community, that we are in need of regular acknowledgment of our sins, a hallmark of a healthy Christian community.

From these opening verses, the rest of the letter unpacks these central claims. First John is notoriously difficult to outline. The varied commentary on the principal foci unfolds without a clear logic, almost like a pastiche of vignettes roughly connected to the overall themes. However, if the preacher keeps in mind the essential issues that 1 John addresses, it will make contextualizing passages easier to negotiate. At stake for 1 John is that particular claims about God should lead to specific kinds of Christian living. What makes the writing somewhat challenging is the interweaving of perceived polemic with moral exhortation.

The second chapter picks up three points to consider: first, Christ as our advocate, or Paraclete, accompanies us in our obedience to Jesus' commandments. As Jesus walked, so does the believer. Second, the primary commandment we are called to obey is to love. "The elder" calls out the hypocrisy of those who say "I am in the light" but then hate a brother or sister. There is an inherent correlation between one's relationship with God and one's behavior, which is always worthy of a sermon or two. Helping people see this correlation, between stated beliefs and actions, remains a critical issue for the church. It is also an urgent subject, as the third point unfolds. Attention to the "last hour" communicates a sense of prioritized living. In this state of realized eschatology, at risk is the very truth itself, which the "antichrists" attempt to derail. Jesus is the Christ, and any claims to the contrary are deceptive and represent a denial of the incarnation itself.

Central to chapter 3 is what kind of difference the "new commandment" of loving one another actually makes in the life of the community. The love of God makes us children of God, and as children of God, we cannot commit sin. While there appears to be differing presentations of the meaning of sin, an overall understanding of sin is not doing what is right, or not practicing one's faith. So strong must be the connection between belief in Christ and behavior that any activity incongruent with the love of God can be perceived as sin. Loving one another means embodying this love in truth and in action (3:18).

Chapter 4 articulates most clearly the theme of the incarnation. The litmus test for discerning the true Spirit and false prophets is whether or not there is a confession that Jesus Christ has come in the flesh and is from God (4:2). The incarnation undergirds the rest of the chapter. "The elder" affirms that the fullest expression of God's love was the sending of God's Son so that we might live through him. The incarnation makes possible the invitation to abide in God's love and to know that God's love abides in every believer.

The final chapter of 1 John reiterates that what we believe about Jesus determines how we understand love and live out love. Once again, the relationship between the new commandment, to love one another, and how one acts and lives takes center stage. The chapter is brought to a close with a reminder of the presence of evil and those who would try to lead true believers astray. This is a real threat. As a result, 1 John is a timeless tract, reminding us of the perennial powers that say things about God that are counterintuitive to the love of God. It is no wonder that the Revised Common Lectionary gives the writing so much attention, especially in the Season of Easter, Year B. This is a lesson for the ages.

2 John

KAROLINE M. LEWIS

Without the preacher's resolve, 2 John would never be the subject of a sermon. It does not appear in the Revised Common Lectionary, and homiletical history has mostly bypassed it, so gleaning its worth for preaching has been hard to justify. And yet, this short communication gives us an important glimpse into the struggles and trials of late first-century followers of Jesus. Second John is one of the three Johannine Letters, typically dated between 90 and 110 CE. Traditionally, along with 1 and 3 John, 2 John is connected to John, the apostle, and therefore, the Fourth Gospel. The only certainty about authorship, however, is the letter's own self-reference to "the elder," who may have held some kind of leadership role within the community. The recipient is an unknown "chosen lady," who could have been an individual with some authoritative role in the congregation or might represent the congregation in general. In either case, consensus is that the letter addresses a specific community of Christ followers, a correspondence prompted by "deceivers" in its midst. As a letter of appeal, 2 John petitions the recipients to love one another, and the primary mark of this love is to walk according to Jesus' commandments.

Compared to other letters in the New Testament canon, 2 John seems more like a modern-day postcard, only thirteen verses long. The structure is simple and follows the standard epistolary format of a first-century Greco-Roman letter: opening, body, and conclusion.

Like most of the epistles in the New Testament library, the salutation

(vv. 1–3) tips the author's hand as to the issue at stake, the knowing of the truth. The truth, as it turns out, has to do with proper doctrine.

Central to this proper doctrine is the confession of Jesus Christ as coming in the flesh (v. 7), and yet there are some who deny this central tenet of the Christian faith. Prior to this revelation is the insistence of the truth's presence in the midst of the congregation. It is no accident, then, that the author asserts the abiding (Gk., *menō*) of the truth, and the truth abides in them (vv. 2, 9). That promise stands in contrast to the claim of the deceivers. The abiding of the truth within the congregation is the promise that Jesus Christ did indeed come in the flesh.

Two other themes stand out in the salutation and are worth the attention of the preacher. First, the elder sees the recipient congregation as a family, addressing the correspondence to the "elect lady and her children" (v. 1). The familial image occurs later in the letter (5, 10, 13), suggesting that the "going out" of the deceivers would have had a significant impact on the community. The loss is real. In the context of first-century Christian churches, a schism such as this would be like the death of a family member. No wonder "grace and peace" will also demand mercy (v. 3).

The reference to "mercy" is a second theme, although less salient throughout the letter. The acknowledgment of the need for mercy as a principle for working out community division functions to moderate the rather strong exhortations in verses 7–11.

At stake for the author of 2 John and the community to which the elder writes is orthodoxy. As believers in Jesus began to transition from a fringe Jewish movement to an established branch of its religious roots, longevity is the primary question on the table. The criteria by which authentic Christian belief would be measured were now at stake. In the case of 2 John, the deceivers have denied that Christ was fully human. Whether an expression of Docetism or gnostic Christology, this confession was a direct challenge to the belief in the incarnation. Anyone who does not say that Jesus Christ came in the flesh is, therefore, the antichrist (v. 7). While the history of biblical interpretation has connected this reference to the antichrist to the famous beast of Revelation 13:18, the term "antichrist" never occurs in the last book of the Bible. For 2 John, antichrists are any persons who do not abide in the "teaching of Christ" (v. 9).

Of course, adjudicating the meaning of the "teaching of Christ" becomes the central issue and is thus the lasting legacy of 2 John. How we judge the central components of the Christian faith has always been a test for the church, in part, because what the church deems central is not, and rarely has been, a uniform decision. This is true even today. At the same time, the church had to argue for core beliefs, such as the true humanity of Jesus Christ. Contemporary readers of the Bible have a tendency to forget how much creedal justification and hermeneutical history surrounds and supports modern conversations about faith. The church of 2 John had no such scaffolding but was rather in the process of constructing the very building itself. As such, any kind of immediate act toward condemnation of the other should proceed with prudence. Second John is not a prescription for eliminating those who make attempts to dissuade or deter from true belief. Rather, it calls attention to this inherent experience and dynamic of the Christian faith.

At stake as well is the very identity of Jesus. The church holds two contradictory confessions together when it articulates who Jesus is: Jesus is fully God and fully human. And the church, over the course of its history, has always erred in weighting one side more than the other. How we manage divergent convictions about our faith within our communities is a constant reality.

The accusation from the elder, calling the deceivers the antichrists, might sound a little over the top in the ears of contemporary hearers. But for the elder, this is a theological emergency. Situated in the context of the beginnings of Christianity, any kind of foothold that heterodoxy might manage to achieve within the community could lead to a deep divide or could result in the deception and demise of the entire congregation. Second John is an important example of how a community measures the core commitments of its faith. And any kind of conversation around matters of this significance and consequence will demand the elder's wise counsel, "I ask . . . [that we] love one another" (v. 5).

3 John

KAROLINE M. LEWIS

Third John, at only 219 words in Greek, is the shortest writing in the New Testament. As one of the three Johannine Letters, it is usually dated between 90 and 110 CE. Traditionally, along with 1 and 2 John, 3 John is connected to John, the apostle, although 3 John will sound the most distant from the Fourth Gospel. Like 2 John, authorship of the letter is the "the elder," who seems to have a relationship with the community as a person in leadership. Similar to its immediate relative 2 John, 3 John would be easy to pass over (as the Revised Common Lectionary does), questioning whether or not this brief late first-century post has much to add to the larger theological themes and tenets of the New Testament. In assessing its contribution to an understanding of the growth of the early church, its brevity should not be held against it.

In fact, 3 John's length is important when it comes to the interpretation and preaching of the letter. A comparison of 3 John to other New Testament letters and the fact that it is a warm address to a single person, Gaius, imply that it is an ancient private letter. As such, we catch a rare glimpse into a very personal relationship between persons trying to lead a community and navigating shared leadership.

Otherwise unknown, Gaius appears to be a dear friend of the author, and the author lauds him for his "faithfulness to the truth" (v. 3). Like 2 John 1, the author is only identified as "the elder" and intimates a certain authority throughout the letter. The reference to "my children" suggests that the author has a leadership role in the congregation, and thus his address of divisions in the community come from pastoral concern. The relationship between the elder and the recipient is not clear, but a common history seems evident, and Gaius's support of other believers is praised (v. 3).

The background for this letter leaves a lot to the imagination, but taken as a whole, the letter gives witness to the practicalities of what it meant to be a church in the late first century, especially when it comes to the topic of church leadership. The evolution of ecclesial traditions around power was a process played out in the smallest of contexts. By including 3 John in the canon, the church advocates that even the seemingly insignificant Christian community is a place where organizational structures best suited for communities in Christ are determined.

Third John is a reminder of the many witnesses that make up the New Testament, a collection of conversations that testify to the diversity of the Christian faith. Before the church was the more established religion of today, even before its efforts toward standardization in the construction of the New Testament canon in the fourth century, the church was negotiating relationships, both personal and communal.

While linked to 1 and 2 John, 3 John does not include the same kinds of concern for "antichrists" or for those who are trying to deceive followers of Christ. The words "truth" and "walk in the truth" are the primary shared vocabulary between 3 John and the other Johannine Letters. However, the attention to the "truth" in 3 John is less about alliance to held convictions of the faith and more about one's loyalties to those who uphold the truth. The leadership is held to certain standards about walking in the truth, and the community is asked to keep to the same values. In particular, the community demonstrates its commitment to the truth by showing hospitality to itinerant preachers who spread the truth (vv. 5–8).

Of primary concern for the elder is the evidence of power struggles within the community, likely the reason why he needs to reassert and reclaim his own authority. Verses 9–12 take up the issue of conflict between persons who appear to be competing for leadership roles within the congregation, or at least are trying to assert some kind of power, perhaps meant to challenge the authority of the elder. Diotrephes is specifically called out as one who seems to have influence in the community but is not acting in the ways of the truth (v. 9). In fact, his behavior is described as evil, antithetical to the good that is from God. In contrast, another unknown individual, Demetrius, is commended for his actions (v. 12). Five issues in particular are noted as demonstrative of behavior that does not represent walking in the truth. While these issues are illustrative of the unique context of 3 John, the critique of leadership qualities is timeless and useful for preaching today. Third John offers a window through which to view perennial matters around authority, leadership, hospitality, and power that have been present in the church since its inception.

First, Diotrephes loves to put himself first. In a small community, trying to survive as a nascent church, such lauding of the self would present difficulties—and still does. Second, Diotrephes does not respect the authority of the other leaders, including "the elder" (v. 1). Third, Diotrephes is condemned for slandering, spreading false charges against "us," presumably the elder and his coworkers. Fourth, Diotrephes is accused of refusing to welcome the friends of the elder. Fifth and finally, Diotrephes stands in the way of those who extend hospitality to other believers, even to the point of casting them out of the church for doing so. Taken together, these acts of evil present a picture of controversy endemic in the church. Furthermore, at the heart of this attack is everything that seems to reject what it means to walk in the truth. While the full extent of the issues that lie behind the critique is not completely clear, there is enough to suggest that adjudicating ways of living in the truth was an active and alive part of discerning Christian community.

The ways in which we speak about how leadership plays out in the church is worth a preacher's efforts. The criteria for good leadership, especially for the health and future of the church, continue to be a critical point of discussion. What are the qualifications for authority in the church? Who gets to decide what those characteristics should be? Where and how is there occasion for mutual discipline among the church's leaders?

The letter's conclusion (vv. 13–15) once again underscores the importance of hospitality in early Christian communities. Expressing the inadequacy of pen and paper for communication, the elder states plans to visit Gaius and sets the stage for being welcomed once again into the community, in direct contrast to the behavior of Diotrephes. Hospitality is essential for these emerging churches, for support, for encouragement, and for survival. This characteristic of walking in the truth has to be reassured and reinforced at every turn.

Jude

WILLIAM F. BROSEND II

Jude is a letter written by an unknown author to an unknown audience for reasons that are far from clear, except this: the author was upset, angry, and at times a little nasty. Questions of authorship are often answered together with questions of dating, and in the case of Jude the suggestions generally run from 70 to 120 CE. Scholars also bring an understanding of what constitutes "early Catholicism" into the conversation about authorship, especially a focus on ecclesial organization, right belief, and a deep emphasis on eschatology. Of these three elements, Jude contains evidence of only a concern for right belief, so the argument for late dating is unconvincing. Preachers will do better, then, to interpret Jude as quite early, from a time when traditions and the use of traditional material was fluid and changing.

The arguments for a later date usually hinge on a specific reading of verse 17: "But you, beloved, must remember the predictions of the apostles of our Lord Jesus Christ." The idea that "predictions" said by "apostles" must be remembered suggests to many that the author is reminding the audience of an apostolic age long past by the time Jude is written. Yet there is nothing in the grammatical construction itself that indicates a distant past. The phrase can simply refer to a prior action, in this case action by apostles. Compare the language to Paul's calling to mind prior teachings (1 Thess. 4:1–2; Gal. 1:9; 1 Cor. 15:1) and how he refers to a central portion of his own teaching as "received from the Lord" (1 Cor. 11:23).These expressions are not thought to suggest a late date for his letters, and neither should verse 17 be read in that manner. What stands out is the sense of being in "the last time" (v. 18), when readers should "look forward to the mercy of our Lord Jesus Christ that leads to eternal life" (v. 21). In other words, the letter contains material that fits with an expectation often seen as evidence for an early date in New Testament literature. While it is not possible to offer a precise date, it is best to interpret the letter as having been written sometime before 70 CE.

An early dating in itself does not answer the question of authorship but it does invite consideration of a biblical "Jude, a servant of Jesus Christ and brother of James" (v. 1). But which one? "Jude" is the conventional English rendering for the author of this letter, but the Greek is actually "Judas"; and there are seven people named Judas mentioned elsewhere in the New Testament:

— Judas "Iscariot," the betrayer (used twenty-two times)
— "Judas of James," one of the Twelve (Luke 6:16; Acts 1:13)
— "Judas Barsabbas" (Acts 15:22)
— Judas who hosts Saul before his sight is restored (Acts 9:11)
— "Judas the Galilean," whose revolt against the census in 6 CE is discussed by Josephus (Acts 5:37; see *Jewish Antiquities* 18.4–10)
— Judas "not Iscariot," a follower who asks Jesus a question (John 14:22)
— Judas, who along with James, Joses, and Simon is a brother of Jesus (Matt. 13:55; Mark 6:3)

The last designation matches most closely with the author's self-designation as "the brother of James" (v. 1), and there is no compelling reason to deny the traditional identification with "a servant of Jesus Christ and brother of James."

The basic movement of Jude—introduction, thesis, two sets of three proofs followed by four exhortations and a benediction—is sermonic in structure. Jude is rhetorically best understood as a riposte to an honor challenge. His authority and standing in the community have been questioned, and he holds nothing back in attacking the credibility of those who oppose him.

Although it would be helpful for contemporary preachers, Jude does not identify the "intruders" nor specify the ways they "pervert the grace of our God" (v. 4) because his original audience knew who they were and what they were doing. Jude considers them opponents and condemns them by comparing them to the vilest and most perfidious beings in his rhetorical repertoire. Some interpreters have tried to discover the nature of the intruders' offense from these comparisons, but be warned: though the author chooses the examples carefully, they also are chosen eccentrically. The comparisons are as follows:

Out of Egypt (v. 5). The reference is half commonplace interpretation, "saved a people out of the land of Egypt," and half innovative, "destroyed those who did not believe."

The angels (v. 6). The tradition, especially that of 1 Enoch 6–19, describes the rebellion and fall of angels to account for the presence of evil on the earth. The reference to the angels being "kept in eternal chains in deepest darkness for the judgment of the great day" is perhaps the strongest apocalyptic image in the letter (cf. Rev. 20:1–3).

Sodom and Gomorrah (v. 7). This example is the most familiar and yet the most ambiguous because of Jude's use of "likewise" and "in the same manner" connecting this example with the previous one (the term angels/watchers is like Sodom and Gomorrah). Because those "strangers" happened to be angelic visitors (Gen. 19:1) and because the sin of the "angels" in Jude 6 was that they "did not keep their own position," is Jude making analogy to the sexual practice or to the violation of angelic/human boundaries? The return to matters angelic in verse 9 suggests the latter.

Cain (v. 11a). After Genesis, Cain is not mentioned again in the Hebrew Bible or New Testament until Hebrews 11:4, 1 John 3:12, and Jude 11. This rare appearance of the murderer makes the comparison all the more striking.

Balaam (v. 11b). Although Balaam is slow to understand the behavior of his donkey, he is considered responsible for the plague deaths of 24,000 Israelites (Num. 22–24). For Jude and his readers, it is a sinister example of evil (Num. 31:16).

Korah's rebellion (v. 11c). In Numbers 16 Korah challenges Moses. The challenge results in a "competition," with God first planning to destroy the whole company and settling, after Moses' pleading, for swallowing up Korah and all his possessions, then destroying his supporters by fire from heaven.

These six examples share a common thread of biblical background, beginning and ending with stories from the exodus tradition (see v. 5). Though their specific offenses vary widely—rebellion, murder, sexual immorality, creating a plague—each is condemned. Even though it was obviously clear to Jude and his first readers, we remain in the dark concerning the sin of the intruders Jude is condemning.

The most common reference to Jude throughout the history of preaching is to the glorious doxology (vv. 24–25). Other than this, the Letter of Jude is best understood as twenty-six insults in search of a target, which makes it no surprise that the Revised Common Lectionary neglects it. One approach to the challenge of Jude would be to preach *against* the text, using it as an example of how *not* to deal with difficulty in the community of believers. Whatever you do, preach it with care, not as a cudgel.

Revelation

DAVID SCHNASA JACOBSEN

Revelation is the final book of the Christian canon and probably the last book from which many preachers would care to preach. Even the Revised Common Lectionary is fairly selective about choosing from among the nicer lections from Revelation. Why all the nervousness about the Apocalypse of John? On one level, the text poses sometimes intractable historical questions (e.g., the name that corresponds to 666 in Rev. 13:18), literary concerns (violent images and mythic narratives), and theological issues (divine vengeance and misogyny) that leave many preachers cold. On another level, preachers are concerned about how to interpret a biblical text that has already generated so much apocalyptic *misunderstanding* in a culture quick to treat the work as if John the Seer were actually predicting the future like some Nostradamus.

Fortunately, the Revelation to John itself offers some helpful cues for preachers negotiating this interpretive problem: it names itself as both an "apocalypse" (1:1, Gk.) and "prophecy" (1:3). Let us begin, therefore, by attending closely to the text of Revelation in context by considering it as both apocalypse and prophecy for its time and place.

The word "apocalypse" in Greek means, in the broadest sense, "revelation" or "unveiling." Here in 1:1, "apocalypse" is qualified by the words "of Jesus Christ." This is an important theological lens for understanding the whole of John's revelation. The verse functions like a superscription.

By the end of this opening paragraph in Revelation 1:3, however,

John refers to Revelation as well as "words of prophecy." The reference to prophecy first reminds contemporary readers that these were intended to be read originally as words from God to that *particular* ancient context. Second, the reference indicates that both hearing and keeping such prophetic words are important to anyone who reads them. Third, it may also indicate that Revelation was meant to be "read aloud" publicly (1:3 alt.) and not just inwardly ingested in silent, subjective appropriation.

For John, this Revelation is an apocalypse of Jesus Christ and a prophetic speaking for God. People who hear it should take note of its claim upon them from the outset: it is not so much a document for reflection as an apocalyptic and prophetic speech act for discerning. This is, by the way, why Revelation also begins with blessings (1:3) and ends with a gift, curses, and a benediction (22:16–21). The apocalypse and its words of prophecy intend to *do* something in relation to Jesus Christ.

HISTORICAL CONTEXT

Revelations and prophecies as well as blessings and curses do not just float detached in the air. These words have a context. Of course, the particular context of Revelation has been a matter of some dispute. Some scholars and traditions have dated Revelation historically as early as the time of the Roman emperor Nero (54–68), or perhaps just after his death. In general, however, scholars now date Revelation to the time of Emperor Domitian (81–96 CE) and thus try to take more seriously the historical problems posed by the emperor worship, which had been taking hold especially in the Asia Minor context (today's Turkey) of the seven cities/assemblies addressed in the opening letters of the book (chaps. 1–3): Ephesus, Smyrna, Pergamum, Thyatira, Sardis, Philadelphia, and Laodicea.

Emperor worship referred to the public activity of praising Caesar as god. While this was not done with serious religious devotion everywhere in the empire, there were places in Asia Minor where it was more vigorously pursued as a way of demonstrating loyalty to the emperor and the Roman Empire alike. There is no evidence of official government persecution of Christians in Asia Minor in this period. It may be, however, that the Christians (who were still closely enmeshed in Jewish identities in Greco-Roman urban life) were experiencing local persecution while trying to discern to what degree they needed to disconnect from the religious/political/economic life of the empire. Refusing to worship Caesar as god in the environment of urban life in imperial Asia Minor was not about intellectual propositions or some optional religious lifestyle choice. Loyalty to the divinity of Caesar was connected to being a good citizen of these cities and just being a part of the religious and imperial economic order.

Jews, as representatives of an ancient religion, enjoyed some exemptions from public life in the Roman imperium. They were not expected to offer military service, nor especially to worship Caesar as a god, given strong Jewish traditions against idolatry. Christians, as members of a Jewish sect that was only beginning to emerge out of Judaism, were faced with a crisis of their own: continue to hew closely to Jewish identity and share the same privilege about emperor worship, or adopt a more distinctive Christian identity of its own in the alluring and yet rough-and-tumble world of imperial Roman urban life.

This context is important for understanding Revelation as a whole: its attitudes about the synagogue, the emperor whose worship is viewed by their non-Jewish fellow citizens as a mark of political loyalty and interpersonal sociability, and the local crisis in Asia Minor that Revelation portrays.

John, the seer and recipient of this revelation and prophecy, communicates this vision-in-context to seven churches in Asia Minor while he himself is in exile on the isle of Patmos (off the coast of present-day Turkey) on the Lord's Day (Rev. 1:9–10). While we do not have evidence from the time of Domitian of a public, official persecution of Christians, it may be that local tumult around emperor worship in the cities of Asia Minor had gotten some upstart religious leader/troublemaker exiled in order to keep the peace. John, as recipient of this revelation/prophecy, wants to make sure that the seven churches know he has gotten this vision "on the Lord's day," not just any day but on the day of the assemblies' common worship of the one God known through Jesus Christ.

REVELATION AMONG OTHER APOCALYPSES (CHAPS. 1–5)

These contextual realities may explain some of the anomalies of John's late first-century apocalypse when compared with other Jewish apocalypses from this period and before (Dan. 7–12, 1 Enoch, 4

Ezra, 2 Baruch, Testament of Levi 2–5, Testament of Abraham). In *Apocalypse: The Morphology of a Genre,* John J. Collins describes an apocalypse as "a genre of revelatory literature with a narrative framework, in which a revelation is mediated by an otherworldly being to a human recipient, disclosing a transcendent reality which is temporal, insofar as it envisages eschatological salvation, and spatial insofar as it involves another, supernatural world." The definition fits Revelation well enough.

Yet unlike all those other apocalypses, John's is not pseudonymous— literally, "written under a false name." Pseudonymous apocalypses were typically written to address something in the author's present time but are attributed to some ancient biblical figure from the past (like Daniel, Enoch, or even Abraham) with enough foresight to see into a much later future. In the Revelation to John, on the other hand, the hearers/ readers in Asia Minor assemblies are presumably aware that a known contemporary (John) is communicating this angel-assisted vision precisely to them in their context. Perhaps this is why Revelation calls itself both an apocalypse *and* prophecy. It is an apocalyptic revelation of Jesus Christ to John, but it is also a living Word of God spoken to the recipients and their context, that is, prophetically.

That said, a yielding of ancient authority in the form of traditional apocalyptic pseudonymity requires some other ground for making the known seer's vision compelling. If first-century John is no ancient, hoary Enoch, Daniel, or Ezra, how else will John be able to convey the authorization of his apocalyptic vision and its prophetic claims? We already know that John calls his work an apocalypse "of Jesus Christ" (Rev. 1:1), a claim that presumably has some local currency for a seer exiled from his communities. Before the seer launches into the cycles of visions that make up Revelation 6–22, however, John does two important things unique to this apocalypse that are uncharacteristically connected with a (contemporary) name.

First, John launches into a series of letters to the seven communities in Asia Minor he hopes to address (chaps. 1–3). The letters address each of the communities prophetically and in some locally differentiated ways. John builds up his apocalyptic credibility on his prophetic relationship to Christians in the seven cities while speaking in the name of the Spirit. Only one other apocalypse in the Jewish tradition uses letters in relation to apocalyptic visions, namely, 2 Baruch, which is roughly contemporaneous with Revelation.

Second, John spends considerable time in Revelation 4–5 developing a typical apocalyptic scene called the "throne-room vision," well known to John's readers from the Hebrew Bible (1 Kgs. 22:19–23; Isa. 6, Ezek. 1–3; Ezek. 10; Dan. 7:9–18) and intertestamental literature (1 Enoch 14.18–16.3; 60.1b–10; 71.5–16; 90.20–22; Testament of Levi 3.4–8; 4.2–6; 5.1–2; 2 Enoch 20–22 [shorter recension]; and Apocalypse of Abraham 18.1–20.5). Some of the language and imagery in John's throne-room vision, however, is not solely of Jewish origin (as is the case with elements throughout Revelation). Sometimes John's songs of praise, even those sung in heavenly regions, sound a bit like the praises for Caesar in the imperial cult! Even then, John as seer, in typical apocalyptic fashion, invokes the throne-room vision to show both the humility of the messenger and the heavenly heights of his sources for what is to follow.

What follows the throne-room vision, of course, are fourteen chapters of apocalyptic battle, death, carnage, and ultimate destruction (chaps. 6–20). Then, at the very end, comes a beautiful vision of the new creation (chaps. 21–22), transformed. For this reason, many prefer to preach from the hopeful visions of the end rather than the rest of the book. However, a critical reading of Revelation, even in those most troublesome sections, might just indicate that it need not be so.

APOCALYPTIC VISIONS (CHAPS. 6–20)

Much of this central section of Revelation 6–20 is taken up with vision cycles: destructive visions of seven seals (6:1–8:1), seven trumpets (8:2–11:18), and seven bowls of wrath (Rev. 16). Some scholars note that the cycles of seven are a bit like looping back over the same thing symbolically again and again. The cycles in succession "loop back" to disclose different aspects of the struggle for faithfulness in Asia Minor (not, by the way, for setting up loopy timetables in each generation throughout church history for the Nostradamus prediction crowd). That said, even the more repetitive cycles of vision are not always about death and judgment.

Amid the carnage of chapters 6–20, John sometimes *breaks* the pattern of a vision cycle, especially between the sixth and seventh visions, as a way of showing how God interrupts judgment to remind of God's salvific actions, persons, and purposes. Thus, the scene with those "robed in white" in 7:9–17, typically read on All Saints' Day, is actually an interruption toward the end of the cycle of seven seals in 6:1–8:1.

This brief vision of salvation interrupts the visionary cycle to offer a glimmer of salvation amid apocalyptic pain and destruction.

Critical readers need also to be aware that not every Revelation text with violent content is prescribing violence. Christians living in times of relative peace or privilege may feel themselves far away from John's apocalyptic vision and assume that such texts may actually advocate violence. Given Revelation's troublesome use throughout church history—especially its binary symbolization of women as brides/whores and the way it sometimes gloats over the disastrous destiny of its enemies—preachers should be willing to deal with such texts critically in the pulpit. It is nonetheless equally important, especially in contexts of privilege, to acknowledge that texts like Revelation also sometimes describe a violence that already afflicts the saints because that is precisely where the goodness of God is being challenged to the utmost. Discerning Revelation for preaching today therefore requires understanding where Revelation *prescribes* violence and where it *describes* a violence that ought to offend us.

NEW CREATION (CHAPS. 21–22)

Why should offense be the measure with Scripture? Well, consider how this Apocalypse ends. The final two chapters of Revelation open up the possibility that such violence may even offend God, the One on the throne. For here in these chapters God's purposes are capped off by a final vision, which ends beautifully with a tree of life whose leaves are ultimately for the "healing of the nations" (Rev. 22:2).